Palgrave Macmillan Studies in Banking and Financial Institutions

Series Editor
Philip Molyneux
Bangor University
Bangor, United Kingdom

The Palgrave Macmillan Studies in Banking and Financial Institutions series is international in orientation and includes studies of banking systems in particular countries or regions as well as contemporary themes such as Islamic Banking, Financial Exclusion, Mergers and Acquisitions, Risk Management, and IT in Banking. The books focus on research and practice and include up to date and innovative studies that cover issues which impact banking systems globally.

More information about this series at
http://www.springer.com/series/14678

Jakub Kerlin

The Role of Deposit Guarantee Schemes as a Financial Safety Net in the European Union

palgrave
macmillan

Jakub Kerlin
Warsaw School of Economics
Warsaw, Poland

Palgrave Macmillan Studies in Banking and Financial Institutions
ISBN 978-3-319-54162-4   ISBN 978-3-319-54163-1 (eBook)
DOI 10.1007/978-3-319-54163-1
Library of Congress Control Number: 2017943384

Cover illustration: Opas Chotiphantawanon / Alamy Stock Photo

Printed on acid-free paper

This Palgrave Macmillan imprint is published by Springer Nature
The registered company is Springer International Publishing AG
The registered company address is: Gewerbestrasse 11, 6330 Cham, Switzerland

For Wiktoria, who always believes

Contents

List of Abbreviations

BCBS	Basel Committee on Banking Supervision
BIS	Bank of International Settlements
BaFin	Federal Financial Supervisory Authority
BFG	Bank Guarantee Fund
DAB	Croatian State Agency for Deposit Insurance and Bank Resolution
DGS	Deposit Guarantee Scheme
BRR directive	Bank Recovery and Resolution Directive 2014/59/UE
DGS directive	Deposit Guarantee Scheme Directive 2014/49/UE
DIA RRI	Deposit Insurance Agency Resolution Readiness Index
DICJ	Deposit Insurance Corporation of Japan
DIF	Deposit Insurance Fund
EBA	European Bank Authority
ECB	European Central Bank
EC	European Commission
ECJ	European Court of Justice
EDPS	European Data Protection
EDIS	European Deposit Insurance Scheme
EFDI	European Forum of Deposit Insurers
EFSF	European Financial Stability Facility
EIOPA	European Insurance and Occupational Pensions Authority
ESM	European Stability Mechanism
ECHR	European Court of Human Rights
FDIC	Federal Deposit Insurance Corporation

FSB	Financial Stability Board
FSF	Financial Stability Forum
G-SIFI	Global Systemically Important Financial Institution
IADI	International Association of Deposit Insurers
IPS	Institutional Protection Scheme
KNF	Polish Financial Supervision Authority
IMF	International Monetary Fund
MPE	multiple point of entry
MREL	minimum requirement for own funds and eligible liabilities
NBP	Central Bank of Poland
NCWO rule	no creditor worse off rule
OECD	Organization for Economic Co-operation and Development
RF	resolution fund
SPE	single point of entry
SRB	Single Resolution Board
SRF	Single Resolution Fund
SRM	Single Resolution Mechanism
SSM	Single Supervisory Mechanism
TLAC	total loss absorbing capacity
WB	World Bank

List of Figures

List of Tables

1

Introduction

The dynamic development of the financial market determines the necessity of creating public institutions responsible for the proper functioning, stability, and safety of market participants. Traditionally, central banks, the government, supervisory bodies, and deposit insurance agencies are all singled out in an institutional perspective as participants of the so-called financial safety net. The evolution of the structure is a frequent subject of thematic research. Times of severe turmoil, such as the global financial crisis that triggered the discussion on necessary reforms, bring constant inspiration for further studies. The experiences derived from the recent financial crisis made it necessary to redefine the role of the financial safety net, along with its deposit guarantee schemes. It also triggered numerous ideas for its further evolvement, questioning the righteousness of current solutions, and inclining possible development paths for deposit guarantee schemes. The establishment of a new, valuable research area for the exploration and evaluation of innovative deposit guarantee schemes' evolvement paths thus may be acknowledged.

In a general manner, the title of the book relates to the financial safety net of the European Union, composed of both national financial safety

© The Author(s) 2017   **1**
J. Kerlin, *The Role of Deposit Guarantee Schemes as a Financial Safety Net in the European Union*, Palgrave Macmillan Studies in Banking and Financial Institutions, DOI 10.1007/978-3-319-54163-1_1

nets and a wide, pan-European financial stability net that is currently under construction. The term "financial safety net of the European Union" declared in the title is a simplified form, as it does, in fact, comprise both national and union-wide nets, the latter of which is in the process of evolving from a simple to a much more complex structure.

The scope of the recent global financial crisis, as well as the bankruptcy of numerous financial institutions, has given rise to the biggest challenge guarantee deposition schemes have ever been presented with since their broad establishment in the 1930s. Having not been provided the proper counter-crisis instruments and sufficient financial potential, deposit schemes are often put in a passive observer role. Still, although reforms are currently being undertaken in the European Union in regard to the evolvement of the institutions mentioned above, the destined outcome remains unknown.

Furthermore, the role of deposit guarantee schemes in postcrisis reality may be perceived as a valuable research area—especially seen through the prism of their new competence scope in postcrisis financial architecture, as well as the identification of the desired role deposit guarantee schemes should take on. In fact, the position is currently evolving in a multidirectional manner. On the one hand, many deposit insurance agencies still hold a traditional guarantor role—namely, the insurer who had been impaneled to indemnify guaranteed financial means. On the other hand, a more significant role of a deposit insurance agency has arisen, where it acts as a fully fledged member of the financial safety net, responsible for maintaining financial stability in the final stages of the process (that is, after supervisory and central bank efforts had already failed). The deposit guarantee system acts as a resolution authority (that is, an organization responsible for carrying out compulsory financial restructuring of an institution by restoring proper functioning or eliminating it from the market) or, at least, is included as a significant player in the process of compulsory restructuring of a bank (as a result of gaining new dominant restructuring and liquidation jurisdiction).

Since the 1990s, the aims of deposit insurance agencies remain binary (that is, the protection of depositors and safeguarding financial stability). Still, there is a great discrepancy between the instruments and competences that are to be achieved. The roles of deposit guarantee schemes within the financial safety net, and their engagement in maintaining financial stability, may differ depending on the conditions and institutional idiosyncrasies of countries in which they function. Despite similar origins of deposit guarantee schemes in the European Union, the level of their engagement in protecting depositors and contributing to financial stability tends to be diversified. This difference became especially apparent in the aftermath of the global financial crisis.

Studies on compulsory financial institution restructuring are an extremely dynamic territory in finances—not only theoretically but also practically and institutionally. Nevertheless, practical experiences of applying compulsory restructuring (resolution) tools are limited, and their use in regard to deposit insurance agencies' engagement currently remains a subject of theoretical debate. Most aspects of potentially enhanced competences of deposit insurance agencies functioning on new terms are not analyzed in literature. Still, the subject is a valuable research territory—especially for those who explore the deposit guarantee schemes area. It may thus be claimed that verifying the legitimacy of deposit guarantee schemes' participation in resolution, as well as the consequences of their actions, is not only possible but also fruitful. Taking the above into consideration, it is therefore important that the possible forms and preparedness of a deposit insurance agency's participation in resolution be clearly inclined.

In light of the outset of new financial architecture concepts, it may be stated that studies concerning deposit guarantee schemes, and their place within the resolution procedure, remain insufficient. The two subjects and related topics are usually studied separately. The new model of deposit insurance agencies and their engagement in the resolution procedure is barely raised in thematic literature, mainly as a side topic of analyzing effects of introducing the Banking Union. Furthermore, research papers analyzing the role of deposit insurance agencies amidst resolution procedures are still lacking.

Studies concerning evolution of deposit guarantee schemes are not currently in an advanced phase. A particularly poorly researched field is the postcrisis development of deposit guarantee institutions functioning according to the new model within the financial safety net, as well as the possible engagement forms deposit insurance agencies may take in regard to bank resolution. Analyzing the field described above as well as demonstrating the evolution of deposit guarantee schemes—especially in regard to the time their role transformed during the global financial crisis—is therefore justified.

The objective of the book was the identification of deposit insurance agencies' weaknesses prior to the crisis, as well as the analysis of deposit guarantee schemes' activities in its aftermath, simultaneously considering their new duties within the financial safety net. The aim was also to verify the extent to which the participation of deposit guarantee schemes in resolution of financial institutions event enhances the process (measured by the scope of potentially effective interventions within a financial institution) in EU member states. Furthermore, the goal was also to check whether the restructuring of the financial safety net during the crisis will, in fact, be an answer to problems and challenges accompanied with liquidating big financial institutions. Finally, the objective of the author was to identify, systematize, and analyze possible forms of deposit insurance agencies' engagements in resolution procedures in EU countries, as well as to propose a method of quantitative measurement of the preparedness of deposit insurance agencies to participate in the process of orderly liquidation.

It has been verified in the publication whether the broadening of deposit guarantee schemes' competences by including them in resolution will impact the strengthening of the financial safety net. It has also been checked whether the process will enhance the protection of the depositor through the existent systems and will thus allow for the enhancement of resolution effectiveness. The above has been expressed through quantitative measures in Chapters 4 and 6. Chapter 4 shows the effectiveness of potential deposit guarantee scheme participation through the prism of his or her initial role of a sole deposit indemnifier, while Chapter 6 tests the code of conduct in case of bank resolution, both with and without the financial supporting participation of the deposit guarantee scheme. The changes required to carry out successful interventions toward financial institutions within the financial safety net have been adopted as a measure of resolution effectiveness.

The book showcases both theoretical speculations and empirical studies. The theoretical analysis comprises the majority of Chapters 2, 3, and 5, which present thematic literature, current academic achievements, the evaluation of country and pan-European legal frames, as well as institutional solutions and experiences of national, EU, and global regulators. Comparative methods are also used as thematic supplement, especially in the form of tabular listings of formal nature. Descriptive analysis has also been applied throughout the publication. Such an approach allowed for the critical, comparative analysis of administrative and legal instruments that lie within the competences of guarantee institutions. The scope presented in the publication also made possible emphasizing significant elements of deposit guarantee schemes, as well as showcasing regulatory deficits that lead to partial weakening or deficiency of depositor protection.

Empirical studies are shown in Chapters 4, 6, and 7, where comparative analysis and selected quantitative measures have been applied. The main source of information on deposit insurance agencies, market structures, and national banking sectors were derived from the Bankscope database. The conducted research focuses on measuring deposit insurance agencies' effectiveness and the process of carrying out compulsory restructuring of financial institutions in chosen scenarios. Chapter 7 provides the reader with Deposit Insurance Agency Resolution Readiness Index (DIA RRI), which measures the preparedness of deposit guarantee schemes to participate in resolution. The index comprises several components that have been ring fenced as a result of legislation and partial database analysis.

The research presented in the book relates to guarantee deposit institutions existent within the EU. They represent a relatively homogenic group, whose legislation—for the most part—is harmonized, thus allowing for an intragroup comparison. Also, the sample size of 28 member states, with a total of over 40 functioning deposit guarantors (all of which have been named in Table A.2 in Annex II) and the potential versatility of particular categories are sufficient requirements for carrying out the analysis. Referring to global experiences and data on non-EU countries (Table A.1 in Annex I) was also necessary for the sake of comparison. This allowed to achieve a proper perspective through showcasing the variety of distinct deposit guarantor roles in the EU and other parts of the world. The timeframe covered in the book spans from the first half of the eighteenth century, when the idea of guarantee deposits was born, until the end of 2015. Special attention is paid to the recent crisis evolvements and changes. Data concerning deposit insurance agencies presented in Chapters 4, 6, and 7, in principle all represent data as of 2012.

According to the author's knowledge, no previous publications have analyzed the functioning of EU deposit insurance agencies along with bank resolution instruments as a complementary data source. It is recommended that eight years from now (that is, at the endpoint of EU financial safety net reforms) the changes to the role and function of deposit guarantee schemes in the EU be inspected. Not until then will it be possible to evaluate which development path will member states have chosen in regard to their appropriate deposit insurance agencies, how the roles of particular safety net members have shaped, and what the degree of successful interventions carried out by the financial safety net in regard to banks will be.

I would like to cordially thank my tutor, Prof. Małgorzata Iwanicz-Drozdowska, Ph.D. for the effort, wonderful didactic care, and the inestimable support provided throughout the process of preparing this text. I would also like to thank Paweł Smaga, Ph.D., for all the granted assistance, and express my gratitude to the reviewers, Prof. Monika Marcinkowska, Ph.D., and Prof. Ryszard Wierzba, Ph.D., for their valuable suggestions and contributions to this work. I would also like to thank the Warsaw School of Economics and the Bank Guarantee Fund for funding the translation of the book, as well as the translator, Anna Rubkiewicz, for her eminent work on this text.

2

Participation of Deposit Guarantee Schemes in Resolution—Literature Review

2.1   Introduction

This chapter introduces terms, which are applied throughout the book, and provides an overview of research achievements in reference to deposit guarantee schemes and resolution of financial institutions. Research output has been analyzed as seen through the prism of two historical time periods—before and after the global financial crisis. The chapter indicates the most important challenges that have been, thus far, perceived as an intersection of resolution and deposit guarantee scheme topics. Merging deposit guarantee scheme and resolution issues is not a thoroughly studied trend. Analyses provided at the end of the chapter concentrate on indicating chosen areas and research deficits, which inspired the writing of this book.

© The Author(s) 2017   7
J. Kerlin, *The Role of Deposit Guarantee Schemes as a Financial Safety Net in the European Union*, Palgrave Macmillan Studies in Banking and Financial Institutions, DOI 10.1007/978-3-319-54163-1_2

2.2   Selected Definition Remarks and Challenges

It must be noted that existent literature demonstrates significant differences in the understanding of deposit guarantee and resolution of financial institutions. In order to avoid misunderstanding, the following section explains the terms used in the book.

2.2.1 Deposit Guarantee Schemes

Deposit guarantee is a topic that remains outside mainstream interest of financial discipline. Taking into consideration the institutional architecture of the financial safety net, deposit guarantee schemes are a relatively new occurrence. Still, their creation, popularization, and functioning had a significant impact on the entire, global financial system. The above-mentioned constructions drew attention of both governing bodies and researchers due to the influence they had on the banking system, depositor behavior, and the occurrence it triggered. Mainly due to the input of American and European scholars, as well as international organization efforts, research papers of both theoretical and empirical nature have emerged in thematic literature. Globally, research focuses primarily on key construction aspects of the organizations, their goals, functioning principles, as well as financing.

The terminology applied depends mostly on the origin of a given research paper. Clear discrepancies may be seen between Europe and North America. Due to unified legislation of the European Union, European researchers most often use the term "deposit guarantee scheme", applied extensively in EU normative acts. Meanwhile, in American terminology (which is also applied in South American, Asian, and African papers) two terms are most popular: "deposit insurance system" and "deposit protection system". In fact, both European and American terms have an identical meaning. Literature on deposit guarantee processes does not pay much attention to providing definitions, as scholars focus on other areas of deposit security. For instance, Garcia states that deposit guarantee schemes are just one of several strategies a country can take on in order to protect bank depositors (Garcia 1999). Demirgüç-Kunt described the scheme as a system created mainly to prevent the occurrence of mass banking sector panic (Demirgüç-Kunt and Detragiache 1999). FSB showed that it is a system responsible for the protection of depositors and the maintenance of financial stability (FSB 2012).

Taking into consideration the scarce sources of definition, for the needs of the following book, deposit guarantee schemes may be defined as an organized set of solutions instated to protect a broadly understood depositor network in case of insolvency of a given financial institution (definition used in the book). The word "scheme" used in the definition indicates the complexity and intricacy of solutions. The more expansive term "financial institution" is necessary, because guaranteed deposits accept not only banks, but also credit unions. Such a definition makes it possible to capture the essence of deposit guarantee processes without including the specificity of other institutional solutions.

The evaluation of existent terminology leads to the conclusion that the definition formulated in Europe is more suitable, as it emphasizes the special guarantee relation approach—namely, its character. It is, in fact, a payout obligation, where the beneficiary is to receive a payment of an agreed amount in case the debtor (bank or other financial institution) is not capable of fulfilling their financial commitments. Where guarantee is present, the safety of locating deposits in a bank is assured by a protecting (guaranteeing) system. The word "insurance" has a much broader connotation. First and foremost, it describes a specific method of paid protection from damage, often an effect of a random incident. Still, it must be emphasized that by paying contributions to a deposit guarantee scheme, banks purchase insurance and provide it to their depositors. Yet, more often than not, insurance is not voluntary. In the context of terminology analysis, it is worth noting that the term "deposit insurance system" is historically older than "deposit guarantee scheme." The first was used in the United States as early as around the year 1829 and was created spontaneously—as a side effect of economical practices development. The second, which relates to guarantee processes, was worked out for the requirements of legislative work and process of coding European law in directives dating back as late as to the 1980s (Thies and Gerlowski

1988, pp. 679–680). The historical meaning of "system" has now changed and it became a more inclusive term. Previously, it indicated its payout functions only, whereas in the aftermath of the global financial crisis, its resolution and financial stability maintenance roles also started being noticed.

The shorter terms "guarantee scheme" and "guarantee system" are also used recurrently in literature. Yet, they have a broader meaning than "deposit guarantee scheme", as they refer to a whole range of guarantee systems. Among other functional systems (existent alongside deposit guarantee schemes) are investor compensation schemes for brokerage homes and insurance guarantee schemes, applied, for instance, in case of bankruptcy of an insurance institution (Iwanicz-Drozdowska et al. 2015a, pp. 201–219).

Terms concerning a specific institution-authority may be encountered while analyzing thematic literature and the conceptual apparatus used by practitioners in the field. The terms include, among others: bank guarantee funds, guarantee funds, bank guarantee institutions, as well as deposit insurers, deposit insurance agencies, and deposit protection funds. Despite its universal connotation, the meaning of the first term is not as broad as that of the initially mentioned "deposit guarantee scheme". The words "fund" and "institution" relate to the foundational character of an organizational unit—namely, its capital or institutional structure (Kulesza 2000, pp. 2–17). For instance, the American FDIC describes itself as "an independent agency created to maintain stability and public confidence in the nation's financial system by insuring deposits, examining and supervising financial institutions for safety and soundness and consumer protection, making large and complex financial institutions resolvable, and managing receiverships". The British Financial Services Compensation Scheme indicates that it is a "compensation fund of last resort for customers of authorised financial services firms, which provide a trusted compensation service for customers, which raises public confidence in the financial services industry". Meanwhile, the French Fonds de Garantie des Dépôts et de Résolution (FGDR) "is a public interest organisation whose mission is to protect customers of a failed bank. By securing customers' assets, the fund helps to ensure the stability of the French banking system."

It is worth noting that as specific institutions, guarantee funds are usually defined functionally. Most often, their elementary task is to maintain the guarantee scheme (that is, the whole of guarantee solutions) in a way that protects its depositors against the consequences of financial institutions' bankruptcy. Its respective functions (assigned after the global financial crisis) usually have a broader meaning, and concern, in particular: offering financial assistance to public institutions in order to reduce the costs of intervention, maintaining financial stability, and participating in resolution. Such a description of the concept, in its broader form, has been adopted in the book.

Overall, as a conclusion to the issue of definition and concept discrepancies, it must be noted that two terms—"deposit guarantee scheme" and "deposit fund"—are often used alternatively, despite it being an erroneous practice. It may be assumed that deposit guarantee scheme is unified and is perceived as such externally by clients and other institutions in the financial safety net. Still, it may be internally complex—for example, it may be comprised of numerous separate funds (multiple institutional guarantee scheme). "Guarantee fund" indicates a specific, elicited institution (in a corporate structure understanding) that governs the whole system, especially the financial means dedicated to the protection of a group of depositors.

Organizations that participate in insurance guarantee schemes also require clarification. First and foremost, banks may be classified as members of this organization group. Yet, a more thorough analysis reveals a much richer variety of such institutions. Narrowing down the analysis to banks only would be inapt due to the existence of entities similar to banks, where repayable deposit funds are also accepted from their customers, thus putting them at risk. Often, they are participants of the guarantee scheme. In the EU, they are mostly credit institutions (commercial and cooperative banks) and credit unions (Kerlin 2014, p. 178). Therefore, the terms "bank" and "credit institution" could be an understatement, because—in the understanding of national legislature of several EU states—they do not cover, for instance, German or Spanish cooperative or building societies that also accept guaranteed funds and put their payback at risk. It must be noted that most often the majority of participants of deposit guarantee schemes are financial institutions that accept deposits. Their creation, functioning, resolution, bankruptcy, and method of liquidation are all regulated by legislature. The "ratio legis" of these specific norms aims at increased control, attentive operation, and maintaining stability and safety of the financial market.

It is necessary to underline that the following publication speaks only of deposit funds located in financial institutions. In some countries, not only does the guarantee institution return lost bank deposits (which are, in itself, a form of savings), but also other types of deposits (for example, apartment security deposits or investor compensation schemes at brokerage homes), as it is in the case of France or Great Britain. The difference between eligible deposits and covered deposits also requires clarification. The first term has a broader meaning, as it is a designation of a deposit in a bank—such that fulfills the requirements necessary for insurance coverage. They extend to all deposits that are not excluded from repayment, as stated in Article 5 of the DGS directive. For instance, among eligible deposits are those that have been instated in banks by a natural person. Meanwhile, deposits of financial institutions and investment companies that are considered as full-fledged members of the market are not examples of eligible deposits and cannot expect repayment from deposit insurers. Among covered deposits are such that have fulfilled the required qualitative and quantitative criteria. Therefore, it means that the value of a given eligible deposit does not exceed the guarantee value declared in legislation. For instance, a natural person who owns a bank deposit of €150,000 does—according to the current legal status—possess an eligible deposit of €150,000. However, the actual level of the deposit's guarantee is only €100,000, because such is the maximum guarantee value a single depositor is entitled to.

In conclusion, it may be stated that a wide variety of deposit guarantee terminology is applied in literature. In order to avoid confusion, the author had decided to use the term "deposit guarantee scheme" for general matters, or—as an alternative—simply "deposit insurer", "guarantee fund", or "insurance agency". Meanwhile, the group of institutions accepting guaranteed funds, for the sake of clarity, will be called "banks" or "financial institutions".

2.2.2   Resolution of Financial Institutions

In relation to the topic of resolution of financial institutions, which is the subject of the following publication along with the concept of deposit guarantee, it may be said that thematic terminology has not yet fully developed. Appropriate nomenclature regarding early intervention, recovery proceedings, resolution, and orderly liquidation of financial institutions is still in the making. In fact, it is not as extensive as in the case of deposit guarantee schemes due to the novelty of the phenomenon and the limited period of time potential solutions have been worked on. One of the most popular phrases used in reference to carrying out reparatory, resolution, and orderly liquidation proceedings of financial institutions is "framework for the recovery and resolution" used in the EU (Directive 2014/59/EU). In short, the sum of these processes is often called "resolution", "resolution framework", or "resolution regime", as used by the FSB (2011). As far as the coordinated liquidation procedure in the United States is concerned, the term "orderly liquidation" is often applied (the Dodd-Frank Wall Street Reform and Consumer Protection Act).

The above terms mean the sum of all the processes that aim at the improvement of a given financial institution, or its elimination from the market in a harmonized, orderly manner (therefore, in a way that will not create financial instability and will maintain real-life financial services' consistency). Another important condition is going through resolution, which is assured and carried out by the public authorities of a given country and is not dependent on the institutions' management consent. Such a solution is designed to be a contradiction to the uncertainty of liquidation bank processes during the global financial crisis. The objective is to protect taxpayers from loss, and to maintain the consistency of important functions of financial institutions. A slightly different definition is used in the EU, where resolution proceedings are described as an action where a set of instruments is used in order to quickly intervene when financial institutions are struggling. The role of resolution is to assure the consistency of critical functions of a given financial institution. At the same time, the procedures should minimize the impact of bankruptcy of financial institutions on the economy. Resolution should result in the avoidance of destabilization of financial markets and the reduction of costs paid by taxpayers.

Along with member-state legislative issues, terminology was also a subject that has been brought up during the transposition works of the European Parliament and of the Council, resulting in Directive 2014/ 59/EU of 15 May 2014, establishing a framework for the recovery and resolution of credit institutions and investment firms (BRR directive). For example, it has been concluded that in the case of Poland, the phrase "orderly liquidation" is in its core contradictory to its legal and juridical nature, because each legally regulated liquidation procedure provides a systematized course of action. Thus, introducing such a term would indicate the existence of additional, imprecise procedures. Therefore, it has been proposed that in Poland resolution should be referred to as "compulsory liquidation" (RCL 2015).

It is important to bring attention to the establishment of an innovative public authority body that has the competences to carry our resolution. Such an event is usually associated with the designation of additional administrative authority. Most often, the body is referred to as Resolution Authority (UE) or Orderly Liquidation Authority (United States).

In regard to resolution, it is important that bankruptcy and liquidation of a financial institution be treated separately. Namely, liquidation does not mean an institution had become bankrupt, but only that a company (financial institution) dissolution decision has been made. The purpose of liquidation is to finalize all ongoing affairs and issues of a given institution, eventually settling all creditor claims and returning surpluses to its respective owners. Liquidation shall therefore be perceived more like privilege, because it is only possible if a liquidated financial institution is in possession of sufficient funds to cover all of its commitments and discontinue operations. It is difficult to indicate any significant role of deposit guarantee schemes in the situation where financial means of an organization are sufficient to reimburse all commitments (including deposits). Still, if liquidation were impossible due to insufficient assets, a more convenient solution (in regard to account settlement) would be for the resolution organ or insurance agency to grant subsidy to the liquidated organization, thus enabling it to reach the budget required for settling all financial claims. Otherwise, standard bankruptcy will have to be declared, the organization's assets will quickly lose value, and—in the end—the financial participation of the deposit insurer (or resolution authority) will still be inevitable. It ought to be remembered that bankruptcy is a procedure commenced in case of insolvency of an institution, and it is mainly based on reciprocal, simultaneous claim recovery of all creditors according to a set hierarchy. Therefore, "bankruptcy" and "liquidation" are not synonymous, and the awareness of the differences is required in order to judge resolution effectiveness. In fact, expectations toward deposit insurance agencies are not the same in case of bankruptcy and liquidation procedures.

In order to avoid misinterpretation, the author will use the short term "resolution" or "compulsory restructuring" (as proposed in the transposition BBR Directive) to refer to recovery proceedings, resolution, or orderly liquidation. Respectively, in regard to organizations responsible for the execution of the procedures mentioned above, "resolution authority" and "compulsory restructuring organ" will be used. Lastly, the terms "procedure" and "proceeding" will be used interchangeably; the only difference worth noting is that "proceeding" is a more specialized, legal term. Both words refer to a process supervised by entities or public authorities within the confines of their administrative competences. It is worth emphasizing that "financial institution", a broader term than "bank", is also used with justification, as—within its jurisdiction—resolution concerns not only banks, but also institutions such as investment companies.

2.3 Mainstream Approach in the Precrisis Period

In the precrisis period, approximately until the year 2007, the issues of deposit insurance and orderly financial institution liquidation were primarily researched as separate topics (for the sake of simplification, the book acknowledges that the global financial crisis took place between the years 2007 and 2009, that is, within the years indicated by the IMF). For a significant period of time, deposit guarantee schemes researchers analyzed only chosen issues regarding their functioning. Among the best explored areas of deposit guarantee schemes are imperfections of the systems (Cull 1998), their financial model (Laeven 2002), and its effective construction (Kane 2000).

Similarly, resolution was most often described together with bank crises analysis (Hawkins and Turner 1999). These publications featured numerous principles of proper bank resolution without paying excessive attention to the allocation of costs of the process (dividing it between taxpayers and shareholders). Still, it was agreed in principle that potential losses resulting from resolution processes ought to be settled primarily at the expense of bank creditors—*de facto* shareholders—who are low in the bankruptcy hierarchy of claims, It would also include their partial expropriation in the process, if necessary. Precrisis literature, where the topics of deposit guarantee schemes and resolution have been spoken of together, is not extensive.

The participation of deposit insurers in the banking sector has been a popular topic in the United States since the late 1980s. However, the specificity of the FDIC lies in the fact that—since the entity had both resolution and deposit guarantee competences—not much attention had been paid to mutual relations of the otherwise separate institutions (FDIC 1997). Deposit insurance agencies showed much less activity in the field. The lesser deposit insurance agency activity was the result of its marginalized role within the financial safety net and the lack of escalated demand due to times of prosperity of the market. Poland is an exemption from the rule due to the fact that the national Bank Guarantee Fund (BGF) supported reform processes of banks in the 1990s, thus allowing the avoidance of deposit payout (NBP 2006).

The joint thread of resolution and deposit insurance agencies' activities is described in literature as the "least cost solution". The term signifies the selection of an administrative path of solving problems of financial institutions at the lowest possible cost. The concept came to life from the initiative of the FDIC in the United States, and was introduced in the 1990s. The core idea of the principle is that the deposit insurer decides, case by case, whether deposit funds shall be paid out and activities of the bank terminated, or the granted funding should be preferably used to assure continuity of the bank and enable its acquisition by a properly functioning entity, capable of providing its financial support. Previously, it was less costly to shut down the bank and carry out guaranteed deposits' payout. Nowadays, however—due to the sizes of banks—it is more economical that the deposit insurance agency carries out resolution proceedings. This has been observed by Helfer (1999), who studied the participation of deposit guarantee schemes in resolution and the costliness of both available solutions.

The IMF published a paper featuring the topic of government attempts at saving banks in specific countries, complemented by number of recommendations (Daniel 1997). The most significant guidance indicated that the least cost solution was to undertake the saving of the bank, not allowing for its unsupervised bankruptcy. It was indicated that creating a timely resolution framework, focusing on the rule of minimizing budget costs spent on saving banks, and providing the transparency of the process, were all crucial. The IMF brought attention to expropriation—a solution that, though unpopular, has been constantly gaining supporters. For this reason, the IMF included a recommendation for using the "bail in" instrument. The solution was supposed to work on the basis of partial claim write-off in return for newly emitted shares and stocks. Therefore, the IMF advised to at least take into consideration the possibilities and potential effects of applying "bail in" as a primary action. Such a procedure was presumably supposed to support market discipline and favor the monitoring of bank situation by all market participants.

Rosengren and Peek (1999) researched the efficiency of pre-resolution intervention, hence, in its early phase. They evaluated prompt corrective action as an early chapter of restorative procedures available in the American system. They noticed that in the United States, institutions that did not meet regulatory criteria, but were covered by the guarantee scheme, were fined by the administrative authority. The authors lauded this approach, emphasizing that the penalty was inevitable and applied through a restrictive procedure. Additionally, such a process takes place with an insignificant legal procedure breach, which—according to the researchers—encourages banks to fight problems in their early phase. It also influences the deposit insurer positively, because he/she may—after being informed about the fine—look into the situation of a specific entity and prepare for payout. Concluding their research, the authors stated that the conflict between the supervisor of entities present on the market and deposit insurance agencies is difficult to overcome. Examinations of extreme conditions and the evaluation of the degree of capital requirements' fulfillment usually lie in the powers of supervisors, but—from the perspective of deposit insurers—are carried out too seldom. Thus, the authors concluded that the existence of prompt corrective actions was desirable and rightful, but the process should be achieved through cooperation of the supervisor and the deposit insurance agency. The authors stated that before resolution takes place, instruments that allow for the timely coping with a difficult financial situation of a bank should be developed before it is too difficult, thus leading inevitably toward bankruptcy. They also indicated the rising significance of deposit insurance agencies and legitimized the sense for their existence since the beginning of a crisis event. They also spoke in favor of an active, deposit guarantee scheme role based on the accumulation of data and the coordination with other members of the financial safety net. Such a guarantee form would potentially allow for the prevention of bankruptcy, and not solely the elimination of its negative consequences.

In a publication relatively ahead of its time, Kaufman and Seeling (2001) draw attention to the important issue of the situation of depositors in resolution that changes depending on the use of different instruments. The authors prepared an innovative formulation regarding the issue of code of conduct while dealing with depositors of significant financial institutions. The research paper written under the auspices of the IMF depicted the extensive problem of discrepancy of deposit guarantee schemes and potential payouts in the case of significant financial institutions' bankruptcy. In effect, applying resolution instruments in the place of payout procedures becomes necessary. The paper was written mainly on the basis of American experiences and speaks of formal and legal guarantees that depositors of resolution-covered institutions are entitled to. The authors noted that often depositors show distrust and, in the case of big institutions, expect difficulties in regaining their funds. The authors recommended a rapid covered deposit payout, and—for the sake of market discipline—a potential withhold of funds exceeding the guarantee level. It must be noticed that at this phase of resolution and deposit guarantee schemes development works, not much attention was paid to the necessity of providing and maintaining the functioning of critical bank operations.

Another relevant publication on resolution is a research paper by Osterberg and Thomson (2002). The authors brought attention to a topic relevant to the following publication's thematic scope, namely "depositor preference"—the priority of settling depositors' claims first in the case of a resolution event. They analyzed the influence of depositor preference on the costs of proceedings. The results transpired that applying the above rule raises resolution costs and determines the choice of its instruments. After introducing depositor preference in the United States, acquisition of the bank with the deposit insurance agency's grant became the more frequently chosen option than the previously popular liquidation. The change was a result of the shift of claim settling hierarchy. The analysis proved that choosing the depositor over others may increase the costs of proceedings and thus shape the resolution strategy altogether. The authors emphasized the necessity of engaging the deposit insurance agency in resolution, as it will naturally care for its best interest and act effectively.

Krimminger (2004) underlined the important role of deposit guarantee schemes in resolution procedures. The author brought to attention that such institutions are a significant part of the bankruptcy process of financial institutions. He also stressed that due to the rising integration of financial markets, often various jurisdictions apply different bankruptcy and liquidation regimes, which significantly differentiate the position of creditors. He claimed that deposit guarantee schemes allow for the unification of creditor protection rules (incarnated in the form of depositors) regardless of the country where protection is being provided, and that the standardization of security rules, including the position of depositors in resolution, has a positive impact on the development and integration of the financial market thanks to the participation of the deposit insurer.

Under the auspices of the World Bank, Beck and Laeven (2006) prepared one of the institution's overview publications. They analyzed a group of 57 countries with a functioning deposit guarantee scheme. The study's aim was to inspect the various forms of deposit guarantee schemes' engagement in the liquidation procedure of banks. The results showcased the different types of commitment and legitimization of various systems. One of the publication's most prominent discoveries was the claim that the engagement of deposit guarantee schemes in resolution has a positive impact on the financial stability of a given country and minimizes the risk of bank functioning within the given system. This applies especially in the case of institutions whose membership in the deposit guarantee scheme may be suspended. Two of the most eminent recommendations of the authors were facilitating access of deposit guarantee schemes to supervisory data and providing independence from political factors. On the basis of their research, the authors concluded that the strengthening of supervisory competences and deposit guarantee schemes' powers has a positive effect on the stability of the banking sector.

Summarizing the achievements of research on deposit guarantee schemes and resolution of financial institutions in the precrisis period, it must be emphasized that their development was not dynamic and was confined mainly to theory. Financial markets did not provide sufficient occasions for the practical verification of financial institutions' orderly liquidation theory, especially in the EU and supranational systems. The issue of low effectiveness of the financial safety net, overlapping of competences of its participants, and the insufficient preparedness for the liquidation of prominent financial institutions were, in fact, noticed, yet necessary reforms were postponed. It was not until the struggles of large banks in 2007 that the trend had turned around, mobilizing governments to implement the new resolution solution—a procedure that lacked practical experiences and studies.

2.4   Change of Approach After the Outbreak of the Crisis

For a long period of time, researchers did not pay much attention to the role of deposit guarantee schemes in resolution. It was not until the financial architecture reforms in 2007 that they started showing interest in both topics and their interdependence. The global financial crisis—especially in the EU—strengthened the previously argued postulates of researchers on the necessity of introducing strong, intervention-enabling instruments that could rescue financial institutions that were going through resolution and were on the verge of bankruptcy. This was due to the fact that traditional payout procedures on behalf of big banks were impossible, because the funds accumulated by deposit insurers in the majority of EU countries were insufficient.

In response to the new procedure requirements, IADI (2009a) prepared a study indicating the role model deposit guarantee schemes should take in resolution. First and foremost, a proper financing of the above institution was expected through the accumulation of funds necessary for carrying out the procedure, prior to the event itself. According to the paper, to ensure the validity of data, it is crucial that the scheme have access to depositor details before the bankruptcy of a bank or the application of resolution. IADI determined that the main changes that need to be made were granting broader authority to control and supervisory guarantee schemes, and the strongly postulated right of unilateral termination of insurance of a given institution by the guarantee fund.

In a publication authored by Tarr (2010), a thesis that the existence of an institution that was too big to become insolvent was declared a myth that supervisors in the EU should face. The author points to an effective FDIC activity that used resolution authority. The analyzed case was the liquidation of Washington Mutual financial holding—a financial company that accepted deposits and granted mortgages. It was the sixth largest financial institution in the United States (measured by the size of its assets) and owned nearly $182 billion in deposits. Thanks to the FDIC intervention, in a short period of time its liabilities were transferred to JP Morgan Chase that provided the continuity of crucial functions and took over Washington Mutual's deposit debt. At the same time, Washington Mutual holding's shareholders and creditors (owners of obligations) lost their respective rights, and their claims were redeemed. Tarr claimed that the size of a bank could not protect it from insolvency, yet, during its liquidation process, basic code of conduct and adamancy of decision makers was needed, in the form of burdening the owners and unsecured creditors of the bank financially.

Simultaneously, the author indicated the necessity of protecting depositors and providing the autonomy of the resolution organ in the United States.

Sharma (2011) researched the development and evolvement of resolution procedures of approximately 140 countries. The author tried to establish whether it was a procedure that lied mainly within the competence of courts (as in bankruptcy of other commercial companies) or was conducted by a separate institution that belonged to the financial safety net (the analysis mainly concerned supervisors). The research outcome showed that, as a general rule, when the supervisor has broad powers to intervene in the market, it also has greater resolution powers. It is usually accompanied by the phenomenon of strong protection of last resort decisions issued by the supervisor in the resolution (with limited opportunity for juridical control). The author pointed out the positive and negative aspects of such a solution, stipulating that there is a global trend of expanding powers of resolution and moving them from the administrative and judicial institutions to the members of the financial safety net, which—most often—takes the form of greater authority of the supervisor.

One of the most valuable publications on the participation of deposit guarantee schemes in resolution is an FSB study (2011) offering guidelines for the preparation for the process. It features an analysis of various resolution instruments, including "bail in", one of the most significant methods, as well as foreign cooperation. The topic of whether depositors of such institutions should in fact be prioritized in the process of settling claims was also included. The paper presented the significance of depositor insurance and the important role of deposit guarantee schemes in financing resolution. The report was later supplemented by an overview of resolution solutions in G-20 countries (FSB 2013a). The analysis of specific deposit guarantee schemes' engagement examples showcased in the FSB report allows for the conclusion that country solutions in 2013 were diversified, and the role of deposit guarantee schemes was imprecise.

Another significant study case is a research paper by BCBS and IADI (2014) that updates the conditions of effective deposit insurance, primarily published in 2009 (BCBS and IADI 2009). The association pointed out that in the years 2005–11 the count of world's deposit insurance agencies increased from 50 to 65 per cent. For this reason, among others, IADI updated its guidelines concerning the conditions of effective deposit insurance, so that they abide by the new postcrisis reality. The association distinguished two options of effective deposit guarantee systems—when the deposit guarantee scheme participates in resolution in a limited, fund-related form only, and when it also holds the position of the resolution organ. In the first variant, where only financial support of the fund was expected, IADI drew attention to several conditions that must be met in order to maintain the efficiency of the resolution process, namely, among others:

– the necessity of making joint decisions with the deposit insurance agency on the time of initiating the resolution procedure,
– the transparency and legal authorization to spend deposit insurance agencies' funds during resolution,
– the principle of protecting the deposit insurer's interest by not requiring depositor payouts after the resolution procedure—even if it fails,
– limiting the financial participation of a deposit insurance agency to the value of an estimated net loss of a standard deposit payout,
– settling losses primarily at the expense of owners of financial institutions and other creditors,
– the use of the deposit insurer's funds is preceded by an independent audit, and after the financing had been used, an *ex post* revealing any potential irregularities of the process is performed.

In the second variant, that is, when the deposit insurance agency is also the resolution authority, the conditions are more restrictive. IADI indicated, for instance, that the deposit insurer needed to be independent and have sufficient powers corresponding to the scope of his or her mandate. Furthermore, the application of resolution procedures ought to be applicable to even the smallest of banks. In the case of multiple resolution authorities, a clear division of roles and responsibilities needs to be established. The deposit insurance agency ought to provide operational independence consistent with its resolution responsibilities, including instating a forced administrator and the transfer of assets or liabilities through a unilateral legal decision (in this case, the competences mentioned above should not be exclusive to a single supervisor). An additional deposit insurance agency should have the right to apply various resolution instruments, while presenting a flexible attitude to the subject matter.

In both variants, maintaining a set hierarchy of settling claims is also a crucial element. Deposits should be among the most privileged (up to the level of covered funds), and their protection should not be limited by their nationality or country of residence. Another necessary rule is making it impossible to cancel the decisions on the form, type, and range of resolution (the finality of decisions). Potential claims on behalf of creditors and owners must be limited solely to compensation. The unavailability of deposits should last the shortest possible time—a condition ensured by the deposit guarantee scheme.

The review of literature on deposit insurance agencies participating in resolution showcases that the engagement of deposit guarantee schemes in the procedure has so far been short-lived, and thus has not been analyzed fully, especially in the EU. It seems that the participation of the deposit insurance system does not require questioning, yet the desired scope and character of its participation remains unclear. The application of least cost solution, which gained significance in the time of hegemony of large banks on the financial market, should be the starting point for the engagement of deposit insurers in resolution procedures.

2.5   New Fields and Research Gaps

It is noteworthy that the global financial crisis changed the views of researchers and decision makers seeking for new solutions. The firmly rooted research achievements do not correspond to recent challenges. Furthermore, global studies on the development of deposit guarantee schemes and their engagement in resolution and orderly liquidation of financial institutions are not in an advanced stage. It is especially visible in the face of new concepts of reshaping the existent financial architecture.

In the past, topics regarding deposit insurance agencies and resolution were most often researched independently. According to the author's knowledge, the topic of deposit guarantee schemes' engagement in resolution is not sufficiently analyzed in thematic publications and usually serves as a complementary source of information on other subjects regarding institutional solutions. What is more, reports that scrutinize the role of deposit guarantee schemes in orderly liquidation of financial institutions, along with its merits and shortcomings, are still missing. Therefore, merging the two topics that have consequently been growing closer together since 2007 is a justified measure.

In light of all of the above, it must be noticed that the activities of deposit insurance agencies and resolution organ are complementary to a certain degree. Both institutions support one another at least in regard to their mutual protection of depositors' interest. The resolution organ has relevant administrative instruments at its disposal, which the deposit insurance agency can support with deposit insurance funds. To a certain extent, the actions of both institutions are also interchangeable, because—from the depositor's perspective—it is not relevant from the technical point of view whether his or her financial means are protected by the deposit guarantee scheme or will be lost as a result of applying resolution instruments. It may be perceived that deposit guarantee scheme participation in resolution exists in multiple forms (Pruski and Kerlin 2015).

Therefore, a more thorough study and evaluation of the influence of deposit guarantee schemes on the effectiveness of resolution is required, along with the analysis of financial repercussions of merging deposit guarantee schemes and resolution (hence, the enhancement of the scope of intervention actions toward banks). Additionally, identification and systematization of possible deposit guarantee schemes' engagement models in resolution, proposition of effectiveness measurement methods, and an evaluation of EU deposit insurance agencies' readiness to act as a resolution organ are all needed. These issues have been revised and covered extensively in the next chapters of this book.

The answers to the questions stated above ought to fill the research gap and inspire the further development of deposit guarantee systems' thematic field. It should also aid the analysis of the evolution of deposit insurance agencies in the EU safety net and define its new role, meaning, and tasks within resolution procedures.

2.6 Conclusion

This chapter provided an overview and systemized current knowledge on deposit insurance agencies and resolution, including their common roles and responsibilities in the financial safety net. In conclusion, it may be acknowledged that development of deposit guarantee schemes is a process that has been taking place at varying paces for many years. Nevertheless, thematic spheres, which have consolidated throughout the years, have been exposed to various changes due to shift in postcrisis reality. The inadequate structure of the financial safety net in many countries—including the EU—forced a change in institutional architecture of safety net members. Since 2007, deposit guarantee schemes have been undergoing a dynamic transformation process into more complex activity forms. Taking into consideration the history of deposit guarantee, it must be underlined that the evolution of the role of deposit insurance agencies is still an ongoing process. The global financial crisis triggered revision of many views regarding their function, as well as approximated them naturally to the topic of bank resolution—the prelude of deposit payouts. Through the analysis of the scope of resolution (created as a response to crisis), as well as the extended deposit insurance agency authority, it may be acknowledged that the merger of both functions has taken place. Thus, their cooperation in the financial safety net in reference to banks may also be observed.

References

BCBS; IADI. (2009). *Core Principles for Effective Deposit Insurance Systems*, Basel.

BCBS; IADI. (2014). *Updated Core Principles for Effective Deposit Insurance Systems*, Basel.

Beck, T.; Laeven, L. (2006). *Resolution of Failed Banks by Deposit Insurers: Cross-Country Evidence*, World Bank, Washington, DC.

Cull, R. (1998). *How Deposit Insurance Affects Financial Depth: A Cross-Country Analysis*, vol. 1, WPS1875, World Bank, Washington, DC.

Daniel, J. (1997). *Fiscal Aspects of Bank Restructuring*, IMF, April.

Demirgüç-Kunt, A.; Detragiache, E. (1999). *Does Deposit Insurance Increase Banking System Stability? An Empirical Investigation*, Policy Research Working Paper no. 2247, World Bank, November.

FDIC. (1997). *Managing the Crisis: The FDIC and RTC Experience*, Washington.

FSB. (2011). *Key Attributes of Effective Resolution Regimes for Financial Institutions*, Basel, October.

FSB. (2012). *Thematic Review on Deposit Insurance Systems. Peer Review Report*, Basel.

FSB. (2013a). *Recovery and Resolution Planning for Systemically Important Financial Institutions: Guidance on Developing Effective Resolution Strategies*, July.

Garcia, G. (1999). *Deposit Insurance: A Survey of Actual and Best Practices*, IMF, WP/99/54, April, Washington, DC.

Hawkins, J.; Turner, P. (1999). *Bank Restructuring in Practice*, Bank For International Settlements, Monetary and Economic Department, Policy Papers, No. 6 - August, Basel, Switzerland.

Helfer, R.T. (1999). *What Deposit Insurance Can and Cannot Do*, "Finance & Development", vol. 36, no. 1, March, Washington, DC. Available at: http://www.imf.org/external/pubs/ft/fandd/1999/03/tigert.htm.

IADI (2009a). *General Guidance for Developing Differential Premium Systems*, BIS, Basel.

Iwanicz-Drozdowska, M.; Kerlin, J.; Smaga, P.; Tomasik, M. (2015a). *EU Guarantee Schemes: Status Quo and Policy Implications*, "Journal of Banking Regulation", vol. 16, no. 3, pp. 201–219.

Kane, E. (2000). *Designing Financial Safety Nets to Fit Country Circumstances*, vol. 1, World Bank.

Kaufman, G.; Seelig, S. (2001). *Post-Resolution Treatment of Depositors at Failed Banks: Implications for the Severity of Banking Crises, Systemic Risk, and Too-Big-To-Fail*, IMF Working Paper no. 01/83, June.

Kerlin, J. (2014). *Zabezpieczenie oszczędności gospodarstw domowych w polskim systemie finansowym*, [w:] *Rozwój nauki o finansach. Stan obecny i pożądane kierunki jej ewolucji*, red J. Ostaszewski, E. Kosycarz, Oficyna Wydawnicza SGH, Warszawa.

Krimminger, M. (2004). *Deposit Insurance and Bank Insolvency in a Changing World: Synergies & Challenges*.

Kulesza, M. (2000). *Bankowy Fundusz Gwarancyjny jako podmiot prawa publicznego – recydywa zapomnianego pojęcia*, "Glosa", 2000, nr 10.

Laeven, L. (2002). *Pricing of Deposit Insurance*, World Bank, July.

NBP. (2006). *Nadzór bankowy 1989–2006*, Warszawa.

Osterberg, W.; Thomson, J. (2002). *Depositor Preference Legislation and Failed Banks' Resolution Costs*, FRB of Cleveland Working Paper no. 97-15, November.

Pruski, J.; Kerlin, J. (2015). *Characteristics of Deposit Insurance Research and the Challenges Ahead*, Safe Bank (Bezpieczy Bank), No. 2(59), Warsaw.

RCL. (2015). *Zestawienie uwag do projektu z dnia 23 pazdziernika 2015 r. ustawy z dnia ... 2015 r. o Bankowym Funduszu Gwarancyjnym, systemie gwarantowania depozytów oraz przymusowej restrukturyzacji*, Ministerstwo Finansów, Komisja Prawnicza, Warszawa.

Rosengren, E.S.; Peek, J. (1999). *Will Legislated Early Intervention Prevent the Next Banking Crisis?* Federal Reserve Bank of Boston, vol. 5, September.

Sharma, M. (2011). *A Study of Bank Failure Resolution*, Indian Institute of Management, PGDM, October.

Tarr, D. (2010). *Why Too Big to Fail is a Myth*, New Economic School, Moscow, July.

Thies, C.F.; Gerlowski, D.A. (1988). *Deposit Insurance: A History of Failure*, Cato Journal, 8, Cato Institute.

3

Development of Deposit Guarantee Schemes and Their Role in the Financial Safety Net

3.1   Introduction

This chapter introduces the subject of deposit guarantee scheme development. It commences with a thorough summary of extensive studies in chosen countries. This, in turn, allowed for the presentation of deposit guarantee scheme data, as well as the distinction of chosen deposit insurance agency differences. The chapter characterizes the process of deposit insurance agency establishment in the world, with special focus on EU member states. The chapter introduces a new classification of deposit guarantee schemes, which includes historical shapes of given institutions, as well as their postcrisis forms, which have not been, thus far, described in literature. Further on, the chapter presents an analysis of key deposit guarantee scheme characteristics as seen through the prism of their evolution in the EU financial safety net. The last part of the chapter introduces the history of deposit guarantee scheme development against EU regulations, which determined the shape of the above institutions in the union.

© The Author(s) 2017   29
J. Kerlin, *The Role of Deposit Guarantee Schemes as a Financial Safety Net in the European Union*, Palgrave Macmillan Studies in Banking and Financial Institutions, DOI 10.1007/978-3-319-54163-1_3

3.2 Research on the Evolution of the Role of Deposit Guarantee Schemes

Data on deposit insurance agencies were gathered in various periods of time, especially during times of crises and reform, or as a supplement to research on other entities of the financial safety net. The first databases dedicated to deposit guarantee schemes were created at the beginning of the 1990s. It was not until the global financial crisis of the years 2007–09 that actions regarding deposit guarantee schemes' funds have been aimed at collating all of the system's characteristics into one, global perspective. The conducted studies focused on differentiating deposit insurance agencies both globally and in specific country groups—especially the EU (due to its harmonized legal standards), and a collective of Asian countries.

The most important comparative publications feature various research scopes:

– 15 world countries (Talley and Mas 1990),
– 47 world countries (Kyei 1995),
– 68 world countries (Garcia 1999),
– 71 world countries (Demirgüç-Kunt and Kane 2002),
– 87 world countries (Demirgüç-Kunt et al. 2005),
– 181 world countries (Demirgüç-Kunt et al. 2008),
– 27 world countries with deposit guarantee schemes that experienced financial crises (Laeven and Valencia 2013),
– 189 countries — members of the IMF and Liechtenstein (Demirgüç-Kunt et al. 2014),
– 28 European Union member states (Iwanicz-Drozdowska et al. 2015a).

The research conducted by Demirgüç-Kunt deserves special recognition, as it popularizes knowledge on global deposit guarantee schemes and belongs to the most cited in thematic literature.

In the previous decade, the process of gathering data was supported by international organizations such as IADI (Annual Surveys), the IMF (2013), and the FSB (2012), which all collect detailed information on deposit guarantee schemes. In recent years, the European Commission also carried out its own, extensive research (2004, 2010, 2011a). It is worth noting that studies may be distinguished into those that analyze the specificity of elements of the financial safety net of countries where schemes are instated, and those where a single deposit insurance agency of a given country is tested, but several others may also be existent (see Table A.1 in Annex I). The fact that the IMF recently incorporated into its regular works the research on deposit guarantee scheme fulfillment of rules presented in the Core Principles for Effective Deposit Insurance Systems (carried out in Malaysia, Uruguay, Poland, Albania, Moldova, Bosnia and Herzegovina, and Montenegro) is an important sign of the growing significance of the topic.

The effects of data synthesis of various studies reveal that—as of the end of 2015—formal, *explicite*-type deposit guarantee schemes were operational in 120 countries of the world (see Table A.1 in Annex I). Comprehensive studies promote the systematization of knowledge and allow for a global comparison, necessary for the determination of various roles of international deposit guarantee schemes. Thanks to the abovementioned research, it is possible to perform an analysis of the evolving functions of deposit guarantee schemes all over the world, along with their respective management institutions. Databases provide historical information on the years deposit guarantee schemes were instated, their guarantee levels, as well as their accumulated *ex ante* funds. Therefore, there is no need to renew or replicate them in regard to previous solutions, for they successfully serve the needs of the analyses carried out in the following book.

3.3 Creation of Deposit Guarantee Schemes

3.3.1 Creation of Deposit Guarantee Schemes in the World

It is crucial to indicate the broader perspective of the evolution of deposit guarantee scheme concepts. A Europocentric approach is not comprehensive enough, and initially a more global overview of the subject matter is needed. The origin of guarantee schemes must be brought to attention, because—although the idea was incorporated by

European legislature in later years—it was subject to other development processes than in the United States.

Despite the extensiveness of thematic literature, researchers have not thus far agreed on when, in fact, was the first formalized guarantee scheme created. A commonly acknowledged date of birth of deposit guarantee scheme concept is, roughly, the year 1934, when the first public deposit insurance agency in the United States was established (Diamond and Dybvig 1986). Yet, after a thorough study of the subject matter, it becomes apparent that the concept of deposit guarantee in banks was known much earlier.

In the United States, the phenomenon of bank insolvency was not known until the year 1809. It was then that the country's first bank— Farmers Bank of Gloucester—declared bankruptcy. Until then, the predominant conviction was that if a bank fulfilled the prerequisites necessary to provide services in the United States, then the return of deposited funds was also guaranteed. At the time, state licensing criteria, though relatively liberal, were perceived as a sufficient protection measure of depositors' interest (Carter 1955, p. 113). In the years of the so-called Free Banking Era (1837–62), banks existed on the basis of state regulations only. As an effect, reserve requirements were inconsistent, and the lack of supervision caused the insolvency of many banks.

In order to avoid severe consequences of bankruptcy of banks, a private initiative of New England banks, Suffolk, was created in 1820 as the first financial liquidity support system for commercial banks. Its primary goal was to protect banks from runs. The expansion and evolvement of these activities took place nine years later. In 1829, the Safety Fund Act was passed as a starting point for deposit guarantee state regulations (Chaddock 1910). In light of the enactment, all New York state banks were obliged to maintain the liquidity of reserves at a level corresponding to 0.5–3 per cent of their equity capital, as a form of securing funds needed to carry out deposit payouts in case of insolvency of a different bank. In later years, the solution was copied and introduced by other American states, but without the introduction of maximum guarantee levels. Similar regulations were also introduced in further states (Vermont, Indiana, Michigan, Ohio, Iowa). Eventually, after the struggles of 1837 and 1842, when bank crises took place, state systems ceased their existence in 1866. This was caused by the formal and legal shift of granting banking licenses from state to federal competences, thus exempting banks from state authority (Holdsworth 1971, pp. 23–26).

In the years 1886–1933, the United States Congress was presented with 150 proposals of legal deposit guarantee regulation. In the year 1907 as many as 30 projects were submitted as a result of multiple events of bank panic, followed by 20 in the crisis year of 1931 (Holdsworth 1971, pp. 23–26). The proposals of a nationwide deposit protection program were as follows:

– 118 assumed the constitution of a joint, nationwide deposit guarantee scheme,
– 22 assumed the assurance of government guarantee for deposits in banks,
– 10 assumed the purchasing of government catastrophic bonds by banks, as a means of depositor claims' settlement guarantee in case of bankruptcy of a bank (bonds would not be purchased in such a situation, or purchased only partially).

Neither of the propositions presented above gained the approval of the Congress until the Great Depression of 1929–33—a time that marked the beginning of a new, more contemporary era of deposit guarantee schemes' development. In one of his first speeches as President of the United States, F.D. Roosevelt, who took office at that tumultuous period in American history, stated that: "After all, there is an element in the readjustment of our financial system more important than currency, more important than gold, and that is the confidence of the people themselves". Due to sufficient political support, a few months later, a deposit guarantee enactment was passed, and the first nationwide deposit guarantee scheme was established and started operation from the beginning of 1934 (Grafton 1999, p. 38). Taking the above into consideration, it may be stated that the first cross-country, joint deposit guarantee scheme was established in the United States and—for a significant period of time—was the only institution of the type in the world. Still, some researchers indicate a different date. For instance, a series of institutional changes carried out in Czechoslovakia in 1920 are often brought up as an example of a scheme established 14 years ahead of its American counterpart (Garcia 2000, p. 5; Litan 1997, p. 26).

A second phase of deposit guarantee schemes' development cannot be acknowledged until many years later, namely 1961–71, when new systems were set up in various parts of the globe. The process took place primarily in developed countries such as Canada, Japan, and West Germany, but also, for instance, in India. These countries derived inspiration for their respectful systems from the American experience.

The third phase started when another rise in deposit guarantee scheme establishment took place within the seven years of 1974–80. It may be stated that the process was dominated by spontaneous system creation, mainly in European countries such as Spain, Belgium, the Netherlands, and Austria, which all followed the path of predecessors in the field. Argentina was a pioneer country in Latin America, with the first up-and-running deposit scheme in the region.

After a two-year break, in the years 1983–89, a fourth phase took place. Similarly to previous times, it was characterized by an influx of deposit insurance agencies' establishment. At the time, they were already popular not only in Europe and North America, but also in Africa.

The fifth and most intensive deposit guarantee schemes' development and establishment phase took place between the years 1991 and 2006. To a significant extent, it was a period of implementing common, pan-European deposit guarantee legislature harmonization solutions, and a time when regulators worldwide showed interest in the development of the financial safety net. It seems that during this period, the number of countries with the potential of creating a functioning deposit guarantee scheme came to an end. In the last years of the mentioned phase, between 2004 and 2006, new systems were created seldom, mainly in Asian countries that adjusted their national financial regulations to global standards. The systems established in the region came to life mainly due to the efforts of IADI, the World Bank, and the IMF, who all popularized the concept of deposit guarantee systems. The global financial crisis gave rise to a new stage of deposit insurance agency establishment and brought time of reform.

The last phase of the years 2007–15 featured another event of significant rise of deposit guarantee schemes worldwide—most probably, an effect of the global financial crisis. The process took place mainly in developing countries, but also in Australia, where—thus far—deposit guarantee schemes were seen primarily through the prism of their disadvantages. Specific data in this regard are shown in Figure A.1 in Annex I, and the influx of countries with operating deposit guarantee systems (divided into groups representing various development levels) is expressed in Fig. 3.1.

Apart from countries where schemes are already existent, a group that expresses its interest in the establishment of a deposit guarantee scheme may also be indicated. According to IADI methodology, they can be divided into two subcategories:

- countries that started legislature preparations in order to establish an *explicite* type of deposit guarantee scheme,
- countries that show interest in building the system, but without the initiation of specific preparation works.

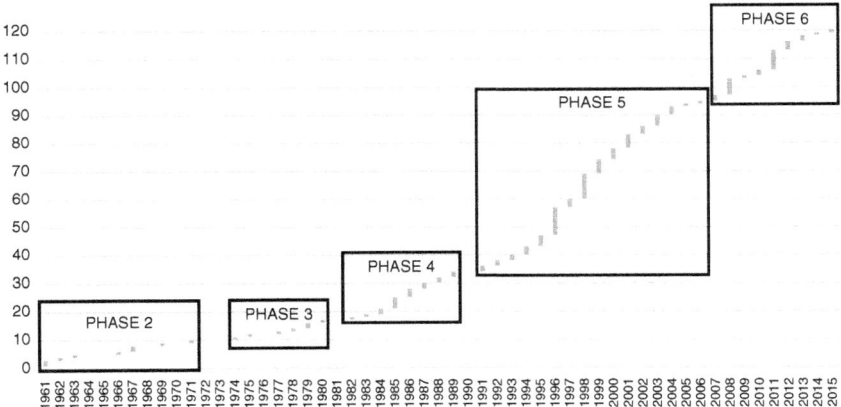

Fig. 3.1 Rise of deposit guarantee schemes in the years 1961–2015 and their division into establishment phases

(For the sake of clarity, the first phase, which took place in the year 1934 only, was omitted. *Source*: Figure prepared by the author on the basis of data derived from IADI (2014a), Demirgüç-Kunt et al. (2014), and own research)

The first subcategory, where the system is currently under construction, includes countries such as Costa Rica, Mauritius, Mozambique, Syria, Turks Islands and Caicos (an overseas territory of Great Britain), and Zambia. According to IADI data from 2014, it may be expected that the countries listed above will have a fully operational system within three years. Still, the organization's information is not complete, as it does not take into consideration the political situation in Syria, and does not recognize that in mid-2016, relevant efforts to create a deposit guarantee scheme were undertaken in China (Linklaters 2015).

The second group, constituted by 29 countries, is a larger collective of entities interested in the formation of a system, but without any specific measures that would have triggered the process. Here, it is worth mentioning several countries of the group that are especially important for world economics: Iran, Israel, Cambodia, Pakistan, and the United Arab Emirates, among others.

Apart from the above mentioned, a group of countries that clearly do not wish to create a formal deposit guarantee system may also be derived. The most prominent among the states are New Zealand and Saudi Arabia. The common argumentation against creating a system in the respective countries is the lack of national banks (New Zealand) and a strong, broad supervisory authority toward financial institutions, with limited significance of courts, and the influence of religion on Islamic banking (Saudi Arabia). Still, the last mentioned group of countries remains a minority (FSB 2014).

As a conclusion, it may be generally said that the historical analysis of the times of scheme establishment shows reoccurring surges since 1961 onward. These influx periods were either triggered (or maintained) by inner or outer shocks. Researchers most frequently refer to bank crises that take place in one country at a time (for instance, Spain or Sweden), but also mention the Tequila crisis in Latin America, the Asian financial crisis, or the political system transformation in Europe in the 1990s, as well as the recent global financial crisis. Most often, this leads to the formulation of the thesis that systems were usually established in times of financial turmoil. Such an assumption does not find clear confirmation in thematic literature (Laeven and Valencia 2013; Rogoff 2009), therefore it would be recommended that additional arguments explaining deposit guarantee scheme creation be sought for. It seems that these may include such events as the natural development of the financial market and the convergence of solutions of neighboring countries.

3.3.2 Creation of Deposit Guarantee Schemes in the European Union

The evolvement of deposit insurance agencies in the EU took place in various paces. The history of deposit guarantee schemes in member states is not very extensive. The first institutionalized schemes in the EU were established in two countries—a private deposit insurance agency in the Federal Republic of Germany (1966) and a public institution in Finland (1969). They were quickly followed by countries such as Belgium (1974), Spain (1977), Austria (1979), the Netherlands (1979), Great Britain (1979), and France (1980). The beginning of the 1980s finalized the period of spontaneous deposit guarantee scheme establishment in the member states.

The next surge in creating deposit guarantee schemes in countries of today's EU took place by the end of the 1980s, when Denmark, Italy, and Ireland established their respective systems. The following years were a time of deposit insurance agency creation in countries that have gone through political system transformation. The first deposit guarantee scheme to be instated in Central and Eastern Europe was the Hungarian deposit insurance agency (1993), followed by the Czech, Polish, and Croatian systems in 1994. Lithuania, Latvia, Slovakia, and Romania followed in their steps in 1996, similarly to Bulgaria and Estonia in 1998. Also, Greece (1995) and Sweden, after the crisis (1996), created their guarantee schemes, though with slight delay in relation to other EU member states. What is more, Germany carried out a revision of its scheme in 1998 and—as an effect—changed its character from optional to obligatory, adjusting it to the newly enacted directive. For many years, the German system was subject to multiple reforms and the segmentation into a greater number of both facultative and obligatory insurance agencies. The last countries to establish their deposit guarantee schemes were Cyprus (2000), Slovenia (2001), and Malta (2003). In effect, such systems are currently up-and-running in all member states of the EU. It may be stated that their establishment process commenced in 1966 and ended in 2003 (Fig. 3.2).

In conclusion, it must be indicated that all EU countries have a functioning deposit insurance agency in place. Even the most recently established agencies have now been operating for over ten years.

What deserves special recognition is the fact that in some EU member states, multiple deposit insurance agencies evolved in a single country. Although the institutions constitute a unified deposit guarantee scheme, it is interiorly diversified. A specific collation of all guarantee institutions functioning in the EU is shown in Table A.2 in Annex II.

By the end of 2015, a multi-entity system was in place in four EU countries—Germany, Austria, Portugal, and Italy. Many guarantee funds have a disjunctive property range—the most common categorization is the division into types of entities. For instance, credit unions, cooperative banks, and commercial banks all have separate guarantee schemes. Most often, it is related to the various risk levels of credit institutions within the guarantee scheme, as well as lower contributions taken from limited

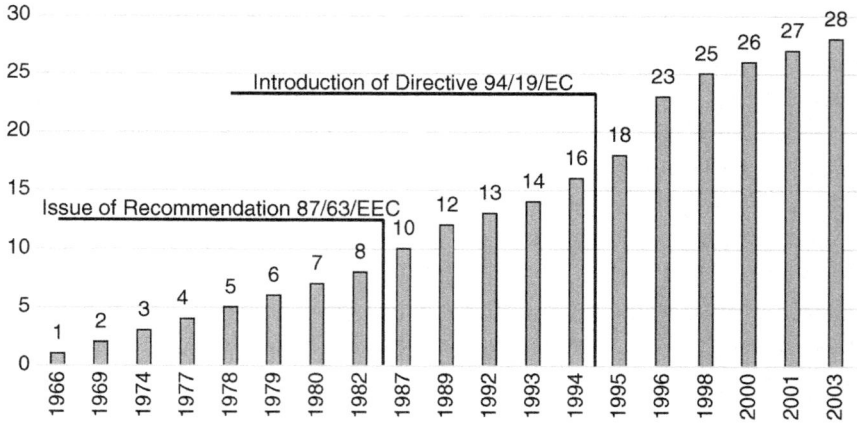

Fig. 3.2 The increase of EU member countries with a minimum of one formally acknowledged deposit guarantee scheme

Source: EC (2011a) and websites of deposit insurance agencies

liability entities. Furthermore, cooperative banks often function as members of associations and participate in the so-calledinstitutional protection schemes that support their liquidity and financial solvency, thus preventing them from bankruptcy (Miklaszewska 2014).

It is worth noting that the popularity of multi-entity systems has been steadily decreasing, and the current trend is to grant governance to a single institution. Countries that previously experienced difficulties in their financial system decided on the concentration of the scheme. Such a situation took place in the case of Cyprus, Greece, Spain, and Poland. Among the reasons behind integrating the funds into one institution was the facilitation of management of the entire scheme, as well as the concentration of guarantee funds in one place, in order to enlarge the emergency, crisis budget. In Spain, it also facilitated the restructuring of the financial sector that initially relied on fund consolidation, and later on their overtaking by banks (both types of institutions were previously protected by separate guarantee funds).

3.3.3   Creation of Deposit Guarantee Schemes Amidst Crises

While analyzing the development of deposit guarantee schemes, it is worth noticing the popular notion, that such systems are usually established during times of crises (Laeven and Valencia 2013). Therefore, a study was carried out in order to verify whether such a statement was true of EU member states. Table 3.1 displays data on countries, where deposit guarantee schemes were brought into force, including the respective periods of crises. The details on the number of schemes were derived from the merged databases of IADI and the World Bank, while the information on crisis occurrence comes from the updated database of the IMF.

The analysis reveals that, as observed by the IMF—from the 28 member states of the EU, where a deposit guarantee scheme is existent—all countries, except for Malta, noted at least one serious bank crisis. Among the 27

Table 3.1 Data on the establishment of deposit guarantee schemes and times of significant crises in EU member states

Country	Year of deposit guarantee scheme establishment	Date of joining the EEC/EU	Year of crisis commencement (according to the IMF)	Year of crisis end (according to the IMF)
Germany	1966	1957	2008	2009
Finland	1969	1995	1991	1995
Belgium	1974	1957	2008	2009
Spain	1977	1986	1977	1981
			2008	2009
Netherlands	1978	1957	2008	2009
Austria	1979	1995	2008	2008
France	1980	1957	2008	2009
Great Britain	1982	1973	1973	1975
			2007	2009
Denmark	1987	1973	2008	2009
Italy	1987	1957	2008	2009
Luxembourg	1989	1957	2008	2009
Ireland	1989	1973	2008	2009
Portugal	1992	1986	2008	2009
Hungary	1993	2004	1991	1995
			2008	2009
Czech Republic	1994	2004	1996	2000
Croatia	1994	2013	1998	1999
Greece	1995	1981	2008	2009

Poland	1995	2004	1992	1994
Bulgaria	1996	2007	1996	1997
Lithuania	1996	2004	1995	1996
Romania	1996	2007	1990	1992
Slovakia	1996	2004	1998	2002
Sweden	1996	1995	1991	1995
			2008	2009
Estonia	1998	2004	1992	1994
Latvia	1998	2004	1995	1996
			2008	2009
Cyprus	2000	2004	2013	2013
Slovenia	2001	2004	1992	1992
			2008	2009
Malta	2003	2004	–	–

According to the IMF, crisis did not take place in Malta

Source: Laeven and Valencia (2013) and author's own research

countries affected, four main phases may be acknowledged in regard deposit guarantee scheme establishment:

1) prior to the occurrence of the first bank crisis in a given country (namely, at least two years before a crisis event took place),
2) during the crisis (exactly at the time of the event),
3) precrisis and postcrisis circumstances (up to two years before and after the event),
4) after the first or subsequent crisis in a given country (after two years from the most recent crisis had already passed).

The results of the simplified analysis presented above indicate as follows: the first group—where a deposit guarantee scheme was existent at least two years prior to the outbreak of the crisis—comprises 14 countries; the second group—where the system was constituted during the crisis—is made of four countries (Spain, Hungary, Lithuania, and Romania); the third group—where the deposit guarantee scheme was created directly before or after the crisis—consists of five countries (Czech Republic, Poland, Slovakia, Sweden, and Latvia). Finally, the fourth group—where countries did not establish a deposit guarantee scheme until two or more years after the crisis—has four countries (Great Britain, Romania, Estonia, and Slovenia). Therefore, well over half of EU member states, where the crisis took place, had a deposit guarantee scheme in place either several years before its commencement or significantly after it had ended. At the same time, ten other countries instated their respective deposit guarantee schemes, immediately before, during, or after the crisis. Hence, it seems that it may not be unilaterally stated that deposit guarantee schemes in the EU were created in response to crisis events. Although in the case of several countries it was, in fact, the case, it was not a dominant practice, and the key role shall rather be attributed to Directive 94/19/EC, as well as the efforts of particular countries striving for the accession to the EU, where officially recognized deposit guarantee is compulsory. Still, it seems that in countries where the schemes are operational, they are reformed during periods of crisis, and—as an effect—evolve dynamically.

3.4 Development of Deposit Guarantee Schemes

The analyses provided in the previous section of the book allow for the classification of the concepts that dominated in respective phases, as well as the models of deposit insurance agencies adopted by particular countries, to separate phases of deposit guarantee scheme development.

Before we carry on to the description of the time key concepts were formulated in, it is worth referring to the data on the number of publications on deposit guarantee schemes, presented in Fig. 3.3. The most prominent amount of papers has been written during two phases—the fourth and fifth. It must be underlined that in the more concise period of the years 2007–12, much has been published on deposit guarantee schemes, and the overall dynamic of research was significantly higher.

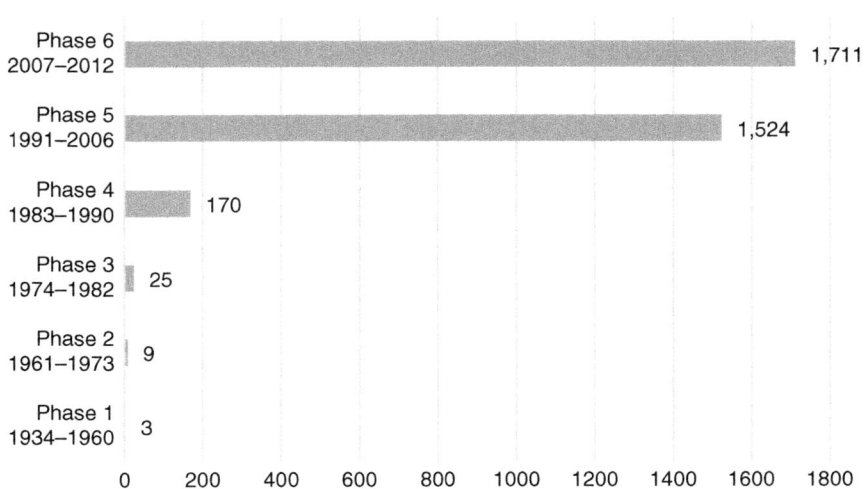

Fig. 3.3 Number of publications on deposit guarantee schemes during particular phases

(Specified phases correspond to the phases of deposit guarantee scheme development, previously identified in Section 3.3.1. *Source*: Figure prepared by the author on the basis of IADI (2012d))

Altogether, the first and second phases lasted from the 1930s till the end of the year 1973. Deposit guarantee schemes were of secondary interest to finance and economy researchers. Such an occurrence does not come as a surprise, for only ten countries had a scheme in operation throughout those years. The most discussed topics on the subject matter referred to the validity of bringing the institutions to life (Taggart and Jennings 1934, pp. 508–516). Up until the mid-nineteenth century, the view that guarantee schemes should exist locally and be ruled by a private entity (as in bank representatives) was prevalent in the United States. The opinion was revised by the fiasco of guarantee schemes in the United States, and verified by the effects of the great crisis that took place at the time. Since then, up until the first years of the 1970s, studies on the aims of system functioning and establishing were scarcely published. The publications that did speak of the subject perceived them through the prism of the utility of the few existent institutions. For the authors, it was indisputable that public management must be impaneled in the deposit guarantee scheme (which, as time showed, was the only form prevalent in the long run in times of bankruptcy in the United States), along with public, emergency funding (Fed 1950). Cooperation with the supervisor was also named as an important element, but introduced in a very limited scope. The subsequent years of uninterrupted deposit guarantee scheme functioning in the United States, and the modest popularity of the systems worldwide, simply strengthened researchers' convictions. In fact, there were few events that would provide the evidence needed for the redefinition of the *status quo* and provoke the birthing of new conceptions (Kreps and Wacht 1971, pp. 605–613).

The third contractual period, between 1974 and 1982, caused the softening of rhetoric regarding regulations toward banks. Researchers postulated the loosening of prudential regulations and granting more freedom to banks, also in regard to the possibility of increasing the risk of their functioning (Horvitz 1975, pp. 589–601). The popularity of deposit guarantee schemes increased, and by the end of the time period, seven additional countries have instated their respective deposit insurance agencies. The interest in verifying establishment legitimacy weakened and was replaced by other thematic concerns. For instance, the relation of bank equity capital and deposit guarantee funding levels provided by deposit guarantee schemes' was analyzed instead (Sharpe 1977; Buser et al. 1981, pp. 51–60). Alternative deposit insurance methods were also sought for—other than establishing a deposit insurance agency. The necessity of proper funding of the scheme was also noticed as a crucial condition for the payout procedures (Bryant 1980). Mainstream researchers called for remaining with the narrow authority scopes for the schemes, preferably in the paybox model (agency is responsible for the transfer of funds for depositors in case the guarantee requirements are fulfilled). Such solutions were most often instated in this particular phase. Research also revealed that deposit insurers function in a specific operational environment, which is also responsible for providing external conditions for the effectiveness of deposit guarantee schemes. Examples include, among others, the quality of regulations, timeliness of supervisory decisions, and the politics of liquidity support, provided by the central bank. By the end of the phase, first accusations toward deposit guarantee schemes concerning the lack of their effectiveness came to light.

They were continued throughout the fourth phase in the years 1983–90, despite it also being a period of new deposit guarantee schemes' rise—as many as 17 countries decided on their establishment during that time. The critics of the newly instated systems inclined that they do not, in fact, serve the depositors, but are means of additional power for governments that seek for protection of their political position in case of a financial institution's insolvency. Even though less than 20 countries with a guarantee scheme were examined, the dominant trend was to prove the systems' ineffectiveness and lack of true protection in the case of bank panic (Pennacchi 1984, pp. 17–84). The multi-thread studies of deposit insurance agencies were built upon the establishment of new guarantee schemes. Yet, the prevalent outlook was critical and unfavorable of systems (Furlong 1984, pp. 31–38). Temptation of abuse, increase of bank risks, weakening of the market discipline, and triggering the principal-agent problem (Thomson 1986a, b) were all named as disadvantageous effects of the creation of deposit insurance agencies. The need for reform was also inclined in the shape of various solutions that were often brought into force. Among them were the loosening of prudential norms (without the deposit guarantee scheme reforms), the introduction of the so-called private system management by banks (due to the fact that public entities are subject to political pressure), and the idea of *ex post* financing of the system. At the same time, other researchers postulated the tightening of cooperation between the central bank and supervisor (Kane 1989). Critics pointed out that the functioning of the scheme became bureaucratized throughout the years, was too costly, and could, in fact, have been financed publicly. Overall, the period may be summarized as a time of continuation of the critical approach toward deposit guarantee schemes and the need of limiting their role, while new institutions with much less authority were simultaneously brought to life. During the phase, it was stated that new institutions may be established, but—if temptation of abuse was properly eradicated—the scheme could provide more profits for the economy.

The fifth phase of deposit guarantee scheme development may be accredited to the years 1991–2006. During this relatively short period, deposit insurance agencies were established in as many as 63 countries worldwide. Although the years were characterized by the creation of new systems, the process was accredited to the global political transformations by various solutions and specific countries (Garcia 1996). It is also when the most dynamic stratification of deposit guarantee scheme authority and significant concepts took place, as well as the time of creation of a whole variety of diversified institutions (Beck 2004; Blinder and Wescott 2001). Side effects of deposit guarantee schemes were also broadly criticized during this period—among them, the often-mentioned moral hazard (Wheelock and Wilson 1993). The government decided that, rather than factual, formal and legal protection of the depositor (on the basis of promise) was important. Therefore, not much thought was given to potential impact of the protection scope on the national budget or bank finances. A two-level system model, consisting of depositor protection (first level) and financial stability protection (second level), was constituted (Goodhart and Schoenmaker 2006). It took on various forms—from specific aiding functions (for example, in the case of Poland), to full supervisory and controlling authorities, among them the possibility of performing receivership supervisory functions, as in the case of the United States (when the existence of synergy between the operations of a deposit insurance agency, liquidator, or the forced administrator had been inclined).

Before the characteristics of the sixth phase are presented, it is worth noting that in previous years, the concept of deposit guarantee did no longer provoke emotions as strong as initially. In most countries worldwide, respective schemes had already been constituted, the topic of negative effects had run out, and—as it seemed—a safe *status quo* was preserved. It was not until the sixth phase, which started in 2007, that the dynamic change in the approach toward deposit guarantee schemes took place. In the few years of 2007–14, deposit insurance agencies have been established in 23 countries. For the first time in over a hundred years, bank panic took place in Great Britain. It became the direct reason behind immediate liquidations of coinsurance in respective systems. The increase of guarantee levels was also postulated as a response to the fact that existent levels were defined relatively long ago. In effect, reforms in the EU and United States were carried out. Still, they were only advisory and intervention actions, calculated for the rapid achievement of expected results. During the crisis, it was revealed that the systems operating in Europe were designed in a procyclical manner. This was accredited to the fact that they deepened the encumbrance of the banking sector during times of financial crisis (the necessity of collecting contributions) and were weakly financed and incapable of keeping up to its challenges.

Since, the key role of deposit insurance agencies in the maintaining of depositor trusts has been accredited, and their inclusion in crisis management, as well as strengthening their position in the financial safety net, postulated. The need to communicate and express the value of proper information exchange with the depositor, in an innovative manner, was also noted. The changes and application of *ex ante* system funding mode were also postulated, as only recapitalized deposit guarantee schemes are capable of working effectively in times of financial turmoil.

Since 2011, studies and legislative research intensified in the topic—with varying results. The dynamic development of the role and authority of deposit insurance agencies throughout the world was most apparent, especially in the case of the United States and Asia. The EU also introduced their respective systems into crisis management practices, leaving, to a certain point, the choice of participating in resolution to specific countries. This had been provided by new directives BRR 2014/ 59/EU and DGS 2014/49/EU. The main focus regarding the functioning of the system was the strengthening of the financial stability and the necessity of participating of the scheme in the financial safety net (Tomasic 2011).

3.5   Key Construction Elements of Deposit Guarantee Schemes

Due to the systematic growth of deposit guarantee schemes (though characterized by leaps), several key characteristics that strengthen the position of deposit insurance agencies in the financial safety net have become apparent. These include the authority scope (mandate), operating capability (related to the number of employees and expenses—own budget), position in the financial safety net, and the financial potential (amount of funds collected for the sake of payouts). The proper collation of all of the characteristics above has an effect on the position of guarantee schemes in national financial safety nets.

3.5.1 Mandate

For a long time, the role of deposit guarantee schemes varied, depending on the scope of their competences. Initially, guarantee insurers functioned as payment agencies (at the beginning of system creation in the twentieth century), but, in time, gained more and more authority and became prominent members of the financial safety net, with competences broad enough to participate in resolution. On the basis of data analysis, deposit guarantee schemes worldwide may be divided into groups (generations) of deposit insurance agencies either in a certain development phase or functioning according to a similar pattern. Model representatives of all groups are present in many countries of the world.

The first and second generations of schemes (presented in Table 3.2) are slowly disappearing in the midst of postcrisis reality, where *implicite* or *explicite* guarantee types are no longer valid. Schemes that have a more complex structure, and are responsible not only for payout of lost deposits, but are also engaged in helping and preventing the fulfillment of guarantee requirements by banks (bankruptcy), have been gaining importance.

Currently, models with extended authority are most popular in the world —namely, *paybox* plus (fourth generation). Their popularity has become clearly distinguished after the crisis and inclines that decision makers acknowledge the broader role of the institutions. In light of current reforms, models with the widest possible authorization that combine traditional deposit guarantee roles with resolution authority are also steadily becoming more popular. The percentage of changes in deposit guarantee scheme mandate worldwide is presented in Fig. 3.4, which expresses the type of authorization as specified in the traditional FSB classification.

IADI data from the end of 2012 provides information on how, in a four-year term, the participation of two broader mandates, *paybox plus* and *risk minimizer*, grew to power. At the same time, the *paybox* model kept loosing its position. Such a trend indicates that most countries have been providing more decision-making authority to their respective deposit insurance agencies through inviting them to participate in crisis management. This procedure is also mimicked by states, where new schemes are currently being established (for instance, African countries).

Still, the situation in the EU in this regard is atypical. Comprehensive, comparative data on member states and the rest of chosen world countries have been presented in Fig. 3.5. Paybox model is present in 29 per cent of non-EU countries, in comparison to 50 per cent of union member states. Similarly, there are few schemes with broad authority in the EU (such as loss of risk minimizer), accounting for only 7 per cent of all schemes, in comparison to 29 per cent worldwide. There are only two systems of the type, in Spain and France. It is also worth noting that resolution authority in Spain is distributed among various institutions and does not belong solely to the national deposit insurance agency.

Table 3.2 Deposit guarantee scheme generations (as at the end of 2015)

Generation	Type	Characteristics	Examples
I	Initial (facultative, private schemes)	Bottom-up initiatives creating deposit guarantee schemes by banks of various types of fund utilization authority (liquidity assistance, financing of takeovers, deposit payout)	Nineteenth-century United States, part of private systems existent in Germany and Austria
II	Public *implicite* guarantee	Informal protection schemes, functioning solely as state promise to pay out funds from an insolvent entity, without the preelection of insurance conditions	Saudi Arabia, New Zealand
III	*Paybox*	Scheme responsible solely for the payout of guaranteed funds. Once guarantee requirements are met, it is responsible for the collection of necessary funds and their potential transfer to depositors	Austria and Germany (official systems), Switzerland, Netherlands, Slovenia
IV	*Paybox plus*	Scheme responsible for the payout of guaranteed funds. It holds additional functions. Capable of providing proper control of data on depositors, gathered in bank systems, tests extreme circumstances, and supports several resolution processes in the sector, without having clear decision-making authorization	Argentina, Brazil, Great Britain

Table 3.2 (continued)

Generation	Type	Characteristics	Examples
V	*Loss minimizer*	Scheme responsible for the payout of guaranteed funds. Actively engaged in the orderly resolution or liquidation of financial institutions. Its representatives are members of entities responsible for decisions on the course of the processes	Canada, France, Indonesia, Japan, Mexico, Turkey
VI	*Risk minimizer—full resolution authority*	Scheme with significant financial sector risk minimizing functions, including resolution instruments and authority of carrying out prudential supervision. Equipped with strong administrative powers. It is properly financed, therefore can strongly support funding procedures	United States, South Korea

Source: Author's own research

Figure 3.5 indicates that paybox and paybox plus models are dominant in the EU. The situation is likely to change once the DGS Directive that, to a certain degree, introduces deposit guarantee schemes into resolution procedures will be fully implemented. Thus, granting broader authority to deposit insurance agencies that will be obliged to participate in resolution may be expected.

Tables A.3 in Annex III presents precise data regarding mandate of schemes in the EU, as well as a description of their additional roles apart from deposit payout.

In conclusion to the presentation of deposit insurance agency competences in the EU, and the comparison to global practices in this

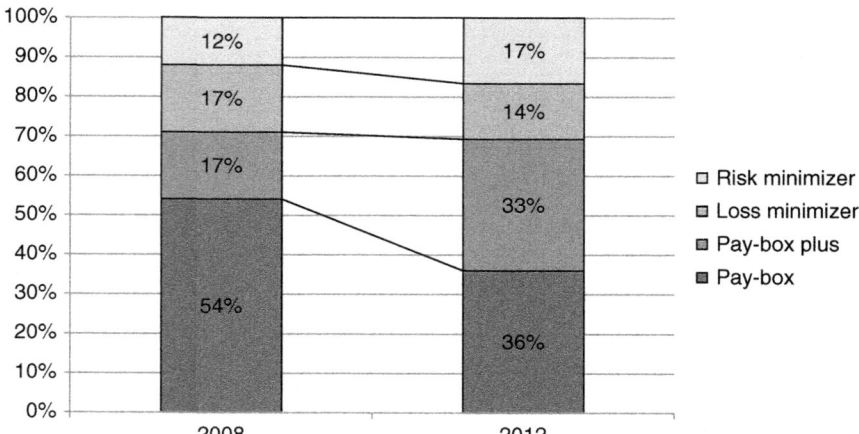

Fig. 3.4 Changes in deposit guarantee scheme mandate
(42 institutions provided data in 2008, compared to 78 deposit insurance agencies in 2012. *Source:* IADI (2008a, 2013))

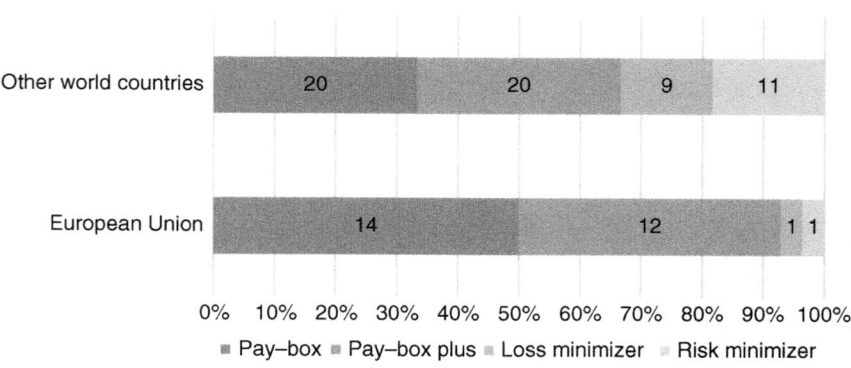

Fig. 3.5 Comparison of number of deposit insurance agencies in regard to the diversification of their mandate authority (data as of the end of 2012)
(28 EU member states and 60 countries worldwide. *Source:* IADI (2013) and author's own research)

regard, several key findings may be named. Firstly, EU schemes operate in a more limited model than their counterparts in other parts of the world. It is most often a result of a different financial safety net structure in member states that initially, for decades, were reliant on the activities of central banks, and later an integrated supervision of a separate entity. Secondly, deposit insurance agencies in the EU were not successful in achieving a prominent role, as in the case of respective institutions in non-European countries, for example the United States, Japan, South Korea, and Canada. This may be accredited to the relatively strict first regulation regarding deposit insurance agencies operating in the paybox model in the EU (Directive 94/19/EC). Also, the rather insignificant number of bank insolvencies caused the marginalization of the given institutions in the EU financial safety net.

3.5.2 Operational Capability

Personnel potential and the size of an annual budget of a deposit insurance agency influence the way it is perceived as a member of the financial safety net. Data analysis regarding specific member states delivers interesting results that leave room for interpretation. Still, the available information refers to the relatively distant years 2007–08. They have been utilized due to their completeness and the fact that they cover nearly all EU countries. The unavailability of current data is an effect of the lack of response on behalf of deposit insurance agencies that do not wish to provide details (IADI 2013). Tables A.4 in Annex III presents comprehensive data.

First and foremost, it must be inclined that deposit insurance agencies are not extensively staffed. The most numerous personnel (that is, employees with a full-time contract) may be encountered in Great Britain, Germany, and Poland. Yet, it is worth mentioning that there are several schemes in the EU that do not have a single staff member hired permanently to administer such a system. An institution model of five or less employees is popular (13 countries). It is therefore justified to say that a scheme comprised of five members only cannot possibly perform an important role within the financial safety net. The personnel count in the so-called new EU countries was 13 employees, in comparison to 24 in the countries of the old EU. Overall, the union's average count was 18 employees, whereas in the United States itself, by the end of 2012, the number was nearly 8,800. Japan accounted for 372 employees, and South Korea for 818 (IADI 2013). Cross-country comparisons in regard to staffing of deposit insurance agencies in the EU are straitened due to diversification of banking sector size across the union, the varying number of credit institutions, and the institutional specificity of the financial safety net. Also, an additional aspect is the performance of traditional deposit insurance agency roles by other members of the financial safety net. France is an example of the above situation, with its insurance agency of four members that may be supported, upon demand, by staff provided by the supervisor. The personnel count range is presented in Fig. 3.6.

It is difficult to clearly evaluate how personnel potential impacts the significance of the institution in the financial safety net, yet the relation between staffing and institutional authority is undoubtedly apparent. Other world countries that may be compared to the EU in regard to their respective schemes (the previously mentioned United States, Japan, and Canada) have a much bigger personnel count in their institutions and, in effect, have more responsibility in the financial safety net.

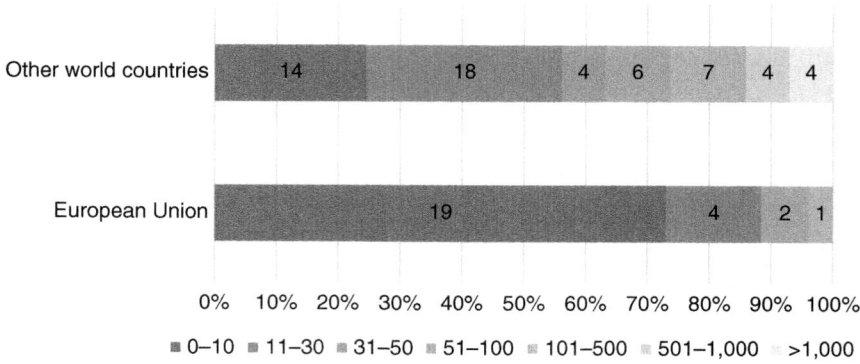

Fig. 3.6 Division of deposit insurance agencies on the basis of their full-time personnel count (as of the end of 2012)

(26 EU member states (except for Croatia and Ireland) and 57 world countries. *Source*: IADI (2013) and author's own research)

Expenses of specific deposit insurance agencies are also diversified. Detailed information is presented in Fig. 3.7. It must be noted that the numbers shown below do not include payout of funds to depositors and are only administrative costs of maintaining the institution. Usually, they are proportionate to the number of employees in a given insurance agency. What is more, although the EU is comprised mainly of highly developed countries and is characterized with high salary levels, they represent some of the institutions with the lowest operational costs. Hence, the significance of these institutions within the financial safety net of the EU is proportionally smaller than in other parts of the world—especially, the previously mentioned United States and Japan.

It is important to notice that there is not a single EU institution among the group of funds that represent the highest global expenditure—that is, above €10 million.

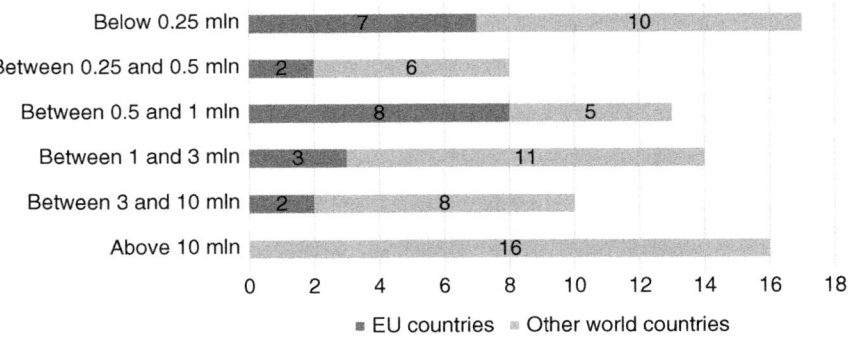

Fig. 3.7 Comparison of annual expenditure of deposit insurance companies in chosen countries of the world and EU member states by the end of 2012 (data expressed in millions of euros)

(22 EU member states and 56 other world countries. Values that fall into certain ranges are worth no less than the range's minimum numeral limit, but less than their maximum limit. For instance, if a value is equal to 0.5 M, it will fall into the range of 0.5–1 M, not 0.25–0.5 M. *Source*: EC (2006b, 2011a), IADI (2008a, 2013), and author's own research)

3.5.3 Position in Financial Safety Net

It is necessary to underline that in the EU the authority of deposit guarantee schemes was not assigned to one body, and member states are at liberty to shape their own national financial safety nets. Previously, a popular trend was to transfer supervisory powers to entities outside the central bank and to integrate supervision altogether (Schoenmaker and Oosterloo 2006). Although EU countries chose different deposit insurance agency establishment strategies, their dominant solution was to grant the above authority to a separate, public entity. In practice, the institution is most often appointed through a legislative decision and, to a certain degree, serves in effect as an emanation of the state and functions as an administrative organ. Also, a popular solution—though seemingly inherited through historical bonds—is the creation of a deposit insurance agency in the form of a commercial law company or association. Leaving the above authority within the competences of the central bank and assigning a supervisor on the financial market is a less common solution. An extremely rare case is the Swedish solution, where deposit guarantee scheme operates in a single agenda in the competences of the Ministry of Finance (*Riksgälden*). Detailed information on the EU is as follows:

- A separate public entity (14): Belgium Bulgaria, Croatia, Czech Republic, Denmark, Estonia, Spain, Lithuania, Poland, Portugal, Romania, Slovakia, Hungary, and Great Britain
- A separate private entity (6): Austria, Finland, Greece, Luxembourg, and Germany
- Part of the central bank (5): Cyprus, Netherlands, Ireland, Slovenia, and Italy
- Part of financial market supervisor (2): Latvia and Malta
- Ministry of Finance Agenda (1): Sweden.

It must be noted that the lack of establishment of an independent entity (with a separate fund and maintenance practices) most often results in the marginalization of deposit guarantee functions and the underestimation of its role as of merely subsidiary nature. Due to the variety of research methodology, it is difficult to compare the results of European Commission studies with the broader IADI research regarding the EU. The latter organization does not differentiate between public and private entities and assigns them to the same category. In an IADI survey (2013) regarding the legal form of deposit insurance agency operation, 61 answers have been received from non-EU countries. It is not known, though, how many among them are public, and how many are privately held. The EU specifies the two categories, which are crucial for the further results expressed in the following book. In chosen world countries, 74 per cent of deposit guarantee schemes exist in a separate institution (of either public or private legal character), 11 per cent are part of the central bank, 5 per cent lie in the competence of the supervisor, and the remaining 10 per cent represent other solutions. The results of EU member countries are similar to those of global nature: 71 per cent of deposit insurance agencies are a separate entity, 18 per cent work within global bank structures, and 11 per cent function in different solutions (hence, lie either in the competence of the supervisor, or the respective Ministry of Finance).

3.6 The Evolution of Regulatory and Legal Framework on Deposit Guarantee Schemes in the European Union

In order to introduce the analysis of the effectiveness of deposit guarantee schemes, apart from the research of the solutions themselves, it is necessary that current legislature and regulation history be referred to. In fact, the two topics have always been the basis of debate on the development of the institutions mentioned above. The relatively apparent discrepancy of deposit guarantee schemes in the EU and the rest of the world is a derivative of European legislature and the history of its regulations.

It must be noted that deposit insurance agencies functioning in the EU are currently regulated on two levels. The first is the European level (directive), second—national (country legislature). It has not been decided to control deposit guarantee scheme functioning through the enactment of a regulation that would cause the direct obligation of all member states to abide to unified norms.

The time of establishment of existent European regulations and their amendments may be divided into two phases: precrisis and postcrisis. Such a division is also referred to in the following section. EU regulations were a crucial, dominant element for the creation of officially acknowledged deposit insurance agencies in the union (all countries of the so-called new EU, prior to the accession to the union, already had such a scheme in place).

3.6.1 Commission Recommendation 87/63/ECC

Initially, deposit guarantee schemes evolved in a spontaneous manner—according to individual initiatives of EU countries. The first country to instate a deposit guarantee scheme was West Germany (1966). The introduced solution, created for banks, was of voluntary nature. Despite the development of the institutions in various EU countries, union-wide regulations in the topic were missing for a long time. It was not until 1986 that EU regulators decided on the provisional formalization of deposit guarantee scheme frameworks. The first voice of approval for the concept of guarantee schemes was heard during the works on the Single European Act. The support for the cause later took form in the European Commission Recommendation 87/63/EEC of 22 December 1986 concerning the introduction of deposit guarantee schemes.

In the recommendation, published toward the end of the 1980s, the necessity of deposit insurance agency existence was justified by the need of protecting the consumer (small depositor), who was the bank's client. Only in time, as a result of ongoing works, did the perspective change (Obal 2004, pp. 53–56).

The European Commission Recommendation 87/63/EEC was not legally binding and was merely of advisory nature. It expressed the desired—and supported—path of the evolvement of guarantee schemes and highlighted general advice to union members. Although it was a clear recommendation that member countries establish their respective schemes, no desired organizational forms were inclined apart from the statement, that the institution must meet basic formal requirements as follows:

- obligatory membership of all credit institutions operating in a given country,
- construction of the system in accordance with the main principle of protecting small depositors' interest,
- consent for the coexistence of several deposit insurance agencies in one country.

Despite its general character, European Commission Recommendation 87/63/EEC was the starting point for deposit guarantee scheme creation in the EU. In time, the document became the cornerstone for further deposit insurance development works.

3.6.2 Directive 94/19/EC

A few years after the Commission's recommendation was enacted, it became apparent that it did not bring the anticipated effects. The revision of deposit guarantee schemes in the EU revealed that its economical reality required reform. The development of the EU internal market that needed harmonization of legislature became the main accelerating force that drove change. The formulation of new solutions was aimed at the protection of competition, the unification of the legal situation of depositors from various member states, and granting broader operational authority to guarantee schemes. The statement was also supported by the theses presented in the ECJ Judgment in case 233/94 Germany versus Parliament and Council. It had been decided that the fundamental differences between deposit insurance agencies in EU countries limit entrepreneurship and service providing freedom. Reforms were to be performed, first and foremost, in regard to institutional structure indication and strengthening the scheme solvency and its responsibility level.

The first proposal of a directive was presented in 1992 and was eventually enacted in 1994 as Directive 94/19/EC. The process of shaping the directive had several recitals. The study of thematic literature, as well as the preamble of the above legal act, brings strong justification for the introduction of regulatory, legal norms specifically protecting bank deposits in the EU. Throughout the legal construction process, many indications and political postulates have been revealed, among them:

- the promotion of bank operations through the abolition of freedom limitations in regard to entrepreneurship and service providing,
- strengthening the stability of bank systems and depositor protection,
- providing depositors of various credit institution branches with unified protection rights,
- acknowledging that costs incurred by banks, resulting from the participation in the scheme, remain in negligible relation to the costs of bank panic and the so-called infection effect,
- agreeing that the minimum coverage level must be defined so that its level covers a high sum of deposits, but would not leave any space for abuse.

The working out of the arrangements above was the direct reason for the enactment of the directive that organized the functioning of deposit insurance agencies for nearly twenty subsequent years.

As an effect of the directive:

- it was restricted that all member states must establish a scheme (change of type of document from recommendation to a legally binding act),
- basic construction and functioning characteristics of schemes were regulated,
- the scope of scheme objectives was broadened (not only in regard to depositor protection, but also the maintaining of financial stability of the bank system),
- the membership of deposit accepting institutions within the deposit guarantee scheme became compulsory (with only very limited exceptions),

- unified regulations of bank membership in deposit guarantee schemes in a cross-border activity was defined,
- the minimum coverage level was set to €20,000,
- terms and conditions of obligatory and facultative exemptions from deposit guarantee schemes were defined,
- payment due dates of guarantee funds were unified,
- basic client-oriented, information responsibilities of banks were defined.

Throughout the works on the directive, it was stated that harmonization of the scheme must be limited solely to key deposit guarantee scheme aspects. Detailed provisions are available in other publications, but—from the perspective of the scope of the following book—three aspects are most important: its function form, financing method, and guarantee level.

First and foremost, Directive 94/19/EC obliged member states (Article 3) to establish at least one deposit guarantee scheme within its territory. Secondly, it regulated that each single depositor shall be covered with an amount of up to €20,000 (Article 7). Thirdly, the directive did not introduce an absolute condition of harmonization of financing procedures of deposit guarantee schemes. The above has been decided, because the costs of financing need to be covered by credit unions, but—on the other hand—the financial capabilities of the schemes must remain in an appropriate relation to its liabilities. Therefore, Directive 94/19/EC harmonized key scheme elements only partially, and the most important of all (financing) was left at the discretion of countries (Baka 2005).

3.6.3   Directive Overview and Amendment 2009/14/EC

Directive 94/19/EC came to life on 31 May 1994 with an implementation date by 1 July 1995. It functioned in a practically unaltered form for nearly fourteen years. During this time, only two amendments were published and were mainly of technical nature. The first of the two was implemented on 1 January 1999 and related to the change of accounting unit from ECU to Euro. The second, dated 13 April 2005, merely harmonized the topic of information obligations of the Commission toward the European Banking Committee.

The European Commission reviewed the solutions applied in the 2005 directive. The end result was the publishing of the Communication from the Commission to the European Parliament and the Council regarding the effectiveness of existent legal solutions (EC 2006a).

During the talks of the Commission, the topic of different funding amounts and methods throughout the union was among the most popular topics. Eventually, the consultation process ended without devising a clear standpoint regarding the directive changes. The *status quo* was upheld in order to avoid costly legal framework changes in light of the so-called infinitesimal economical justification for change (EC 2006a, pp. 2–4). On the other hand, the communication stated that:

> However it is the Commission's view that [...] the lack of standardised rules contribute to the inability of the supervisory safety net to function adequately in a cross-border crisis situation. The costs to the economy and the undermining of confidence in the single financial market could ultimately prove far higher than the level of investment needed to ensure satisfactory functioning of the pan-EU safety net. (EC 2006a, p. 3)

Eventually, after the crisis events, Directive 2009/14/EC amended the thus far binding Directive 94/19/EC, and:

– National authorities were obliged to work more effectively and time efficiently. The amendment inclined that state authorities need to make binding decisions in the fastest manner possible, but "in any event no later than five working days after first becoming satisfied that a credit institution has failed to repay deposits which are due and payable" (Article 1(3)).

– It was said in regard to countries that they "shall ensure that the coverage for the aggregate deposits of each depositor shall be at least €50,000 in the event of deposits being unavailable". The level of coverage was set as the minimum guaranteed value for deposits.

- It was noted that in the transitional period from 16 March 2009 to 31 December 2010, during the crisis, countries were obliged to provide a higher coverage level in regard to the aggregate deposits of each depositor. The sum was set at €100,000 in the event of deposits not being available (Article 7(1) and (1a)).
- On the basis of Icesave experiences (EFTA Court 2013), the entity directly responsible for ensuring that guarantee funds in regard to the aggregate of deposits of each depositor have a sufficient level was changed. Prior to the directive amendment, it was the deposit guarantee scheme (most often, the guarantee fund). After the amendment, the state itself became the entity, thus moving the potential financial responsibility directly to the country's budget (Article 7(1)).
- The time for payout of unavailable deposits was changed to 20 working days (from the initial three months), with the possibility of extending the time limit for another ten working days in case of "wholly exceptional circumstances" (Article 10(1)).
- The necessity of submitting a report to the European Parliament and to the Council was also introduced, regarding such issues, as: "the harmonization of the funding mechanisms of deposit-guarantee schemes, the appropriateness and modalities of providing for full coverage, possible models for introducing risk-based contributions, the benefits and costs of a possible introduction of a Community deposit-guarantee scheme, [and] the link between deposit-guarantee schemes and alternative means for reimbursing depositors" (Article 12(1)).

3.6.4 Proposal of New Directive from 12 July 2010

The crisis experiences of the years 2007–09 and their unfavorable market conditions triggered the decision on changing the content of Directive 94/19/EC provisions. The decision on preparing a proposal of long-term system changes was presented in the directive project of 12 July 2010. The crisis events of 2007 caused depositor concerns regarding the effectiveness of deposit guarantee schemes. As it was later revealed, due to the potential value of payouts, it could not have been expected of deposit insurance agencies to be capable of meeting financial requirements. Several schemes functioning in countries that did not experience crisis so strongly did not have properly adjusted deposit guarantee schemes.

The wave of deposit guarantee scheme changes was also initiated by the Iceland versus Great Britain and the Netherlands conflict on the responsibility of providing financial potential necessary for guarantee insurance agencies directly by the state. It eventually resulted with Iceland submitting redress to the EFTA Court (EFTA Court 2013). For this reason, a new EU deposit guarantee scheme harmonization project, included in the above-mentioned directive proposal of 12 July 2010, was presented (Bełdowski and Kantorowicz 2011). In the final draft of the document proposal, it was noticed that materialization of risk was possible, thus causing the endangerment of financial stability and the mass withdrawal of deposits. It was also noticed that deposit insurance agencies in the EU are very different from one another. Several issues were named as most important in the works of the Commission, among them:

– the simplification and harmonization of the scope of coverage,
– the reduction of the time limit for payouts,
– the elimination of deductible,
– the unification of information responsibilities,
– the unification of approach toward financing deposit guarantee schemes (high level of harmonization).

The above-listed points were all reflected in the new regulation proposals. Some of the solutions presented in the 2010 paper require an in-depth analysis—especially, the proposed financing plan and target levels of funds.

In order to fulfill the financial requirements, all deposit insurance agencies in the EU would need to aggregate funds of the 1.5 per cent value of eligible deposits. Such a level was described as the target. The possibility of introducing a special *ex post* contribution of 0.5 per cent of eligible deposits was also an additional opening for enhancing the financial potential. It was therefore planned that aggregated *ex ante* funds would be responsible for 75 per cent of deposit insurance agency financing (standard procedure), and ex post, for the remaining 25 per cent (additional action of extraordinary character). As an additional form of protection of deposit guarantee scheme funds, an implementation of a new instrument was planned—the so-called mutual borrowing between deposit insurance agencies. If needed, a given deposit guarantee scheme would have the possibility to take a loan from a different scheme functioning in the EU. The institutions functioning in the union had, among its compulsory elements, the obligation to provide a loan equal to 0.5 per cent of eligible deposits (proportionally to the level of eligible deposits in particular countries). The last line of defense against exhaustion of funds from private sources was the possibility of using alternative financing mechanisms by deposit insurance agencies, including guarantee and government loans. A four-phase mechanism of financing was to begin its operations ten years after the enactment of the directive.

Table 3.4 shows the financial consequences for the banking sector in case the proposal from 12 July 2010 was implemented. A large majority of countries (22) showed fund deficit in comparison to levels specified in the directive. Very significant amounts would be needed to be aggregated in countries with the greatest banking sectors, such as Germany and France, where the deficit would be equal to €33 and €20 billion, respectively. The implementation of the decisions would therefore mean enormous financial burden for the banking sector.

Other widely commented concepts regarded conditioning contributions of banks to risk (Article 11), based on risk profiles of credit institutions. In its core, the regulation aimed at encouraging cautious management of risk in a banking activity. Other proposals regarded cross-border communication (Article 12) and unified, extended information responsibilities (Article 14).

Still, the directive proposal of 12 July 2010 caused controversy and had multiple opponents due to the strong burdening of the banking sector. One of the most questioned spheres was the level of dues transferred to insurance agencies, as well as the shortened lost deposit payout time limit (maximum seven days long). The introduction of such a proposal would mean a multiple increase in payment levels. In an evaluation of potential effects of the regulation, it was shown that it would decrease bank profit by approximately 2.5 per cent (EC 2012; Table 3.3).

Table 3.3 Influence of the proposal of 12 July 2010 on the banking sector (data as of the end of 2012, expressed in millions of euros)

Country	Fund size in 2012	Fund size in the proposal of 12 July 2010 (1.5% ex ante)	Fund size in the proposal of 12 July 2010 (0.5% ex post)	Fund size deficit in 2012 in relation to the proposal of 12 July 2010 (ex ante funds only)
Austria	0	3,634	1,211	−3,634
Belgium	2,064	5,141	1,714	−3,077
Bulgaria	1,580	396	132	1,184
Croatia*	185	562	187	−377
Cyprus	22	1,165	388	−1,143
Czech Republic	983	1,473	491	−490
Denmark	770	1,863	621	−1,093
Estonia	172	129	43	43
EU—altogether	21,457	157,931	52,644	−136,474
Finland	910	1,927	642	−1 017
France	2,111	23,054	7,685	−20,943
Germany**	2,363	35,418	11,806	−33,055
Great Britain	−969	32,616	10,872	−33,585
Greece	3,979	2,105	702	1,874
Hungary	265	663	221	−398
Ireland	403	2,100	700	−1,697
Italy	0	10,872	3,624	−10,872
Latvia	262	216	72	46
Lithuania	−660	150	50	−810
Luxembourg	0	2,410	803	−2,410
Malta	16	142	47	−126
Netherlands	0	8,632	2,877	−8,632
Poland	1,789	2,635	878	−846
Portugal	238	2,472	824	−2,234
Romania	661	496	165	165
Slovakia	194	403	134	−209
Slovenia	0	261	87	−261
Spain	855	14,014	4,671	−13,159
Sweden	3,264	2,981	994	283

*Data on Croatia (as of 2010) and all deposits (instead of eligible only).
**Data on Germany based on FSB evaluations

Source: Iwanicz-Drozdowska et al. (2015a), EC (2011a), FSB (2012), IADI (2008a, 2013), Cannas et al. (2014, pp. 9, 12) and DAB (2015), and author's own research

Furthermore, the directive project imposed a loan-granting obligation equal to 0.5 per cent of covered deposits' value on all institutions. Unfavorable opinions inclined the possibility of snowball effect creation and the weakening of single insurance agencies' stability.

The adoption of directive proposals would result in the tightening of country deposit guarantee schemes' relations in the EU. The Commission enacted the document on 12 July 2010. It was decided that consultations with the European Central Bank (ECB 2011) and the European Data Protection Supervisor (EDPS 2010) were needed. The document was later forwarded to the European Parliament and to the Council. The Committee on Economic and Monetary Affairs of the European Parliament (ECON) worked on the directive project and its amendments. The works were finalized on 14 June 2011 by the adoption of the document in its first reading. The very same day, the Commission also expressed a similar statement in this regard and accepted part of the Parliament's amendments in the first reading.

Still, the planned course of legislative works on the directive proposal was disturbed by the idea of creating integrated financial frameworks for the union (the so-called banking union) with a common deposit guarantee scheme as one of its pillars.

The concept was presented by the Commission at an informal Council session in May 2012. In June, a report titled "Towards a Genuine Economic and Monetary Union" was presented, where three future pillars of the EU were pinpointed (European Council 2012):

- the establishment of a single, bank supervisory scheme,
- creating EDIS,
- preparing a European procedure for resolution and orderly liquidation of banks (European Council 2012).

Simultaneously, it was inclined that the integrated financial framework interferes with the works that were performed thus far in regard to the deposit guarantee scheme in the EU. As a result, a new deposit insurance agency vision was outlined, stating that: "A "European deposit insurance scheme" could introduce a European dimension to national deposit guarantee schemes for banks overseen by the European supervision. It would strengthen the credibility of the existing arrangements and serve as an important assurance that eligible deposits of all credit institutions are sufficiently insured" (European Council 2012, p. 5).

The Council decided that a new agreement in regard to the deposit guarantee scheme directive that would include the banking union provisions and provide a just balance between the country of origin and receiving state was absolutely necessary. It was also brought to attention that these mechanisms needed to provide taxpayers with protection throughout bank crises, rely on the contributions of the financial sector, and prepare necessary, effective protection instruments (European Council 2013, p. 11).

3.6.5 Directive 2014/49/EU and Chosen Provisions of Directive 2014/59/EU

After the initial placation of the economical state of the EU, as well as the decision on building and designing the shape of the banking union, works aimed at bringing to life new deposit guarantee scheme directive solutions were initiated. At this stage, efforts to create the third banking union pillar (pan-European deposit guarantee scheme) were abandoned; eventually, they were renewed in November 2015. After the first reform attempts in 2010, finally, in 2014, the new directive was enacted. Directive 2014/49/EU is similar in terms of shape to the 2010 proposal, but the requirements regarding financing and charging the banking sector were mitigated. Most of its provisions (with some exceptions) were to be incorporated into national legal order by mid-2015, with several exemptions (Article 20). It may be expected that the directive will have a decisive role on the shape of deposit guarantee schemes in the EU for many years to come.

The most important provisions of Directive 2014/49/EU refer to new financing methods for deposit insurance agencies. Banks will be obliged to regularly pay contributions to the guarantee scheme (*ex ante* financing) until the 0.8 per cent threshold of guaranteed funds will be reached. This amount will also be the target level. It must be noted that the proposal is less ambitious than the initially assumed 1.5 per cent (in the directive proposal of 12 July 2010). Additionally, by way of derogation, the 0.8 per cent level may be lowered to 0.5 per cent. Such a decision must be approved by the European Commission and supported either by a low probability of utilizing a prominent amount of funds for the needs of protecting depositors of guaranteed funds, or a banking sector characterized by a high concentration level (namely, where a number of assets belongs to a small number of credit institutions). Furthermore, other exemptions are also possible due to the fact that payment commitments may also be counted when calculating the target level. Their total participation can reach as much as 30 per cent of the total number of available funds. Formally, a minimum level of 0.8 per cent of covered deposits was introduced as part of funds used for deposit guarantee.

Still, at the same time, through special European Commission permissions that allow for the lowering of accumulation levels and the acquisition of a mere "obligation for payment" (which may be hard to utilize in case of a system crisis), countries were allowed to avoid aggregating funds. What is more, introducing new solutions regarding the accumulation of funds was phased over extended periods of time, and the financing mechanism in the form described is scheduled to come into force on 3 July 2024, with the possibility of further postponing its implementation.

Table 3.4 demonstrates information on aggregate funds and the changes that will take place once the directive provisions are enforced with direct financial consequences. Data as of the end of 2012 show that current lack of funds in EU deposit guarantee schemes equals to a total of approximately €44 billion and should be satiated throughout the next decade.

The analysis of data presented in Table 3.4 shows that 17 EU member states have a deficiency of funds needed for aggregation purposes in the 0.8 per cent accumulation worth model. Among the countries with the highest deficiency are several large economies, such as Great Britain (−€10.7 billion), Germany (−€10.2 billion), France (−€6.7 billion), Spain (−€4.5 billion), Italy (−€3.9 billion), and the Netherlands (−€3.6 billion).

On the other side are countries with funds aggregated above the level required by Directive 2014/49/EU. Among them are Greece (€3.1 billion), Sweden (€2.1 billion), Bulgaria (€1.4 billion), and Poland

(€0.9 billion). What deserves special attention is the fact that EU member states will be obliged to collect the previously mentioned €44 billion in the form of contributions within ten years. Still, the burden will not be distributed evenly among member states, because part of them—namely, 11 countries—has already met the requirements. The remaining 17 countries will have to reach the assumed levels gradually.

It is hereby worth mentioning the relation between Directive 2014/49/EU, regarding deposit guarantee schemes, and Directive 2014/59/EU, regarding resolution procedures. The provisions of the latter document set a compulsory cooperative of resolution financing mechanisms in a deposit guarantee scheme. Guarantee schemes are, in light of Article 109

Table 3.4 Data on aggregate funds in deposit guarantee schemes and the target coverage level expressed in Directive 2014/49/EU (data in billions of euros)

	1.	2.	3.	4.	5.
Austria	766	0	866	1,386	−1,386
Belgium	108	2,064	1,145	1,833	231
Bulgaria	31	1,580	91	147	1,433
Croatia	29	185	187	299	−114
Cyprus	141	22	259	415	−393
Czech Republic	58	983	326	522	461
Denmark	161	770	527	843	−73
Estonia	17	172	26	42	130
Finland	327	910	388	622	288
France	660	2,111	5,517	8,827	−6,716
Germany	1,898	2,363	7,876	12,601	−10,238
Great Britain	373	−969	6,093	9,750	−10,719
Greece	58	3,979	523	838	3,141
Hungary	189	265	151	242	23
Ireland	480	403	400	640	−237
Italy	754	0	2,452	3,923	−3,923
Latvia	31	262	29	47	215
Lithuania	92	−660	33	53	−713
Luxembourg	141	0	152	243	−243
Malta	26	16	35	56	−40
Netherlands	287	0	2,235	3,576	−3,576
Poland	700	1,789	516	825	964
Portugal	155	238	551	881	−643
Romania	41	661	137	219	442
Slovakia	31	194	121	193	1

Table 3.4 (continued)

	1.	2.	3.	4.	5.
Slovenia	25	0	74	119	−119
Spain	335	855	3,374	5,399	−4,544
Sweden	175	3,264	704	1,126	2,138

Data as of the end of 2012, and the 0.5 per cent and 0.8 per cent benchmarks were calculated in reference to the worth of deposit guarantee schemes at the end of 2012

1 – Number of banks registered in a given country as of the end of 2012

2 – Value of aggregate funds in the deposit guarantee scheme as of the end of 2012 (expressed in millions of euros)

3 – Minimum value of aggregate funds in the deposit guarantee scheme with the assumption of the first benchmark equal to 0.5 per cent of covered deposits (expressed in millions of euros)

4 – Minimum value of aggregate funds in the deposit guarantee scheme with the assumption of the first benchmark equal to 0.8 per cent of covered deposits (expressed in millions of euros)

5 – Missing or surplus funds, resulting from the comparison of the amount of available funds in 2012, and the projected level from the directive, equal to 0.8 per cent of covered deposits (expressed in millions of euros)

Source: Author's own research and Iwanicz-Drozdowska et al. (2015a), EC (2011a), FSB (2012), IADI (2008a, 2013), Cannas et al. (2014, pp. 9, 12), and DAB (2015)

of the BRR Directive, obliged to participate in the financing of resolution under specific conditions. It is worth signaling the problem, because the risk of utilizing deposit guarantee scheme funds is much higher due to this obligation. It may result in frequent financial shortfalls in deposit insurance agencies, the prevailing negative balance in budgets, as well as the need for a rapid compensation of budget shortage through the rise of contributions.

Several limitations have been introduced to the subsidiary financing mechanism of resolution from deposit insurance agency funds. First and foremost, the insurance agency must participate in resolution, but only under the condition that it guarantees uninterrupted availability of deposits on behalf of depositors of a given financial institution. Secondly, it was decided that deposit guarantee scheme participation could not exceed the amount of losses it would be exposed to, if the institution were to go through a standard bankruptcy procedure. Other limitations include that in no situation will the financial responsibility of deposit insurance agencies exceed 50 per cent of the target level. This is also the maximum amount that may be dedicated to resolution purposes in a single operation.

The risks that were not mentioned in the directive deserve special recognition. As a result of uneven breakdown of decisiveness within the national financial safety net, the decision on the participation in resolution (and its legitimacy) may be made with the omission of the institution. What is more, it may also be revealed that resolution procedures financed without the authorization of deposit insurance agencies will not bring any anticipated effects. In a negative scenario, the deposit guarantee scheme may be charged twice (Mazhenova 2014): initially, while granting capital support, and secondly—again at the same financial institution—while paying out covered funds to respective depositors, if such a necessity arises. Therefore, such relations between financing mechanisms may result in several, potential risks, which are analyzed broadly in Chapters 5 and 7. As a conclusion, it is worth noticing the basic differences between the two most important directives regarding deposit guarantee schemes in the EU, enacted 20 years apart from one another. The discrepancies have been presented in Table 3.5.

Summarizing the key aspects of both legal documents, it must be noted that the current directive—due to the significant changes in national legal order—requires longer implementation dates and designates a nearly decade-long transitional period (mainly, in regard to the aggregation of capital in deposit guarantee schemes). Difference may also be seen in the reasons for implementation of documents. The center of gravity during works on Directive 2014/49/EU was put on the elimination of disparities in legislature of member states after the global financial crisis. Meanwhile, 20 years before, it was merely aimed at caring for the harmonious development of credit institutions. Objectives of both normative acts remain convergent. Among them are the strengthening of the stability of the bank system and providing depositor protection. Still, obligations of member states, included in the character of the obligation of bringing deposit insurance agencies to life, are worth noticing.

Although it has not been specified, an obligation of establishing deposit guarantee schemes as the sole executor of deposit payouts was introduced in 1994. Member states, through the establishment of a deposit guarantee scheme itself, became exempt from the responsibility of maintaining the

Table 3.5 Overview of chosen differences in EU regulations regarding deposit guarantee schemes

	Directive 94/19/EC	Directive 2014/49/EU
Year of enactment	1994	2014
Date of implementation of provisions	1 July 1995	3 July 2015 3 July 2024 (accumulation of funds)
Reasons for the implementation	Harmonious development of credit institutions in all parts of the EU	Unification of legislature in member states after the global financial crisis – Enforcing the concept of the EU Internal Market for credit institutions' sector
Goal	Strengthening the stability of the bank system Increasing the safety of depositors Promoting the development of bank operations Abolishment of liberty limitations Providing depositors with unified protection rights	Increasing the stability of the bank system and depositor protection Providing depositors with a unified protection level while maintaining identical system stability of deposit guarantee schemes Protection of depositors from repercussions of credit institutions insolvency
Obligation of establishing the scheme	Obligation of establishing schemes in all EU countries (change from recommendation to legally binding document)	Necessity of providing the functioning of an officially acknowledged deposit insurance agency, as well as the country's responsibility for its proper operation
Coverage level	€20,000 with the option of applying coinsurance franchise	Setting a harmonized coverage level of €100,000 (with possible exemptions)
Payout date of guarantee-covered funds	Three months with the option of extending for an additional three months	Seven days (possible transitional period until the end of 2023)

(*continued*)

Table 3.5 (continued)

	Directive 94/19/EC	Directive 2014/49/EU
Exemption of entities from protection	Several depositor or deposit categories may be exempted from protection	Unified criteria of exempting depositors from protection
Obligatory exemptions from protection	Interbank deposits Money laundering Own funds of credit institutions	Strictly defined (including deposits of public authority or other financial institutions)
Coinsurance franchise	Loss coverage must be equal to at least 90 per cent	Not permitted
Information obligations	Minimal	Informing depositors is a crucial element of protection (specific conditions)
Establishment of financing mechanism	Lack of provisions	Until 3 July 2024, funds from the deposit guarantee scheme will be responsible at least for the target level of 0.8 per cent of covered deposits
Method of solving conflicts among insurance agencies	General terms in the form of legal actions	The European Banking Authority (EBA) should have the possibility of binding conflict solving among insurance agencies

Source: Author's own research

proper, formal functioning of the institution. Meanwhile, the solutions from 2014 caused that member states themselves were put in charge of proper functioning of the so-called formally acknowledged deposit guarantee scheme, and became financially responsible for the credibility and effects of the institution's actions. Thus, the perspective of member states on potential budget obligations, which may arise as an effect, has changed.

Shorter deadlines for the payout of deposits, currently set to seven days (with a prolonged transposition period), were introduced, and the coverage level unified to €100,000. Harmonized, previously nonexistent exemption conditions for the above levels were implemented. Deposits resulting from the temporary high balance of a bank account, caused, for instance, by the sale of a real estate, are also thus protected. The conditions of protection and its exemption were also unified, enabling the security of deposits of public organs. Deriving from the negative British experiences, the possibility of applying coinsurance franchise (the participation of the depositor in loss, named as one of the triggers of bank panic) was no longer available. The information obligations of deposit insurance agencies were extended, as the communication with depositors was recognized as a crucial guarantee scheme activity.

The harmonization of the minimum accumulation level of funds in member states and its normative inclusion on an unimpressive level of 0.8 per cent of guaranteed funds, with the simultaneous support in the form of resolution procedures, is a true milestone. It is also important to determine that the European Banking Authority (EBA) will, in fact, have the competences to resolve conflicts between deposit guarantee schemes from various member states, as well as current, quickly escalating disputes (for instance, as in the court case of Iceland against the Netherlands and Great Britain).

3.7 Proposal for EDIS

Construction works on the banking union were initiated by the creation of a first, supervisory pillar, Single Supervisory Mechanism (SSM), followed by the establishment of a second, responsible for the resolution and orderly liquidation of banks—Single Resolution Mechanism. According to the procedure logic, the next anticipated step is the creation of the EDIS, perceived as the completion of the banking union. The institutional financial safety net in the EU is comprised of the following: ECB, European Supervisory Authorities (EBA, ESMA, EIOPA), Single Resolution Board (SRB), and European Systemic Risk Board. The supportive functions of the financial safety net are also performed by the European Stability Mechanism (ESM) and the European Financial Stability Facility. In its framework, the banking union built upon three pillars is expected to allow the creation of unified competences of institutions functioning in the financial safety net. Still, thus far, the target goal of the third pillar remains unknown.

3.7.1 Key Assumptions

The proposal of establishing EDIS appeared first as one of the ideas presented in "The Five Presidents' Report" (EC 2015b, p. 11). According to the proposal of the European Commission dated 24 November 2015, EDIS is designed as a common, supra-national deposit guarantee scheme for credit institutions belonging to the banking union (Euro+ Pact). As accredited by Regulation 806/2014, SRB is anticipated to become the executive organ of EDIS as an organization managing the resolution and orderly liquidation procedures of financial institutions in the banking union. The tasks of EDIS will be the same as those designated to country deposit insurance agencies in Directive 2014/49/EU. The legal basis for the establishment of EDIS is provided in Article 114 of the Treaty on the Functioning of the European Union. Its scope is anticipated to be coherent with the remaining banking union pillars and will cover deposits existent in all banks functioning in its range, regardless of whether they are covered with ECB or state organ supervision. It does not signify the liquidation of country deposit guarantee schemes, for—through their intermediation—EDIS will fulfill its tasks, such as the payout of deposits and collecting contributions from banks.

The EDIS proposal assumes the creation of the institution in three phases—by gradually increasing its responsibility scope—and the mutualization of country deposit guarantee funds (progressive combining of funds aggregated by country insurance agencies into one common fund for banking union states). First, a reinsurance phase will take place, followed by coinsurance, eventually leading to full depositor protection. The main task of EDIS will be providing financial support to country deposit guarantee schemes. Depending on the construction phase of EDIS, this support will take on various forms. At the beginning, it will function as liquidity support and help in covering extraordinary losses (namely, after resources of the national fund run out). Eventually, they will be applied as coverage of payouts of lost deposits or financial support for the participation of the national guarantee scheme in resolution. During the initial phase of EDIS, significant differences in aggregated funds for payout purposes will be visible in member states. The disproportion of accumulated funds for deposit guarantee purposes between EU countries is significant, which is further described in Chapter 4. In such a situation, the support of EDIS will have to be proportional and nondiscriminatory for all banking union countries. That is why it was foreseen during the reinsurance phase that EDIS would participate in national guarantee schemes' interventions only to a certain degree. The financial participation of EDIS will be confined to covering part of shortages—the lack of financial means of national deposit guarantee schemes. However, they will not be factual shortages of a given national deposit guarantee scheme, but shortage calculated hypothetically for the needs of mutual settlement between the national deposit guarantee scheme and EDIS. Shortage or extraordinary loss was described in the Commission proposal as a result of the comparison of deposit guarantee scheme target fund levels (required in the given year by Directive 2014/49/EU), along with the amount needed for individual payouts throughout a bank's bankruptcy process. In the second phase, EDIS will take over limited responsibility for "standard" expenses of national deposit guarantee schemes, related to payouts or resolution proceedings. EDIS responsibility will gradually rise until it reaches the third phase, when it will have become fully obliged to incur costs of payouts and participation in resolution. Benefiting from EDIS support by a national deposit guarantee scheme requires full implementation of DGS and BRR Directives at each stage, as well as proper and consequent application of certain provisions of Directive 2014/49/EU, which will be verified during the support-granting preparation procedures of EDIS. These include Articles 4, 6, 7, and 10 of Directive 2014/49/EU, regarding the conditions of qualifying for deposit protection, levels of coverage, payout amount evaluation, and the financing of deposit guarantee schemes. Maintaining the discipline of collecting contributions from banks will be of particular importance.

As proved in the analysis above, one of the most important tasks awaiting EDIS, enabling its operational activities, will be the accumulation of financial means required for covering potential interventions. According to the EC proposal, national guarantee schemes will annually pay fixed amounts to EDIS directly from their own financial resources. These contributions will not be an additional burden for banks, because they already fulfill the requirements that, according to Directive 2014/49/EU, should be achieved by national deposit guarantee schemes. As a result and effect of establishing EDIS, part of national contributions will be simply transferred to a higher, cross-union fund—namely, Deposit Insurance Fund (DIF). It will allow, in theory, for maintaining cost neutrality during the creation of EDIS. The target level of aggregated funds in DIF equals to 0.8 per cent of the value of covered deposits, and by the end of 2024, is expected to reach approximately €44 billion euros. As an effect, EDIS will gradually take over national funds, until the full insurance of EDIS is achieved in the year 2024.

3.7.2 Potential Benefits

The idea of creating a pan-European deposit guarantee scheme in the banking union itself potentially creates multiple advantages. Due to the relatively high level of financial integration of the Eurozone, a common, supra-national solution in regard to deposit guarantee schemes is justified. Through the gradual mutualization of national funds of deposit guarantee schemes into DIF, EDIS will become a solution providing scale benefits and a more effective deposit protection than an unrelated net of national deposit guarantee schemes. Therefore, due to the high potential of spreading the "contagion effect" inside the Eurozone, as well as in its relations with the rest of the EU, EDIS would limit the system risk and promote trust for financial schemes existent in banking union states. EDIS will also permit the limiting of cross-border financial shocks and support their absorption into the banking sector. This, in effect, will also improve the mechanisms of transmission of a unified monetary policy, better risk diversification in the banking union, and the limiting of financial market fragmentation (Kerlin and Smaga 2016).

Moreover, EDIS would allow for the effective minimizing of trust decrease risk, related to the insolvency of a cross-border functioning bank, whose deposits would thus far be paid out by deposit guarantee schemes in different countries. In this regard, EDIS will also support the harmonization of code of conduct and the cooperation between national deposit guarantee schemes. The risk of negative external effects and the defect of coordinating national deposit guarantee scheme activities will thus be minimized. The rise of harmonization of national deposit guarantee scheme functions will allow for free capital movement within the banking union, promote the development for cross-border banking services, and lower the risk of regulatory arbitrage proceedings.

In case a given country's deposit guarantee scheme funds run out, for instance, as a result of a local crisis, EDIS creates the opportunity for limiting the need for governmental support. This would, in effect, lower the negative feedback loop between the condition of banks and governments (Davies and Ng 2011). Introducing EDIS creates the opportunity for the decoupling of a bank's deposit safety from the fund resources of countries in the banking union, as well as increases the credibility and public financial condition of a given country. In effect, the stability of banks incorporated in the banking union would be strengthened, and the scale of uncontrollable deposit flow between countries of the banking union, representing various scenarios of public financial condition, would be limited. The support of a national deposit guarantee scheme by the DIF would promote the extension of intervention capabilities of the country scheme, which would itself be connected with the DIF. Thus, the level of burdening banks with additional *ex post* contributions will be limited in the case of national deposit guarantee schemes funds' exhaustion. It is worth comparing the above situation with such, where EDIS is nonexistent.

Thanks to EDIS, the risk of disturbing equal freedom of action of banks representing a similar risk profile within the banking union will be lowered, but through the already existent differing levels and guarantee scopes in particular countries. As a result, the fragmentation of the banking sector in the banking union will be limited, thus contributing to the reduction of disparities in bank financing costs caused, thus far, by various financial potential of national deposit guarantee schemes.

The thus far high financial potential of national deposit guarantee schemes could have an impact on the choice of bank activity models' shape (branch vs subsidiary). In countries belonging to the banking union (with EDIS and SSM as a sole supervisor) the role of the criterion above will be deprecated. The condition of public finances and the macroeconomic situation of the member state in the banking union shall, in such a situation, have lesser influence on trust for the bank operating in the given country. It would, in turn, depend more on trust to EDIS itself.

Perceiving the obligation of implementing and meeting all requirements of the DGS Directive (including the necessity of possessing significant financial potential by the national deposit guarantee scheme) as crucial prior to using DIFs shall be evaluated favorably. It may promote the development of financial potential of funds in banking union countries, in accordance with the path indicated in the above directive.

Granting management of EDIS and DIF to SRB, in contrary to creating a separate institution for administering EDIS, is justified from the operational perspective. In theory, it will allow a single organ to execute decisions regarding a bank on the verge of bankruptcy and provide it with a choice of instruments, namely, either resolution or declaring insolvency and paying out deposits. On the one hand, such a situation will support reaching effects of synergy of both functions, as well as ensure a cohesive approach toward banks in a banking union, a more effective management of situations, and lower the "budding of authorities". Ultimately, in the long term, this may also lead to the merging of DIF and SRF funds (Gros 2013). Yet, on the other hand, lack of sufficient DIF for the payout of deposits from a bank of systemic importance may cause the SRB to lean toward resolution, not bankruptcy, at a time of crisis. Furthermore, the decisive and operative capabilities of resolution in the banking union in light of time-consuming decision-making processes were not yet fully tested.

In conclusion, EDIS shall positively affect the financial stability and support the rebuilding of trust toward the banking sector in the banking union, as well as lower the risk of bank panic. Furthermore, through a better diversification of local shocks, the endurance of the banking union would rise in case of future crises. The gradual implementation of EDIS allows for the preparation and adjustment to new rules—on behalf of not only banks, but also national deposit guarantee schemes. Still, it must be kept in mind that the possible environment and scale of potential benefits of EDIS functions remains unclear.

3.7.3 Potential Flaws and Their Minimizing

The EC proposal regarding the establishment of EDIS will undoubtedly be subject to changes in union negotiation procedures, though certain questions may already have been asked, and partial scarcities of proposed provisions pinpointed.

The establishment of EDIS will most probably lead to convergences of Eurozone target levels of respective guarantee funds, but only to a minimal, required degree. Thus far, only the minimum level of 0.8 per cent of covered deposits' value had been harmonized. Still, national calibration of the indicator in a manner that would enable the potential payout for average-sized banks at least is crucial. Yet, this is dependent on internal, national political decisions. In effect, a situation is created where—depending on the concentration of the banking sector in a given country and the size of a banks—some countries (for example, Germany, France, and Italy) must accumulate much more than the required 0.8 per cent of covered funds. Aggregating such an amount in the countries above will not allow for payouts of even medium-sized banks. Other countries (for instance, Sweden, Finland, and Ireland) may accept the 0.8 per cent level as sufficient for the execution of proper, effective interventions toward the majority of its entities. Therefore, the sole fact of establishing DIF discourages the collection of higher contributions and—in consequence—the further works on enhancing the financial potential of a country's deposit guarantee scheme funds (above the minimum required for benefiting from DIF). It may result in temptation of abuse, expressed through dependence on external support for financing deposit payouts. This is especially true for countries belonging to the banking union that represent a weak financial system condition. In an extreme situation, it will create relatively higher costs (due to participating in EDIS) for "more stable" countries, at the advantage of those that generate expenses resultant from crisis management flaws and insolvency of their banking sectors. Setting a minimum target level for country funds, exceeding the 0.8 per cent of covered deposits value, would provide a partial solution to the problem. What is more, in the transitional period until the year 2024, the degree of DIF access of countries shall take into consideration the input level of their respective, national fund in DIF.

EDIS presents vague criteria of offering financial support from its own resources. The Commission proposal declares that EDIS assistance will not be provided to countries that shy away from certain provisions of the DGS Directive (2014/49/EU). However, neither the criteria of directive requirements' fulfillment nor the verification procedures (especially regarding Articles 4, 6, 7, and 10 of Directive 2014/49/EU) are yet clear. These ought to be clarified during the EDIS construction works phase.

The investment policy of EDIS that will gradually replace national politics is a next reason for concern for EU countries. According to new conditions of deposit guarantee, funds taken from deposit guarantee schemes of member states to satiate EDIC deposit guarantee activities will need to be allocated at the local market in size proportional to what it was at the time when investment policy was still executed on the country level. This, in effect, may mean the outflow from financial markets of some banking union countries. Consequences of the regulation must therefore be analyzed—namely, it must be determined whether it will have a significantly negative effect on the liquidity of country's financial markets and especially, the bond market.

Another objection is the change of risk profile evaluation methodology for banks that are obliged to pay contributions. Currently, the methods of designating contributions for deposit guarantee schemes are set individually by member states (based on the EBA provisions specified in Article 13(3) of the DGS Directive). It means that the level of risk of a given bank is evaluated from the perspective of a given country's entities. If the proposals come to life, this state will change. In the second phase of EDIS creation, since 2020, the contributions for various entities will be assigned jointly, on the basis of comparison of all entities of the banking union—not only those from the specific country. Consequences of such reforms in regard to contribution levels are not yet known. Although it is cohesive with the concept of the banking union, the situation requires an in-depth analysis of the effects of burdening banks in the banking union with deposit guarantee scheme contributions.

What is more, the Commission's proposal lacks analyses that would specify the circumstances EDIS resources will be used in. One of the key concepts of resolution, competitive in regard to guaranteed fund pay-outs, is taking action only when it is absolutely necessary for the sake of public interest. One of the elements of fulfilling the rule is analyzing the indications for carrying out bank liquidation through a standard insolvency procedure (that is, payout from deposit guarantee scheme funds in paybox mode). Payout capabilities of deposit insurance agencies are a fundamental factor taken into account during evaluation. If DIF gathers funds of a value approximate to the target level of €44 billion euros (comparing to €55 billion in SRF), it will be theoretically capable of carrying out payout procedures of big entities, which will be less favorable for them than resolution. Yet, it seems that in the case of the most prominent entities, resolution should be given precedence, because it is considered more effective (FSB 2013a). Establishing EDIS may result in a lower number of entities covered by resolution (due to lack of public interest factor). This may, in effect, promote the use of traditional payout procedures. It is not clear what the relation between resolution and covered deposit payout procedures will be once EDIS has the power to carry out both. However, one of the most serious flaws of EDIS proposals is the issue of insufficient DIF funds size in comparison to that of European banks. As far as it is known, DIF-accumulated funds will not be sufficient in case most major banks become insolvent—that is, if DIF will not cover even middle-sized banks. As a result, the "too big to fail" concept becomes popular among banks of the banking union. The EDIS Regulation project does not assume either a faster accumulation of means or a higher value of the unified fund than that expected by the DGS Directive. The target €44 billion may be insufficient, because the effects of thematic analyses incline that even the joint value of country deposit guarantee funds, and the resources from guarantee schemes from other sectors, will not satiate the budget needed for payouts of a global bank's deposits, worth well over €44 billion (Iwanicz-Drozdowska et al. 2015a). Simultaneously, the effective resolution and orderly liquidation procedures, as well as the successful use of amortization or bail-in, provide a chance for limiting the needs of deposit payout, hence the requirements regarding the size of financial potential of DIF.

Therefore, it is also crucial that—in case DIF runs out of funds—a reliable security of DIF be instated in the form of emergency financing, strengthening in effect the credibility of EDIS. The European Commission proposal is much too vague in this regard. Capitalizing DIF via ESM or in the form of credit lines of particular countries in a manner similar to that of SRF seems like a natural solution. Another option is providing DIF with short-term liquidity assistance on the basis of an autonomous EBC decision (as a sole SSM supervisor), if financial stability is threatened. An alternative DIF financing mechanism shall be established before the EDIS Regulations are brought into force.

3.8   Conclusion

The chapter provided an analysis of deposit guarantee scheme evolution and their increasing role in the financial safety net. Data on deposit insurance agencies, which aggregated their key characteristics, were collected on an irregular basis. Historical data, both for the EU and globally, allowed for the division of deposit guarantee scheme development into stages. What needs to be noted is that it would have been difficult to analyze the role of deposit guarantee schemes in the EU safety net without the consideration of the global context. The world financial crisis allowed for the systematization of deposit insurance agency functioning models from a previously unknown perspective—its increasing responsibility and new roles and tasks. Among key institutional deposit guarantee solutions named by the author are the scope of scheme authority, its organizational potential, and position of deposit insurers in the institutional financial safety net. Even an analysis confined only to the above solutions allows for the conclusion that deposit guarantee schemes in EU countries vary greatly, despite the partial harmonization of solutions attempted by the directives. As a result, two functioning models of deposit insurance agencies evolved in the EU, with varying competences and contradictory positions within the financial safety net. Due to ongoing legislative works in the EU, the evolution of deposit guarantee schemes took place at varying paces, dependent on the situation on the financial market. Varying approaches toward the shaping of deposit insurance agencies, as well as views, which eventually received recognition, were hereby underlined. These included, among others: necessity of calling systems to life in 1994, harmonization of guarantee levels in 2009, and, lastly, indication of target levels which shall be achieved by guarantee funds, and the obligatory collection of *ex ante* contributions on behalf of banks in 2014.

References

Baka, W. (ed.). (2005). *Systemy gwarantowania depozytów w Polsce i na świecie. Dziesięć lat Bankowego Funduszu Gwarancyjnego*, PWE, Warszawa.
Beck, T. (2004). *Deposit Insurance as Private Club—Is Germany a Model?* World Bank.
Bełdowski, J.; Kantorowicz, J. (2011). *Nowa propozycja harmonizacji systemu gwarancji depozytów w Unii Europejskiej—uwagi na tle projektu dyrektywy z 12 lipca 2010 r.*, "Bezpieczny Bank", nr 1(43), BFG, Warszawa.
Blinder, A.S.; Wescott, R.F. (2001) *Reform of the Deposit Insurance. A Report to the FDIC*, FDIC, March.
Buser, S.; Chen, A.H.; Kane, E.J. (1981). *Federal Deposit Insurance, Regulatory Policy, and Optimal Bank Capital*, "Journal of Finance", vol. 36.
Bryant, J. (1980). *A Model of Reserves, Bank Runs, and Deposit Insurance*, "Journal of Banking & Finance", vol. 4, no. 4.
Cannas, G.; Cariboni, J.; Veisari, L.K.; Pagano, A. (2014). *Updated Estimates of EU Eligible and Covered Deposits*, JRC Technical Reports, Report EUR 26469 EN.
Carter, H.G. (1955). *Origins of Deposit Insurance in the* Middle West, *1834–1866*, "The Indiana Magazine of History", vol. LI, June, no. 2.
Chaddock, R.E. (1910). *The Safety-Fund Banking System in New York State, 1829–1866*, Government Printing Office, Washington D.C..
DAB. *Deposit Insurance, Numbers at a Glance*, State Agency for Deposit Insurance and Bank Resolution. www.dab.hr (access 24.08.2015).
Davies, M.; Ng, T. (2011). *The Rise of Sovereign Credit Risk: Implications for Financial Stability*, "BIS Quarterly Review", BIS September.
Demirgüç-Kunt, A.; Kane, E. (2002). *Deposit Insurance Around the Globe: Where Does It Work?*, "Journal of Economic Perspectives", vol. 16, no. 2, Spring.
Demirgüç-Kunt, A.; Karacaovali, B.; Laeven, L. (2005). *Deposit Insurance Around the World: A Comprehensive Database*, WPS3628, Washington.

Demirgüç-Kunt, A.; Kane, E.; Laeven, L. (2008). *Deposit Insurance Around the World: Issues of Design and Implementation*, MIT Press, July.

Demirgüç-Kunt, A.; Kane, E.; Laeven, L. (2014) *Deposit Insurance Database*, IMF Working Paper, no. 14/118.

Diamond, D.W; Dybvig, P.H. (1986). *Bank Runs, Deposit Insurance and Liquidity*, "Journal of Political Economy", vol. 91.

EC. (2004). *Report on the minimum guarantee level of Deposit Guarantee Schemes Directive 94/19/EC*, Brussels, 2004.

EC. (2006a). *Communication from the Commission to the European Parliament pursuant to the second subparagraph of Article 251 (2) of the EC Treaty concerning the common position of the Council on the adoption of a Decision of the European Parliament and of the Council laying down guidelines for trans-European energy networks and repealing Decisions No 96/391/EC and No 1229/2003/EC*, Brussels.

EC. (2006b). *Screening Report. Financial Services. Croatia*, 28 November.

EC. (2010). Proposal for a DIRECTIVE . . . / . . . /EU OF THE EUROPEAN PARLIAMENT AND OF THE COUNCIL on Deposit Guarantee Schemes [recast], COM/2010/0368 final – COD 2010/0207.

EC. (2011a). *JRC Report under Article 12 of Directive 94/19/EC as amended by Directive 2009/14/EC*, JRC, Unit G09, Ispra (Italy).

EC. (2012). *Commission Staff Working Document, Impact Assessment. Accompanying Document to the Proposal for a Directive . . . / . . . /EU of the European Parliament and of the Council on Deposit Guarantee Schemes [Recast] and to the Report from the Commission to the European Parliament and to the Council Review of Directive 94/19/EC on Deposit Guarantee Schemes* {COM(2010) 368} {COM(2010) 369} {SEC(2010) 835}.

EC. (2015b). *Completing Europe's Economic and Monetary Union*, report by J.C. Juncker in close cooperation with D. Tusk, J. Dijsselbloem, M. Draghi and M. Schulz, June.

ECB. (2011). Opinion on a proposal for a directive of the European Parliament and of the Council on deposit guarantee schemes (recast) and on a proposal for a directive amending Directive 97/9/EC of the European Parliament and of the Council on investor-compensation schemes (CON/2011/12), OJ C 99, 31.3. 2011, p. 1.

EDPS. (2010). Opinion of the European Data Protection Supervisor on the proposal for a Directive of the European Parliament and of the Council on Deposit Guarantee Schemes (recast) (2010/C 323/03), OJ, C 323/9.

European Council. (2013). Conclusions, EUCO 23/13, CO EUR 3, CONCL 2, Brussels, 14 March.

Fed. (1950). *Staff Study on Assessments and Coverage for Deposit Insurance*.

EFTA Court. (2013). Judgment in Case E-16/11 – EFTA Surveillance Authority v Iceland, delivered in open Court on 28 January.

FSB. (2012). *Thematic Review on Deposit Insurance Systems. Peer Review Report*, Basel.

FSB. (2013a). *Recovery and Resolution Planning for Systemically Important Financial Institutions: Guidance on Developing Effective Resolution Strategies*, July.

FSB. (2014). *Towards Full Implementation of the FSB Key Attributes of Effective Resolution Regimes for Financial Institutions*. Report to the G20 on Progress in Reform of Resolution Regimes and Resolution Planning for Global Systemically Important Financial Institutions *(G-SIFIs)*, 12 November.

Furlong, F.T. (1984). *A View on Deposit Insurance Coverage*, "Economic Review".

Garcia G. (1996). *Deposit Insurance: Obtaining the Benefits and Avoiding the Pitfalls*, IMF Working Paper, August.

Garcia, G. (1999). *Deposit Insurance: A Survey of Actual and Best Practices*, IMF, WP/99/54, April.

Garcia, G. (2000). *Deposit Insurance and Crisis Management*, IMF Working Paper, March.

Goodhart, C.; Schoenmaker, D. (2006). *Burden Sharing in a Banking Crisis in Europe*, "Penning—Ochvaluta Politik", no. 2.

Grafton, J. (ed.). (1999). *Franklin Delano Roosevelt—Great Speeches*, Dover Publications, New York.

Gros, D. (2013). *Principles of a Two-Tier European Deposit (Re-)Insurance System*, CEPS Policy Briefs no. 287, Centre for European Policy Studies, Brussels.

Holdsworth, J.T. (1971). *Lessons of State Banking Before Civil War*, "Proceedings of the Academy of Political Science", vol. 30, no. 3, Control or Fate in Economics Affairs, May.

Horvitz, P.M. (1975). *Failures of Large Banks: Implications for Banking Supervision and Deposit Insurance*, "Journal of Financial and Quantitative Analysis", vol. 10, issue 4.

IADI. (2008a). *Annual Survey*, BIS, Basel.

IADI. (2013). *Annual Survey*, BIS, Basel.

IADI. (2012d). *Transitioning from a Blanket Guarantee or Extended Coverage to a Limited Coverage System*, January.

IADI. (2014a). *Annual Survey*, BIS, Basel.

IMF. (2013). *Deposit Insurance. Technical Note*, Washington, March.

Iwanicz-Drozdowska, M.; Kerlin, J.; Smaga, P.; Tomasik, M. (2015a). *EU Guarantee Schemes: Status Quo and Policy Implications*, "Journal of Banking Regulation", vol. 16, no. 3.

Kane, E. (1989). *How Incentive-Incompatible Deposit-Insurance Funds Fail*, NBER Working Papers 2836, February.

Kerlin, J.; Smaga, P. (2016). *Europejski System Gwarantowania Depozytów jako trzeci filar unii bankowej, Przełamywanie dysonansów poznawczych jako czynnik stymulowania rozwoju nauk o finansach*, Karmańska, A.; Ostaszewski J. (eds.), Szkoła Główna Handlowa w Warszawie, Warszawa, pp. 213–231.

Kreps, C.H.; Wacht, R.F. (1971). *A More Constructive Role for Deposit Insurance*, "The Journal of Finance", vol. 26, no. 2, Papers and Proceedings of the Twenty-Ninth Annual Meeting of the American Finance Association, Detroit.

Kyei, A. (1995). *Deposit Protection Arrangements: A Survey*, IMF, WP/95/134.

Laeven, L.; Valencia, F. (2013). *Systemic Banking Crises Database: An Update*, IMF Working Paper, WP/12/163, IMF.

Linklaters. (2015). *China Formalises Broad Parameters of Deposit Insurance Scheme.* www.linklaters.com, 10.04.2015 (access 23.08.2015).

Litan, R. (1997). *What Should Bank Do?* The Brooking Institution, Washington.

Mazhenova, B. (2014). *The Basic Challenges for DIS in Bail in Application. Kazakhstani Bail in Experience*, Kazakhstan Deposit Insurance Fund, 25–26 June, Warsaw.

Miklaszewska, E. (2014). *Small Banks in Post-crisis Regulatory Architecture: The Case of Cooperative Banks in Poland*, Governance, Regulation and Bank Stability, Palgrave Macmillan Studies in Banking and Financial Institutions, pp. 129–150.

Obal, T. (2004). *Podstawowe cechy systemów gwarantowania depozytów i dzialalnosci pomocowej w panstwach Unii Europejskiej – wnioski dla Polski*, "Bezpieczny Bank", Nr 1(22), BFG, Warszawa.

Pennacchi, G. (1984). *Partial Deposit, Bank Runs and Private Deposit Insurance*, Center for Financial.

Rogoff, R.C.K. (2009). *This Time Is Different: Eight Centuries of Financial Folly*, Princeton University Press.

Schoenmaker, D.; Oosterloo, S. (2006). *Financial Supervision in Europe: Do We Need a New Architecture?*, European League for Economic Co-operation, Cahier Comte Boël, no. 12, Brussels.

Sharpe, W.F. (1977). *Bank Capital Adequacy, Deposit Insurance and Security Values*, Part I, NBER Working Papers 0209.

Taggart, J.H.; Jennings, L.D. (1934). *The Insurance of Bank Deposits*, "Journal of Political Economy", vol. 42, no. 4, The University of Chicago Press, Chicago.

Talley, S.; Mas, I. (1990). *Deposit Insurance in Developing Countries*, World Bank Policy Research Working Paper no. 548, November.

Thomson, J. (1986a). *Alternative Methods for Assessing Risk-Based Deposit Insurance Premiums, Economic Commentary*, September.

Thomson, J. (1986b). *Equity, Efficiency, and Mispriced Deposit Guarantees*, Federal Reserve Bank of Cleveland.

Tomasic, R. (2011). *The Emerging EU Framework for Bank Recovery and Resolution*, Corporate Rescue and Insolvency, April.

Wheelock, D.C.; Wilson, P.W. (1993). *Explaining Bank Failures: Deposit Insurance, Regulation, and Efficiency*, Federal Reserve Bank of St. Louis, Working Paper Series 002.

4

Financial Capabilities of Deposit Guarantee Schemes

4.1   Introduction

This chapter visualizes the effectiveness of deposit guarantee scheme interventions in their most common form—standard deposit payouts from insolvent banks (paybox). Factors that influence the effectiveness of deposit insurance agencies were verified along with the scope of successful interventions in light of the global financial crisis. Additionally, the reasons behind their ineffectiveness were also indicated. The chapter describes two components—psychological and financial—which are crucial to deposit guarantee scheme effectiveness. Special attention was brought to the scope of successful deposit guarantee scheme intervention, which mostly depends on financial means at the disposal of a given institution.

© The Author(s) 2017   **91**
J. Kerlin, *The Role of Deposit Guarantee Schemes as a Financial Safety Net in the European Union*, Palgrave Macmillan Studies in Banking and Financial Institutions, DOI 10.1007/978-3-319-54163-1_4

4.2   Capabilities of Deposit Guarantee Schemes

Deposit insurance agency potential is expressed either by its capability of preventing bank panic, or the effectiveness of its interventions. Two basic components, psychological and financial, decide about the effectiveness of deposit guarantee schemes (Iwanicz-Drozdowska et al. 2015, p. 201–219). The first aims at promoting rational point of view and convincing the depositor about the safety of financial means located in the bank (returned in case of insolvency of the financial institution). The above factor is not easily measurable, and most often is seen through the prism of a small percentage of consumers, who are aware of protection system existence. The second component described as "financial" is the factual agility and capability of the scheme to carry out payouts in case guarantee requirements are fulfilled (the so-called financial potential). It is most often measured by a so-called coverage ratio or fund-to-deposit ratio (the percentage of accumulated and available funds in total liabilities of deposit insurers), or the scope of possible intervention (highest possible payout amount) (Iwanicz-Drozdowska and Lepczyński 2011, p. 20).

The above components may exist independently with success. It is possible to create a psychological component of such prominence, that it limits the need of constructing a credible financial component. Until the year 2007, rarely did both components fail simultaneously during a bank's insolvency to an extent that would harm depositor interest. Still, payout proceedings that resulted in partial financial loss of protected depositors took place in Chile between the years 1980 and 1983; Venezuela and Bolivia in 1994 and 1995; Lithuania, Latvia, and Estonia between 1990 and 1996; and in Thailand between 1997 and 1979. Despite runs on the Northern Rock bank, the British deposit guarantee scheme managed to settle all claims. A similar situation took place in Cyprus despite the initial bank panic—depositors did not suffer from loss exceeding the fund coverage level. In the past, trust in the stability of the EU financial sector prevented bank panic events, and deposit insurance agencies dealt with incidental bank bankruptcies flawlessly. Thus, the second component was never formally verified (Laeven and Valencia 2012).

4.2.1 Psychological Component

Public awareness of deposit guarantee scheme existence was a rather marginalized issue by researchers working in the field, and the topic does not have long heritage. The erroneous practice of omitting the topic was brought to attention by FDIC, which was the first to carry out analyses regarding the importance of a functioning psychological component (FDIC 2010). A common perception during the first phase of deposit guarantee scheme existence was that introducing and communicating to depositors the existence of legal guarantee was sufficient. Deposit insurers noticed that a high level of public awareness of guarantee existence has an influence on the entire scheme (FSF 2000, p. 20). As it turned out, the often disregarded topic was of colossal importance during the recent global financial crisis. Orderly management of the psychological component of deposit guarantee schemes, dependent on the maintenance of high nominal guarantee and proper information policy, allows for the appropriate functioning of schemes—even despite low levels of factually aggregated funds. Although the topic does not lie directly within the scope of this book, it must be underlined that deposit guarantee scheme effectiveness is not influenced solely by legislative solutions and formal and legal concepts, but also the way society learns about the protection it is entitled to in this regard. Communicating the undisputed value of deposit insurance has a tremendous influence on the majority of processes a given deposit guarantee institution is engaged in.

Significant problems with the psychological component of the functioning of EU deposit guarantee schemes have taken place as early as at the beginning of the global financial crisis in Great Britain, in 2007. Due to information on financial malfunctioning of the Northern Rock bank, clients lost faith in the enhancement of the situation, and the majority of customers decided on withdrawing funds from their accounts (Ungureanu and Cocriş 2008). It was the first event of bank panic in Great Britain since 1866, and one of the first in the EU during the global financial crisis (Shin 2008, p. 2). Among countries that also witnessed failure of the component were Iceland (with its branches in the Netherlands and Great Britain, present on foreign markets due to cross-border activities), Baltic States (Estonia, Lithuania), as well as Cyprus and Bulgaria. Still, in these above cases, the origin of bank panic was quite different. Detailed information on chosen bank panic events during and after the global financial crisis is presented in Table 4.1.

While analyzing the events presented in the Table 4.1, it must be emphasized that bank panic, which took place in several countries in 2007, was triggered by various reasons, but some have common roots. In the United States, the reason behind such customer behavior was the information on financial struggles of institutions, caused by the sub-prime crisis. In time, the problem also emerged on the British market and concerned banks such as Northern Rock and Bradford & Bingley (the latter of which was liquidated despite lack of client runs). In Great Britain, problems mainly concerned banks that financed transactions on the real estate market (Iwanicz-Drozdowska 2016).

Iceland, the Netherlands, and Great Britain all experienced problems of Icelandic banks that struggled with maintaining their financial liquidity. Due to the fact that Icelandic banks provided services in the Netherlands and Great Britain through their cross-border agreements, deposit insurance was provided, but by the Icelandic deposit guarantee scheme (in accordance with Article 4(1) of Directive 94/19/EC). Once guarantee requirements (lack of deposit availability) were fulfilled, the Icelandic deposit insurance agency *Tryggingarsjóður* did not provide assistance for the bank's non-Icelandic depositors. It would not have been capable of carrying out the procedure even with the assistance of the Icelandic government, because the value of foreign deposits exceeded all aggregated financial resources, potentially available for the purpose.

Events that took place in the Netherlands (DSB Bank), Latvia, and Bulgaria shall be treated separately and incidentally. A clear, common cause may not be acknowledged. Panic breakout was either caused by clients' unusual behavior (Netherlands), bad reputation and suspicious transactions (Bulgaria), or, simply, bad financial condition (Latvia).

As for Cyprus, it may be said that the government behaved mistakenly by communicating to depositors their intention of taxing or nationalizing part of their covered deposits. Clients' savings were to be remitted in

Table 4.1 Chosen bank panic events since 2007

Time of occurrence	Country	Institution	Genesis
August 2007	United States	Countrywide Financial	Information on the worsening financial situation of the institution due to subprime crisis, and the significant engagement in low-quality mortgages.
September 2007	Great Britain	Northern Rock	Disclosure of information on bank struggles related to acquiring funding on the market, turning to the Bank of England for emergency liquidity assistance.
September 2008	United States	Washington Mutual	Disclosure of information on the bank's poor condition, resultant from mortgage granting improprieties. Within a few days, clients withdrew nearly $17 billion from their accounts.
September 2008	United States	Wachovia	Disclosure of information on the bank's poor condition, resultant from mortgage granting improprieties. Within a few days, clients withdrew nearly $5 billion dollars from their accounts. It was an example of the so-called silent bank run by institutional investors.
October 2008	Iceland, Great Britain, Netherlands	Landsbanki, Icesave, Kaupthing Edge	Disclosure of information on poor condition of Icelandic banks by British press. Bank panic took place both in Iceland and abroad, in foreign branches of Icelandic banks present mostly in the Netherlands and Great Britain (where online services were

(*continued*)

Table 4.1 (continued)

Time of occurrence	Country	Institution	Genesis
			provided). Panic was deepened by refusal of paying out funds by the guarantee fund to depositors who did not hold an Icelandic passport.
October 2009	Netherlands	DSB Bank	Public appeal for withdrawal of funds, authored by a client of the bank who justified the call by the bank's aggressive politics. As a result of the plea, approximately €600 million were withdrawn within a few days.
December 2011	Latvia	Swedbank	Release of information on the poor condition of the bank and its liquidity problems. As an effect, depositors withdrew nearly €20 million—an amount prominent in relation to the size of the bank in Latvia.
March 2013	Cyprus	Cyprus Popular Bank, Bank of Cyprus, Hellenic Bank	Release of governmental proposal of utilizing all depositor-owned funds as an instrument of restructuring the financial condition of the country. The proposal also applied to depositors who owned less than €100,000.
June 2014	Bulgaria	CorpBank First Investment Bank	Disclosure of information on the improprieties in the bank, namely, transactions of questionable nature with the bank's main shareholders as participants.

Source: Author's own research

the amount of 6 to 9 per cent of their value (based on varying concepts) (IBP 2012, p. 202). Thus, panic was triggered and Cypriot clients flocked into banks in an attempt of withdrawing their funds. An *ex post* European Parliament analysis noticed that the situation when depositors are not provided the minimum covered amount of €100,000 is unacceptable and breaches current legislature provisions (EP 2013).

Modern bank panic no longer resembles its traditional shape and is hardly noticeable. The outflow of funds no longer happens only through client visits of at a bank's branch, but also through online transfers. Silent runs, the process of large deposit withdrawals by institutional or commercial depositors, are also of great importance. They may, in fact, have an enormous impact on the liquidity of a bank, as in the case of situations that took place in the United States.

On the basis of errors specified above, the following may be named as elements that support the psychological component of deposit guarantee schemes:

– proper communication of protection conditions, provided by deposit insurance agencies,
– ensuring the appropriate level of formal protection,
– maintaining credibility and confidence in scheme's functions (government support, declaration of certainty of statutory protection),
– liquidation of coinsurance (participation of depositor in losses) and ensuring rapid deposit payout.

In conclusion, it is worth noting that even the best designed psychological component model for deposit guarantee schemes cannot provide a hundred per cent effectiveness, and the necessity of verifying the actual capability of a deposit insurance agency cannot be ruled out. Although the component prevents bank panic, the situation when guarantee conditions will be fulfilled by other factors than loss of solvency also remains possible. When the guarantee payout requirement (unavailability of deposits) is fulfilled, the deposit guarantee scheme becomes reliant mostly on its own financial potential, which is also a supporting and strengthening factor of the psychological component.

4.2.2 Financial Component

When the psychological component fails, or the situation of the bank requires suspension of activities and carrying out payouts, the guarantee scheme relies mainly on the strength of its financial component. It was not until the risk of multiple bankruptcies of banks that researchers and rulers began analyzing whether current construction and financial potential of deposit insurance agencies allowed them to perform payout procedures of guaranteed funds on behalf of insolvent banks. A rapid banking sector rise in relation to real economy, with its extreme circumstances and a genuine insolvency risks for major banks (that took place at an unprecedented scale since 2007 onward), inclined that insufficient accumulation of the guarantee fund may result in catastrophic events, as in the case of Iceland, where covered funds were not paid out to clients of their foreign branches after insolvency of local banks took place.

Coverage ratio is an often encountered form of deposit guarantee scheme financial potential. It is a factor often applied, for instance, by the European Commission in its deposit guarantee scheme sector, IADI and EFDI in their annual surveys, as well as the IMF and World Bank in analyses, cited extensively in this book. Coverage ratio is a quotient of funds accumulated by a deposit insurance agency (fund size), divided by the overall worth of financial commitments (potential liabilities), hence, deposits with a set guarantee limit (covered deposits). Coverage ratios in the EU are shown in Fig. 4.1, and specific data in Table 4.2. The data present information as of the end of 2007 and 2012. Due to difficulty with access to current data and varying periods of reporting by deposit insurance agencies, for the sake of the study it may be assumed that three years delay is acceptable. In its analysis from mid-2014, the IMF presents financial data on deposit insurance agencies as of the end of 2010 (Demirgüç-Kunt et al. 2014). Similarly, IADI—with one of the world's best accesses to deposit guarantee information—needs about two years to collect, formulate, and publish data. This means that reports regarding 2012 are published in 2015 (IADI 2014).

Data in Table 4.2 and Fig. 4.1 present the readiness of deposit insurance agencies, as of the end of 2007 and 2012, to carry out payouts

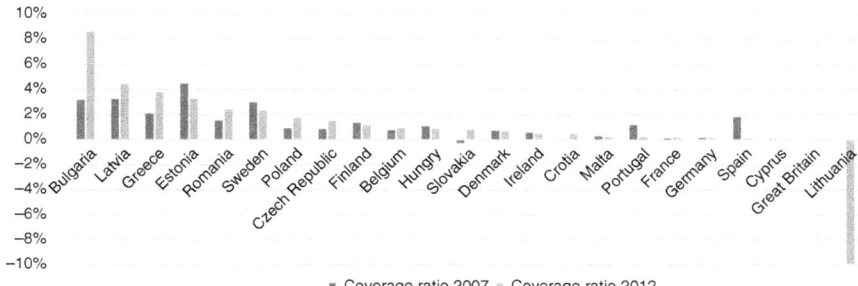

Fig. 4.1   Coverage ratio of deposit insurance agencies in 2007 and 2012 Austria, the Netherlands, Luxembourg, Slovenia, and Italy were omitted due to their ex post schemes (with coverage ratio equal to 0). Data on Poland and Portugal come from 2005, while that on Croatia from 2006 and 2010. Data on Germany was derived from 2012 FSB estimations

Source: Author's own research and Iwanicz-Drozdowska (2011a), Iwanicz-Drozdowska et al. (2015), EC (2011a), FSB (2012), IADI (2008, 2013), Cannas et al. (2014)

in specific EU countries (measured by coverage ratio). The highest ratio levels were found in countries with a relatively small banking sector, namely, Bulgaria, Latvia, Greece, and Estonia. These countries, with the exception of the latter mentioned, accumulated funds in their respective schemes during the crisis period. Still, most EU countries did not have prominent funds at their disposal. With the exemption of countries with an *ex post* scheme, the majority of states had an insignificant coverage ratio, not exceeding 0.2 per cent. The group included countries such as Great Britain, Cyprus, Spain, Germany, and France. Some schemes lost their higher coverage ratios from 2008; among them are Portugal, Spain, and Lithuania, where the depletion of financial resources of deposit insurance agencies took place due to banking sector struggles.

Financial potential is characterized by its long accumulation period and quick utilization, once a financial institution becomes insolvent. Rebuilding the potential after payouts is difficult, as the guarantee fund often begins the process with significant delay (Slovenia, Lithuania, Latvia, and Great Britain). In these countries, before funds are being accumulated again, debt must be covered fully. Nevertheless, it must be noted that many countries applied an *ex post* solution, which means that

Table 4.2 Collation of coverage ratios in EU member states as of the end of 2007 and 2012

Country	2007 coverage ratio (%)	2012 coverage ratio (%)	Financial variant
Austria	0.00	0.00	ex post
Belgium	0.73	0.90	ex ante
Bulgaria	3.16	8.60	ex ante
Croatia	0.00	0.49	ex ante
Cyprus	0.06	0.04	ex ante
Czech Republic	0.84	1.50	ex ante
Denmark	0.71	0.3	ex ante
Estonia	4.44	3.27	ex ante
Finland	1.34	1.17	ex ante
France	0.13	0.19	ex ante
Germany	0.15	0.15	ex ante
Great Britain	0.00	−0.08	ex post
Greece	2.08	3.80	ex ante
Hungary	1.07	0.88	ex ante
Ireland	0.58	0.50	ex ante
Italy	0.00	0.00	ex post
Latvia	3.23	4.40	ex ante
Lithuania	NDA	−9.90	ex ante
Luxembourg	0.00	0.00	ex post
Malta	0.30	0.23	ex ante
Netherlands	0.00	0.00	ex post
Poland	0.90	1.73	mixed
Portugal	1.20	0.22	ex ante
Romania	1.51	2.41	ex ante
Slovakia	−0.26	0.80	ex ante
Slovenia	0.00	0.00	ex post
Spain	1.81	0.13	ex ante
Sweden	2.98	2.32	ex ante

Poland's mixed variant signifies obligatory use of aggregated funds, both ex ante and ex post (to a certain level). Data on Croatia shown as of 2010. Assessments for Germany based on FSB (2012)

Source: Author's own research and Iwanicz-Drozdowska (2011a), Iwanicz-Drozdowska et al. (2015), EC (2011a), FSB (2012), IADI (2008, 2013), Cannas et al. (2014)

their schemes do not aggregate funds for emergency situations. Detailed information on the financial component of EU member states is presented in Table 4.2.

During the global financial crisis it became apparent that aggregated funds of deposit insurance agencies were insufficient for deposit payouts, even those of medium-sized banks. European Commission assessment data show that 1.96 per cent value of eligible deposits is needed in order for a deposit insurance agency to carry out deposit payouts for a single, medium-sized bank. Accumulating 0.6 per cent of eligible deposits is necessary in order to enable the scheme to pay out deposits of a small bank. Detailed information regarding the analysis is featured in Table 4.3.

Calculations show that majority of deposit insurance agencies in 2010 were not ready for successful interventions (with ex ante resources), even of minor banks. As many as 15 EU countries did

Table 4.3 Scope of successful interventions of deposit insurance agencies in 2010

Scenario	Countries capable of carrying out successful interventions with *ex ante* funds only	Countries capable of carrying out successful interventions, while using *ex ante* funds and submitting extraordinary contributions (*ex post*), equivalent to the maximum value permitted by country legislature
High value payout (1.96 per cent of eligible deposits)	Bulgaria, Estonia, Greece, Latvia, Lithuania, Romania, Slovakia (7)	Bulgaria, Cyprus, Czech Republic, Denmark, Estonia, Hungary, Latvia, Lithuania, Malta, Portugal, Romania, Slovakia, Spain (14)
Medium value payout (0.6 per cent of eligible deposits)	Bulgaria, Czech Republic, Estonia, Finland, Greece, Hungary, Latvia, Lithuania, Poland, Portugal, Romania, Spain, Sweden (13)	Bulgaria, Czech Republic, Denmark, Estonia, Finland, Greece, Hungary, Latvia, Lithuania, Poland, Portugal, Slovakia, Spain, Sweden (15)

Source: EC (2011a)

not have a deposit guarantee scheme capable of carrying out payouts of even the smallest of institutions.

4.3   Scope of Successful Intervention of a Deposit Guarantee Scheme

4.3.1 Measurement Method

As elaborated in Section 3.5, various accumulation levels were proposed in regard to deposit guarantee scheme intervention funds. Eventually, the DGS Directive, effective from 3 July 2015, declared the minimum value as 0.8 per cent of the overall worth of covered funds. As shown in the analysis in Section 3.6.5, the above threshold has already been reached in some EU states, while others still need to initiate the accumulation procedure, starting from either very low or negative levels (for instance, Lithuania).

The analysis objective was the comparison of deposit guarantee schemes' effective intervention scope in case deposit payouts from an insolvent bank were necessary. It concerns procedures that took place prior to the introduction of DGS reforms, and those after fund accumulation requirements specified in the directive had been fulfilled. It allowed for the evaluation of introduced postcrisis solutions, as well as the measurement of financial potential of specific funds.

A significant amount of analyses rely on deposit guarantee scheme financial potential evaluation only, based on the coverage ratio presented in Section 4.2.2. Testing the above factor only is not enough to assess the true effectiveness of deposit insurance agency intervention. In order to evaluate an institution's true capability of protecting depositor interests, the scope of successful interventions in the national banking sector, in which it operates, must be analyzed. The scope may be measured either by numbers or percentage of banks covered by a successful deposit guarantee scheme intervention in a given country. It may be achieved through the verification of the number of banks a given deposit insurance agency is capable of carrying out payouts for in a mode that will allow for covering all depositor claims from previously accumulated, own funds. Such a measure is applied in part of theoretical divagations (Bartkowiak 2005). Still, showcasing results of empirical studies is not an easy task—usually, as a rule, they are not carried out, because detailed data required for the analysis are either difficult or impossible to acquire, for they are not provided by banks or deposit insurance agencies (particular banks do not disclose in their periodic reports the amount of accumulated funds). In several EU member states, deposit insurance agencies do not monitor deposit liabilities of specific banks, because they do not analyze current banking sector data. Institutions with a less intricate organizational structure calculate payout amounts (hence, also covered funds of a given bank) only after guarantee requirements had been fulfilled, when the list of depositors entitled for payouts is created.y

The key issue of the study was evaluating the cost of carrying out payout proceedings in a given bank. Information on costs is important, because its value determines whether a guarantee fund is capable of carrying out payouts (intervening successfully). A simplified assumption was applied, that the cost of payment is equal exactly to the value of deposit guarantee schemes accumulated across the whole institution. In reality, the cost is usually lower, because the deposit insurer reclaims part of liabilities during insolvency proceedings, from its bankruptcy estate. The amounts are diversified in the union and vary from country to country. The recovery rate in case of Great Britain often exceeds 80 per cent, thus creating a favorable position of the deposit insurer, who ultimately regains the majority of funds that have been paid out previously. Still, in other countries—especially those from the former Communist Bloc—the recovery rate often reaches only up to 20 per cent, and proceedings are carried out before court and are lengthy. Due to lack of current data regarding recovery rates of various countries, as well as the fact that payouts oblige deposit insurance agencies to provide funds immediately, and recovering funds from bankruptcy estate can take many years, a simplified assumption was made, that the cost of payouts is equal to the value of covered deposits.

A single scenario was applied, where a bank, which is covered by the deposit insurance agency, becomes insolvent (for the sake of simplicity, all available funds were summed up in case of countries that feature a multi-entity deposit guarantee scheme model). Such a case would be favorable from the deposit insurance agency perspective, because insolvency of a bigger number of financial institutions in a short time would drain its funds significantly, thus limiting its intervention scope.

Each financial institution's covered funds were compared separately with the current financial potential of the deposit insurance agency, and the hypothetical financial potential resultant from the DGS Directive (0.8 per cent). For the sake of clarity of the method applied, a graphic presentation of course of events of an effective intervention in Poland is showed in Fig. 4.2.

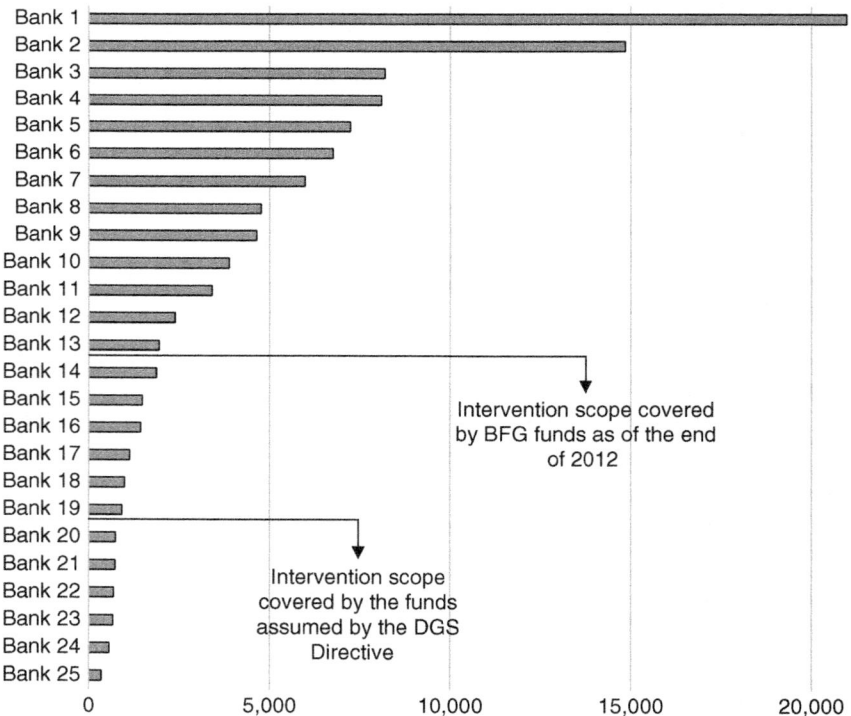

Fig. 4.2 Scope of successful interventions of the deposit insurance agency on the example of Poland in 2012

Value of covered deposits in banks as of the end of 2012, expressed in millions of euros

Source: Author's own research and Bankscope (2015)

Figure 4.2 presents 25 biggest banks based in Poland, sorted by the value of their aggregated, covered deposits. The comparison of the hypothetical deposit insurance agency budget—resultant from DGS Directive provisions—and the factual level of funds accumulated in BGF in relation to covered deposits of particular banks lead to the conclusion that reforming the deposit guarantee scheme so that it abides to the rules of the DGS Directive will not have a greater meaning in the case of Poland. This is caused by the fact that the initial state provided a better intervention scope than required by new, EU legislature. By the end of 2012, the Polish deposit guarantee scheme was capable of carrying out payouts for the 14th biggest bank, while—if it abided to DGS Directive provisions—it could only do so for the 20th. Nevertheless, a significant part of the sector remains outside the effective deposit guarantee scheme intervention scope.

The method above calculated a successful intervention scope for all EU member states. Due to the size of the table and its numerical data, as well as an extensive description of the interpretation method, it may be found in Tables A.6 and A.7 of Annex V, and the further part of this chapter presents the study results.

4.3.2 Data Sources

Data used for the study were derived from several sources. Data of the European Commission (aggregated by Joint Research Center), collected as a side topic of works on deposit guarantee directives or their revisions (Cannas et al. 2014), as well as the BRR Directive (EC 2012), may be named as the main source. Originally, European Commission data were derived from the European Central Bank and surveys sent to deposit insurance agencies. To a significant degree, European Commission data were supplemented by the Bankscope database, especially when data on single, specific banks were needed. The difficulty of acquiring complete, up-to-date information from deposit insurers, who rarely collect and aggregate information, is also worth noting. Other researchers, who carried out similar analyses at an earlier time, also noticed the obstacle (Demirguc-Kunt et al. 2014 or Cannas et al. 2014).

The first column of Table 4.4 presents EU member states as of the end of 2012, but—for the sake of completeness—Croatia was also included in the study, despite its accession in 2013. The second column presents the value of the deposit insurance agency's fund as of the end of 2012, derived from its earlier, yet updated studies. The third column demonstrates hypothetical funds required for reaching the accumulation levels described in DGS Directive provisions, equal to 0.8 per cent of national banking sector covered deposits. For the sake of comparison, it was assumed that deposit insurers, by the end of 2012, already had at their disposal the levels described in the DGS Directive. Still, the directive requires accumulating funds throughout a much longer period of time.

The fourth column includes credit institutions based in EU countries that lie within the competences of deposit guarantee schemes and accept guaranteed funds from depositors. The number of studied entities was limited to that of the Bankscope database from the end of 2012. Bankscope has at its disposal data on approximately 8,000 financial institutions existent in the EU and, as a rule, has information on the biggest and medium-sized credit institutions in each member state (Bureau van Dijk, 2015). Bankscope is evaluated positively in terms of validity of its data, because they come from annual reports. An extraordinarily high quality of data evaluation may be encountered in the case of European and American institutions, which is also favorable for the research (Bhattachyra 2003). Therefore, even if several deposit-accepting entities (mainly cooperative banks) were omitted in the study, most possibly it was due to the size of their activity (small value of covered deposits) and their insignificance from the study's perspective. The line separating banks—those which qualify for successful intervention of deposit insurance agencies, and those which do not—runs through the big and medium-sized bank group. The number of evaluated entities reached a total of 3874 credit institutions. Estonia represents the smallest number of analyzed entities (8), while Germany—the largest (1730).

The fifth column of Table 4.4 shows the covered-to-eligible deposits correction ratio. While the study analyzes the possibility of carrying out payout proceedings for individual entities, there is no capability of acquiring data on the value of covered deposits of any of the nearly

Table 4.4 Data used for the study of successful intervention scope of deposit guarantee schemes, based on payout of guaranteed funds in specific member states

Country	Factual fund size (in millions of euros)	Fund size assumed by the DGS Directive (in millions of euros)	Number of analyzed entities	Correction ratio (%)
Austria	0	1,387	248	72
Belgium	2,064	1,833	46	67
Bulgaria	1,580	147	25	70
Croatia	185	175	34	67
Cyprus	22	416	16	67
Czech Republic	983	523	27	67
Denmark	770	844	83	85
Estonia	172	42	8	61
Finland	910	622	32	61
France	2,111	8,828	315	72
Germany	2,363	12,602	1,730	67
Great Britain	−969	9,750	178	56
Greece	3,979	838	13	75
Hungary	265	242	25	69
Ireland	403	640	23	57
Italy	0	3,924	571	68
Latvia	262	48	17	41
Lithuania	−660	53	9	67
Luxembourg	0	244	71	19
Malta	16	56	10	74
Netherlands	0	3,576	50	78
Poland	1,789	826	38	59
Portugal	238	882	28	67
Romania	661	219	24	83
Slovakia	194	194	15	90
Slovenia	0	119	19	85
Spain	855	5,399	130	72
Sweden	3,264	1,127	89	71

Data on Croatia presents the value as of the end of 2010; a medium correction ratio for the EU was applied

Source: Author's own research and Cannas et al. (2014); DAB (2015) and Bankscope (2015)

4,000 banks. Still, in order to approximate to the value, the correction ratio, whose use is thoroughly described below, may be applied.

Data that have not been included in Table 4.4, but are mentioned in Table A.5 in Annex IV and were used in the study, concern the value of covered deposits accumulated in particular banks in all EU countries. The value of deposits for each bank was acquired through the Bankscope database, which collects information of five categories of banks. They are as follows:

- customer deposits,
- bank deposits,
- municipalities/government deposits,
- other deposits,
- certificates of deposits.

Neither of the categories above expresses the value of covered deposits worth up to €100,000. Therefore, a decision on which of the categories above were to be included in the scope of the analysis had to be made. The first step was evaluating deposit categories that qualified for the privilege of protection—hence, eligible deposits. Accepting all deposits as such would be erroneous, because not all deposits are protected (in accordance with Art. 5 of the DGS Directive, those include deposits of financial institutions, other deposits—among them non-nominal—and deposits of part of public/municipality units). For the sake of clarity, in order to select the category of eligible deposits, customer deposits (represented mainly by natural persons and entrepreneurs) were mentioned in the analysis. Considering all five deposit categories in regard to EU banks, the above group is significantly dominant in terms of its liabilities. Due to difficulties in access to certain data, some analyses regarding deposit guarantee schemes were left by other authors at the peripheries of eligible deposits and based on approximated values (Cannas et al. 2014).

In the next step, after information on eligible deposit value of specific banks had been acquired, actions aimed at learning the approximate value for eligible deposits' category (namely, worth up to €100,000 euros) were initiated. Thus, the category was corrected and the value of a country's eligible to covered deposits ratio was subtracted. The ratio was calculated and published by the European Commission and was presented in the fifth column of Table 4.4 (EC 2011a).

Two flaws of such calculation method of covered deposits' value for each of the banks may be named. Firstly, individual preferences of depositors regarding the value of deposits may vary significantly from bank to bank. It may be expected that deposits in big financial institutions will have a high value—for instance, those owned by commercial law companies. Secondly, the situation when a small-sized bank manages only several deposits of significant value, while the remaining do not exceed coverage limits, may not be ruled out. Hence, from the perspective of a single bank, correcting the category of eligible deposits through applying the ratio measured for the whole sector will provide a misleading view of potential liabilities of deposit insurance agencies. Still, even a flawed correction, as mentioned above, provides a better understanding of reality and the potential responsibilities of the deposit guarantee scheme toward particular banks, especially for countries with an extensive banking sector.

Applying the correction of eligible to covered deposits is of special significance to countries, where the covered to eligible deposits ratio is relatively low (below 50 per cent), as in the case of Luxembourg and Estonia. It is most often related to the modest size of the banking sector of these countries, as well as high value of deposits of foreign depositors. Such a correction alters the view of the situation, as well as potential intervention capabilities of deposit guarantee schemes (in their favor). A similar methodology was applied by the European Commission for the needs of guarantee scheme research in 2009 (EC 2011b).

The method described above allowed for the adopting of covered deposit value calculation for each bank and was later used for evaluating possible interventions of the deposit guarantee scheme. Bankscope information on client deposits, as a rule, expresses data as of 31 December 2012 (in case of a different reporting date, the annual report of 31 December 2012 was taken into account). European Commission data regarding covered deposit values in each country and the covered to eligible deposit ratio also present the state as of 31 December 2012. Data on accumulated funds of deposit guarantee schemes were derived from the author's own research, statutory studies of Warsaw School of Economics, of which he was a participant (Iwanicz-Drozdowska et al. 2015), information acquired directly from deposit insurance agencies, as well as data published by the European Commission and IADI, that mirror the state as of 31 December 2012, unless otherwise inclined.

4.3.3 Analysis and Evaluation of Successful Intervention Scope

Studies of successful interventions—according to the state of being before the enactment of reforms that unified the accumulated fund levels for deposit insurance agencies—incline that EU member states may be divided into four groups, as presented in Table 4.5 (as of 31 December 2012). It must be highlighted that the scope is expressed numerically. For instance, a result of 20 of a given country means that, in case of fulfillment of guarantee requirements, payout of covered deposits would be possible for the credit institution with the 20th biggest number of covered deposits. 19 entities with a higher amount

Table 4.5 Division of EU member states on the basis of the scope of successful deposit guarantee scheme interventions prior to reform (as of the end of 2012)

Evaluation of payout scope	Countries	Group size
Good (1–10)	Bulgaria, Estonia, Finland, Greece, Latvia, Malta, Romania, Sweden	8
Sufficient (11–20)	Belgium, Croatia, Cyprus, Czech Republic, Hungary, Ireland, Poland, Portugal, Slovakia	9
Insufficient (above 20)	Denmark, France, Germany, Spain	4
None	Austria, Great Britain, Italy, Lithuania, Luxembourg, Netherlands, Slovenia	7

For instance, a range of 1–10 means that a given insurance agency is capable of carrying out payout procedures for a bank from the group of ten institutions with the highest value of covered deposits.

Source: Author's own formulation, based on analysis results presented in Annex V

of deposits will be excluded from payout procedures of the country guarantee scheme. Detailed information may be found in previously presented for the case of Poland Fig. 4.3.

Eight countries may be accredited to the group representing good intervention and payout capabilities. These countries were capable of carrying out payout procedures for the top ten banks of their respective banking sectors. It is worth noting that the positive evaluation is

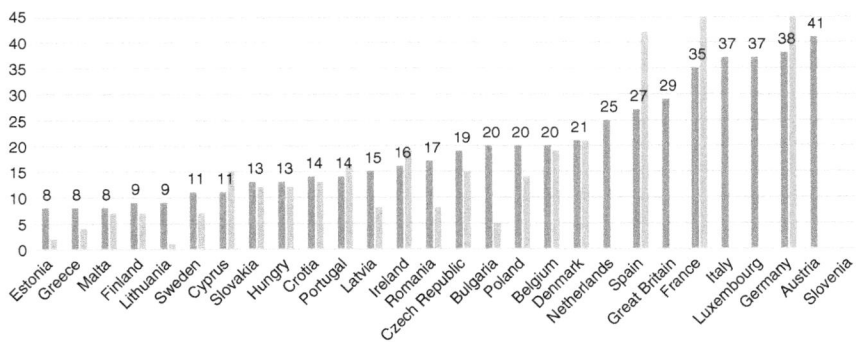

■ Scope of intervention in accordance with DGS Directive 2014/49/EU (0.8% of covered deposits)
▪ Scope intervention—country levels as of the end of 2012

Fig. 4.3 Scope of successful deposit guarantee scheme intervention—data as of the end of 2012, and the assumed levels of Directive 2014/49/EU

The scope is expressed numerically. For instance, a result of 20 for Poland means that—in case of fulfillment of guarantee requirements—payout of covered deposits would be possible for the credit institution with the 20th biggest number of covered deposits. 19 entities with a higher amount of deposits would be excluded from payout procedures of BGF. Lack of intervention scope (expressed by absence of the bar) means that funds of the country deposit guarantee scheme are not sufficient for successful intervention toward any entity (applicable mainly in regard to ex post systems). Results for France and Germany exceed the scale of the chart and are, respectively, 97 for France, and 145 for Germany

Countries, where the darker bar (to the right) is lower than that to the left (lighter bar), are potentially endangered with an unfavorable result of DGS Directive introduction in regard to the amount of funds accumulated in the guarantee fund

Source: Author's own formulation, based on Annex V, where detailed calculations and result interpretation may be found

exaggerated in case of several states—for instance, Estonia, Malta, and Greece all had small-sized banking sectors, and their sample sizes were 8, 10, and 13, respectively. The omission is seen clearly in Annex V, where coverage of the banking sector with successful deposit insurance agency interventions is shown. It is especially worth noting that in 2012 Greece had already been in the midst of financial sector reform, and the deposit level in banks decreased significantly. Despite the examples above, it may be assumed that deposit guarantee scheme financial potential was high—especially in countries such as Sweden or Finland.

The group whose intervention scope was evaluated as sufficient is comprised of countries, whose deposit guarantee schemes were capable of carrying out payments for banks numbered 11–20 in regard to the sizes of their covered deposits. Once more, countries with a relatively small sector found themselves in the group—among them, Slovakia and Cyprus. Still, the sample size in the group was bigger, ranging from 15 in Slovakia, to 46 in Belgium. The fact that several countries constituting the group were close to the lower limit of interventions (with a result of 19) deserves special recognition. Hence, a large group of banks did not qualify for payout procedures.

Countries that aggregated a small amount of resources in their deposit insurance agencies, but had a prominent banking sector, belong to the third group. The presence of Germany, with a result of 145, and France, with 97, is especially worth noting. Effectively, Germany's deposit guarantee scheme would not be capable of fulfilling its responsibilities toward 144 banks, based on their deposit values. Although the result was more favorable for France, 96 banks would not be given the possibility of benefiting from guaranteed funds. In practice, it means that in several EU countries funds accumulated by deposit insurance agencies have a symbolic meaning only and are insufficient for interventions in multiple banks.

The last group represents countries, where deposit guarantee scheme funds are collected in the *ex post* model, or the scheme itself is in debt (Lithuania). As an effect, the deposit guarantee scheme does not have any operational authority. It does not mean a total lack of capabilities, but—as shown in the British or Lithuanian example—it causes indebtedness of the scheme and necessity of using public finances, which are subsequently paid off by banks present in the system.

Decision makers have noticed that the above situation created multiple risks, such as the deepening of country debt or threats to the financial stability. Therefore, it has been decided that a directive obliging EU member states to accumulate funds equivalent to 0.8 per cent of covered deposits of a given banking sector was necessary. A detailed collation of intervention scopes under the DGS Directive is presented in Table 4.6.

The analysis of specific groups leads to the conclusion that the size of the group showing broad intervention competences will decrease for eight to five as a result of DGS Directive enactment. What is more, majority of countries will note a worsening of their results (for instance, Finland will gain two, and Greece four points in addition to their previous results). The second group representing sufficient intervention capabilities is comprised of 13 countries—an additional four, than prior to DGS Directive introduction. Still, these are countries that fell from the favorable group representing a good intervention scope, such as Bulgaria, Romania, or Sweden. Therefore, it must not be mistaken as a positive effect of reform introduction.

The group of countries with insufficient deposit insurance agencies' payout potential became broader, but their number is simply no longer

Table 4.6 Division of EU member states on the basis of the scope of successful deposit guarantee scheme interventions; prognosis of DGS Directive target levels' achievement

Evaluation of payout scope	Countries	Group size
Good (1–10)	Estonia, Finland, Greece, Lithuania, Malta	5
Sufficient (11–20)	Belgium, Bulgaria, Croatia, Cyprus, Czech Republic, Hungary, Ireland, Latvia, Poland, Portugal, Romania, Slovakia, Sweden	13
Insufficient (above 20)	Austria, Denmark, France, Germany, Great Britain, Italy, Luxembourg, Netherlands, Spain	9
None	Slovenia	1

For instance, a range of 1–10 means that a given insurance agency is capable of carrying out payout procedures for a bank from the group of ten institutions with the highest value of covered deposits

Source: Author's own formulation, based on analysis results presented in Annex V

evaluated as zero. Countries with an *ex post* scheme model appeared in the group, among them the Netherlands, Great Britain, and Italy. Despite favorable assumptions (achieving target levels), national deposit insurance agencies are not capable of carrying out payouts for major deposit acceptant institutions and achieved results of 25, 29, and 37, respectively, in reference to the size of the bank (measured by their covered deposit value).

Only Slovenia remained in the last group. In case of the country, even an accumulation of funds on the 0.8 per cent threshold would not allow for payouts of the last institution covered by the study—namely, Slovene Export and Development Bank, which held approximately €135 million in covered deposits, while the Slovene deposit guarantee scheme would only be capable of providing €119 million. Therefore, the issue of high concentration of the sector in Slovenia was not resolved by the enactment of the European deposit guarantee scheme reform.

Table 4.7 presents a summary of successful interventions of deposit guarantee schemes, resultant from the introduction of the DGS

Table 4.7 Division of EU member states on the basis of influence of the DGS Directive on successful deposit guarantee scheme interventions

Influence of reform on successful intervention scope*	Countries	Group size
Potentially negative	Belgium, Bulgaria, Croatia, Czech Republic, Estonia, Finland, Greece, Hungary, Latvia, Malta, Poland, Romania, Slovakia, Sweden	14
Neutral (0)	Denmark, Slovenia	2
Minimal (1–4)	Cyprus, Ireland, Lithuania, Portugal	4
Average (15–34)	Luxembourg, Netherlands, Spain	3
Significant (62–534)	Austria, France, Germany, Great Britain, Italy	5

As an example, reform influence scaled from 1 to 4 means that the given insurance agency expanded the scope of its successful intervention by another 1 to 4 deposit accepting institutions

Source: Author's own formulation, based on analysis results presented in Annex V

Directive. In case of half of EU countries, applying the minimum level of 0.8 per cent value of funds had a unfavorable influence on deposit insurance agencies' intervention scope. For several other states, it did not bring any change (Denmark, Slovenia). Four countries noted a slight improvement of deposit guarantee scheme intervention capabilities. It is worth noting that in 2012, Lithuania's insurance agency was in debt and—according to the methodology of the study—was not capable of carrying out payouts for even a single bank. After DGS Directive implementation, the ninth biggest bank (out of a sample of nine) will be within deposit guarantee scheme implementation reach.

As it seems, reform has a positive impact on countries with a large banking sector, where many covered deposits' aggregating institutions are present. Scope of intervention in the case of Spain, the Netherlands, and Luxembourg would be broadened by another 15, 25, and 34 banks, respectively. Therefore, after implementing reform in the above-mentioned EU states, deposit insurance agencies would better fulfill their duties in regard to a total of 74 banks. Prior to reform, funds were missing for the payout of such a number of lost deposits. It may be perceived a positive result, as it increases the capabilities of deposit guarantee schemes in the above countries significantly. An even more favorable result may be noted for countries that, thus far, applied the *ex post* deposit guarantee scheme model (with the exception of France, where resources from banks were already reserved, and the Netherlands that belonged to the previous group). The above is a result of analysis methodology and the effect of low base (lack of intervention capabilities for all entities).

Detailed financial potential comparative results for deposit guarantee schemes are presented in Fig. 4.3.

A broader evaluation of DGS Directive influence on successful interventions of deposit guarantee schemes may be achieved through the analysis of the second and fifth columns of Table A.6 in Annex V. They represent the percentage of the finance sector, which stayed beyond specific deposit insurance agencies' competences. The analysis may only be treated as a supplementary source, because the key to a deposit insurance agency's effectiveness is not the percentage of institutions that payouts may be carried out for, but the value of covered deposits that are protected by the scheme. The fact that countries with a small banking sector demonstrate positive, yet partially ostensible effects (for the accumulation levels of deposit insurances agencies in 2012) is another supplementary conclusion of the study. Results that provide deposit payout capabilities for the seventh and eighth banks in Malta and Latvia, or even—as in the case of Greece—the fourth biggest credit institution (in terms of its covered deposits) are misleading, because they might not be as favorable if compared to the percentage of banks remaining under genuine successful intervention scopes of guarantee schemes. In such countries, a considerable percentage of their banking sectors are beyond successful intervention capabilities and are, as follows, 70, 47, and 31 per cent. Contradictory dependencies may be noted, for instance, in Germany and Italy, where deposit guarantee scheme reform scenarios present 37 and 36 banks, respectively, outside their intervention scope. It is a scarce percentage of the respective banking sectors—namely, accounting for only two and six per cent.

It is difficult to clearly evaluate deposit guarantee scheme reforms introduced by the DGS Directive. On the one hand, it will not be of significance to several countries (16), because their national approach toward shaping financial security had already provided guarantee schemes with at least one financial backing, similar to that introduced by the DGS Directive. On the other hand, it will be a positive change to payout efficiency of twelve member states. What is most important is that countries with an ex post scheme will begin fund accumulation for the necessities of their deposit guarantee schemes. An important change will be noted in Germany, France, Spain, Italy, and Great Britain, hence—from the perspective of financial stability—important EU members with large banking sectors. Improvement will be very apparent in their case, for hundreds of banks will be found within the scope of successful deposit guarantee schemes' intervention.

In conclusion, it seems that the changes introduced by the DGS Directive are not of ambitious nature. It is profitable from the perspective of deposit guarantee scheme scope that obligatory fund accumulation in an *ex ante* model will be introduced, but for many countries the current situation is more favorable than that foreseen by the directive. Yet, analysis inclines a different, significant problem. Even with the use of currently accumulated funds, or those foreseen by Directive 2014/49/EU, in case of insolvency of a single bank, intervention scope of the deposit guarantee scheme will be ranged from the eighth (Malta, Estonia, Greece), up to the 41st bank in the sector (Austria).

The question of what shall be done with banks that will not find themselves within the scope of interventions remains unanswered. The concepts presented in the study show that 516 banks (including the total lack of intervention capabilities, as in the case of Slovenian institutions) will not be covered by intervention procedures. The above entities do not comply with the requirements for standard deposit guarantee scheme intervention in EU member states (out of nearly 8,500 banks in the union) (EC 2012). Although the above account for 6 per cent of all EU banks, they are also some of the largest institutions of tremendous meaning for financial stability. Another fact worth noting is that worse scenarios are possible—such, where two banks become insolvent in a short time, or rebuilding funds in the guarantee scheme is not complete before the next intervention becomes necessary. A government loan or issue of bonds by the deposit insurance agency may be the answer, yet it is only a partial solution the society does not approve of, which is limited by strict European public aid conditions. Regulatory reforms of the financial sector were, in fact, created in order to limit public fund use. It is worth mentioning that the above analysis reveals the ineffectiveness of deposit guarantee scheme solutions in regard to banks with a prominent deposit base, even after DGS Directive postcrisis reforms will have been instated. Deposit insurance agencies will not have at their disposal full intervention competences, despite the enhancement of the situation in several countries. It is therefore crucial to indicate why deposit guarantee schemes are ineffective in regard to certain banks, and what way can the inefficiencies be dealt with.

A conclusion revealed through the analysis of potential deposit guarantee scheme intervention scope is that part of financial institutions remain beyond deposit insurance agencies' assistance range. Still, apart from insufficient resources of deposit guarantee schemes, the weaknesses of the system are of external nature and are unrelated to deposit insurance agency actions. It seems unlikely that a long-term setback of the EU banking sector will take place, nor is it probable that bank increase or deposit base development will be limited. On the other hand, the impact of perseverance of low-level interest rates and search for alternative location forms for financial surpluses are unknown. Therefore, it is crucial that regulatory solutions are adjusted in a way that they become capable of managing these deficits. Most likely, banks that will not benefit from deposit payout assistance will still be existent in the EU for many years to come. Under the rule of new Directive 2014/49/EU, there are still 500 institutions of the type. Such organizations require alternative intervention instruments of the financial safety net (such as bail in), but applied in cooperation with the deposit guarantee scheme.

4.4   Causes of Deposit Guarantee Scheme Inefficiency

Previous studies reveal that the situation when a prominent number of banks and depositors are not protected by deposit insurance agency interventions is still common in many EU member states. Such circumstances were not present when the concept of deposit guarantee schemes came to life in the Unites States, nor was it as unfavorable as it is today, when first guarantee schemes were implemented on European ground. The banking sector was transformed, despite years of maintaining the *status quo* and not implementing any important deposit guarantee scheme reforms. The changes that took place were not responded to by the institutional construction of deposit insurance agencies. As an effect, several basic reasons behind ineffectiveness—created both directly and passively—may be indicated. Low accumulation of funds may be named as the main cause of deposit insurance agency weakness, as shown in the analysis in Section 4.2.3. Still, it is not the only factor, for many banks—despite their favorable position in the guarantee fund—will stay beyond deposit insurance agency protection, and collecting high amounts of contributions is unjustified from the economical point of view.

Passive reasons (described in Sections 4.4.1–4.4.3), influencing the ineffectiveness of deposit guarantee schemes and the remaining of certain banks outside intervention scope, include the fast-paced development of the banking sector in the EU, increase in deposit value of financial institutions, and the rise in foreign capital in banking sectors (especially in small economies of the Union). Several factors that have direct influence on deposit guarantee schemes may be named: the rising concentration in the banking sector (created, for instance, by fusion and acquisition), guarantee levels' rise without guarantee scheme reforms, and the low return rate from assets of an insolvent bank (shown in Sections 4.4.4–4.4.6).

4.4.1   Banking Sector Size

Throughout the shaping of deposit guarantee scheme concepts in the 1930s and the later period of 1970–80s, the banking sector played a comparatively lesser role in the economy than it does today. Bank assets in relation to GDP of a country were still not close to today's levels. Previously, a relatively modest banking sector meant that a single bank's insolvency would not be able to undermine the financial stability of the country and did not truly influence the real economy. Still, the situation was subject to change. Since the 1990s, the banking sector of the EU changed greatly and was influenced by various trends, mostly upward. The increase in value of bank assets in relation to a country's GDP was the basic change, which gradually made the stability of the economy dependent from the condition of the sector (ESRB 2014). The relation of assets of the biggest banks to GDP of countries is shown in Table 4.8.

Although the increase in bank assets' participation in country GDP was observed globally, the most spectacular changes may be accredited to EU

Table 4.8 Assets of the largest banks in relation to GDP of chosen countries in the years 1990, 2006, and 2009, expressed in percentages

Country	Three largest banks			Five largest banks		
	1990	2006	2009	1990	2006	2009
Germany	38	117	118	55	161	151
Great Britain	68	226	336	87	301	466
France	70	212	250	95	277	344
Italy	29	110	121	44	127	138
Spain	45	155	189	66	179	220
Netherlands	154	538	406	159	594	464
Sweden	89	254	334	120	312	409
Japan	36	76	92	59	96	115
United States	8	35	43	11	45	58

Source: EC (2012), p. 97

countries. Japan and the United States noted must less dynamic rises. In countries such as the Netherlands, Sweden, or Great Britain, assets of the greatest banks exceed GDP of the country even several times.

In the last decade, banks increased the value of their assets noticeably, which is presented in Fig. 4.4. It is especially apparent in the European Union. In the year 2011, banking sector assets stood for 90 per cent of GDP, while in Japan the rate was 196 per cent (EBF 2011). At the same time, the EU accounted or 284 per cent, and the Eurozone itself—323 per cent. Still, such comparative measures require specifying the banking sector model present in the given country. As a general rule, the Anglo-Saxon model adopted by the United Kingdom and the United States shows a lesser participation of assets in the country's GDP, because part of bank activities are being taken over by the better developed capital market.

The EU is characterized by a certain anomaly; namely, assets of the banking sector exceed GDP levels of several countries. It is especially important in regard to smaller states, such as Luxembourg and Malta. In

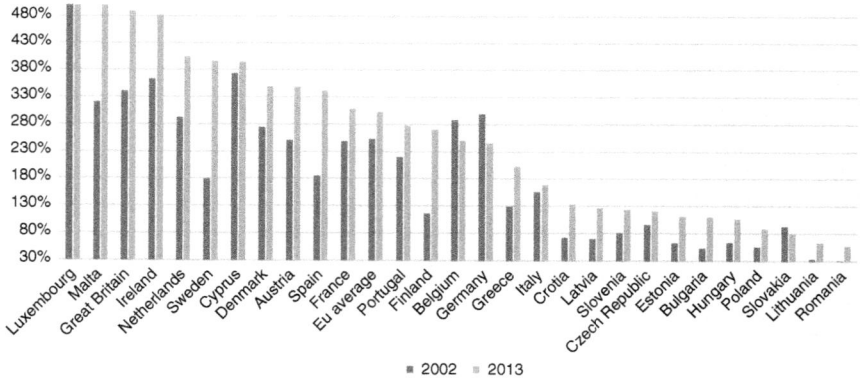

Fig. 4.4 Value of banking sector assets in relation to nominal GDP of EU countries in 2002 and 2013

For the sake of clarity, the scale displayed on the vertical axis starts from 30%. In Luxembourg, the ratio was equal to 1596% and 2753%, respectively, and for Malta—714% in the year 2013. Data on Romania and Bulgaria express the state as of 2004 (instead of 2002)

Source: ECB (2006, 2008, 2014); CNB (2015); Eurostat (2015)

nominal terms, countries with more prominent banking sectors, such as Great Britain, Germany, France, and Italy, also possess a high level of banking sector assets' to GDP ratio.

The average value of banking sector assets in the EU was 253 per cent in the year 2002, and 302 per cent in 2013 (the value dropped in the years that followed 2011 as a result of the financial crisis). For the last 15 years, a trend of banking sector asset increase may be observed in relation to GDP of certain EU member states. Apart from the already mentioned Luxembourg and Malta, extraordinarily large banking sectors were present in Great Britain, Ireland, the Netherlands, and Sweden. Only in the case of four EU countries (Luxembourg, Belgium, Germany, and Slovakia) did the ratio decrease; other countries noted a contrasting trend. Some states—such as Sweden, Spain, or Croatia—noted a very dynamic rise of the banking sector in terms of its GDP value. Detailed information in this regard is shown in Fig. 4.4.

A general rise in EU banking sector assets conveys important implications for deposit guarantee schemes. The initial guarantee concept had not been reformed for many years, while the banking sector, its meaning for the economy, as well as its relation to GDP rose notably. Such a situation burdens deposit insurance agencies with bigger responsibilities, because it became in charge of a much broader, more significant economy sector than ever before. What is more, several EU countries with small economies created a banking sector, whose assets' value greatly exceeds the country's GDP. As a result, potential deposit payouts for clients of the banking sector will be virtually impossible, and the supportive intervention of the state (even if public resources are used) will also be insufficient due to the scope of banking activities of a given country. The EU lacks reforms that would adjust current deposit guarantee scheme regulatory legislature and prepare the institutions for successful interventions of banking sectors of the sizes present in certain countries. A pan-European institution that would be capable of intervening at a supra-national level is also missing (Smaga 2013). The relatively insignificant financial potential of guarantee schemes, analyzed in Section 4.2.3, has an influence on the entire shape of the banking sector in the EU.

4.4.2 Deposit Value

An increase in deposit value in relation to GDP of respective countries took place in EU member states. This may be seen in Fig. 4.5, which shows data starting from the year 1960 onward. At the beginning of the 1960s, the value of deposits in a banking sector in relation to GDP of EU countries was 40 per cent; in the record-breaking year 2009, the ratio was already at 96 per cent.

Figure 4.6 presents data on the nonfinancial sector's deposit share in relation to GDP of specific EU countries. Since 1995, the share had been rising and reached its highest values in Spain, Portugal, the Netherlands, and Germany—as far as the biggest EU economies are concerned. Therefore, nonprofessional participants of the financial market (the nonfinancial sector) increased their participation and deposited more and more funds in the banking sector. This is also confirmed by the rising responsibilities of deposit guarantee schemes that not only,

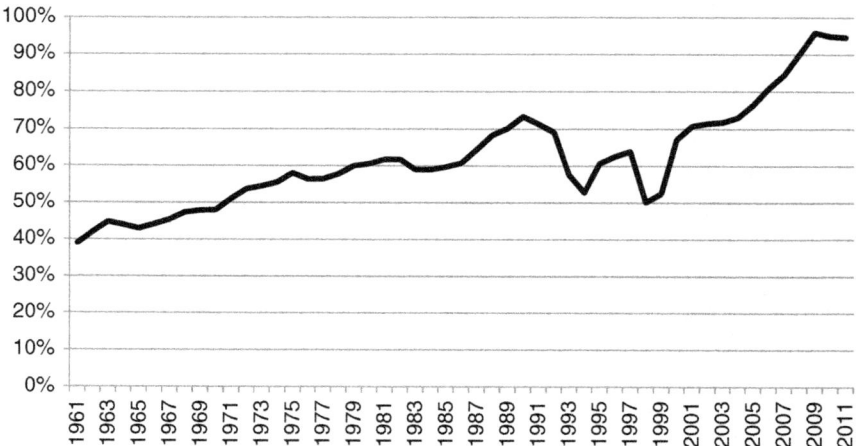

Fig. 4.5 Value of deposits in banks in relation to GDP of current member states of the EU

An arithmetic, annual mean of deposit value in relation to GDP of current EU countries is shown on the chart (if such data was available)

Source: World Bank (2014)

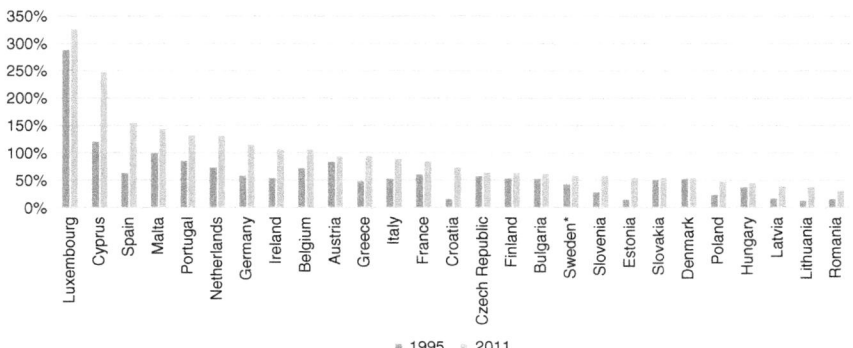

Fig. 4.6 Banking sector deposits owned by the nonfinancial sector, shown in relation to GDP of a given country in 1995 and 2011
Data on Great Britain is not available

Source: Author's own formulation on the basis of World Bank (2014)

year after year, constituted a more prominent part of the market, but also guaranteed the sound functioning of households.

4.4.3 Foreign Capital Share

As a result of implementing the common market concept, the EU banking sector started undergoing internationalization. This translated into the creation of transnational corporations and holdings comprised of banks simultaneously functioning in several countries. These, in turn, are connected to one another through country nets and other banks. Most often, problems of a single institution result in difficulties of other, interconnected entities (contagion effect). Struggles of the parent company may create drainage of its subsidiaries (banks in other countries). In many of the so-called New EU countries, foreign bank assets account for 70 per cent of total bank assets' value (World Bank 2014). In this regard, an unfavorable situation is present in Luxembourg (99 per cent of banks with foreign capital), Hungary (92 per cent), Ireland (90 per cent), Slovakia (87 per cent), Romania (81 per cent), Estonia (71 per cent), Lithuania (70 per cent), and Poland (69 per cent). In the case of Luxembourg and Ireland, though, it must be noted that the countries are considered as financial hubs and are also beneficiaries of big foreign banks' presence on their respective markets. The criteria show a clear division between countries of the so-called New EU (big foreign capital share in the banking sector) and the Old EU (a relatively low level of foreign capital share).

As a rule, the deposit insurance agency of a given country is responsible for payouts of deposits of a bank based in the given country. Still, if the bank is present on a market through its branch (the entity is not registered in the host country), then the home country deposit guarantee scheme is responsible. As proved by previous experiences, institutions did not always fulfill their duties (as in the case of Iceland). Instead of Iceland, Great Britain carried out payouts from its own resources, despite not being obliged by any form of law. The rise of banks with foreign capital and local branches, especially in New EU countries, is clearly visible. Therefore, it is possible that a foreign bank operating through its branch on a given market will accumulate a prominent value of deposits, and the deposit scheme of the country, where the entity is officially registered—not the host state—will be formally responsible for the protection of accounts. Such a situation is possible even in the case where a given country does not have sufficient financial potential, refuses to carry out payouts, or does not initiate intervention proceedings.

4.4.4 Banking Sector Concentration

The above-described reasons behind the passive weakening of deposit guarantee schemes' position may be characterized as an overall rise of deposit insurance agency responsibility scope. Three factors may be hereby named.

The first is a rising concentration of the banking sector. In the 1990s and later years, a consolidation of the EU banking sector took place. A trend of building big structures—financial groups—became apparent. As a result, in the majority of EU countries, three to five biggest banks own half or more of overall banking sector's assets.

It may be said of the EU that an average of five banks comprised 83 per cent of its banking sector. In 13 states (for example, Denmark, the Netherlands, Sweden, and Belgium) the rate was even higher—90 per cent, and for another ten, it was above 70 per cent (among them Germany and Ireland) (World Bank 2014). The relation was of similar shape in case of three biggest banks of the 15 states that were characterized by ratio above 70 per cent, and the EU average was equal to 71 per cent. The most concentrated banking sectors are present in Estonia, Cyprus, Malta, and Sweden, and the least, in Luxembourg, Poland, Latvia, and Slovenia (World Bank 2014). The state of concentration of the banking sector has serious implications on deposit insurance agency activities.

A dispersed banking sector encourages the effectiveness of deposit insurance agencies and was the warrant of depositor protection concept fulfillment in previous years. Initially, insolvency of one financial institution was not difficult to control by the guarantee scheme. The financial component of the fund was usually designed in a way that equipped the deposit guarantee scheme in sufficient funds for payouts from a liquidated institution.

In time, guarantee schemes in EU countries became less and less prepared for insolvencies in highly concentrated banking sectors. The basic financial construction of deposit insurance agencies, as well as accumulation method of funds, has not changed in many years. The progressing process of banking sector concentration systematically lowered the scope of successful deposit insurance agency interventions in regard to a greater number of banks. The rise of banking sector concentration also causes deposit concentration at a single financial institution, thus putting them at risk of loss.

The scope of potential deposit insurance agency intervention is set on a certain level, resultant from the earliest projected hedge ratio (for example, 1 per cent of covered deposits' value of a given banking sector). Still, an increasing number of banks have more and more covered deposits, than those present in the whole guarantee fund. Hence, it is highly probable that several banks will remain beyond successful intervention scope of the guarantee scheme. An example of Poland is shown in Fig. 4.7.

The line indicating potential intervention scope of BGF separates banks with a high concentration of covered deposits from those that are within successful intervention capabilities. Still, the increase in

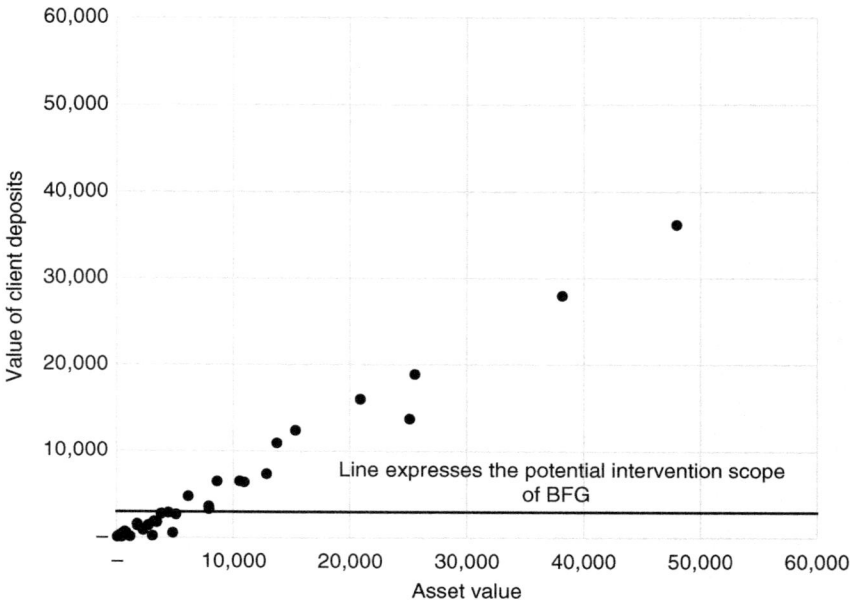

Fig. 4.7 Concentration of the banking sector on the example of Poland in 2013, and intervention capabilities of deposit insurance agencies (value expressed in millions of euros)

Black dots symbolize assets' and client deposits' value of a given bank

Source: Bankscope (2015)

banking sector concentration causes the relocation of a constantly rising number of banks above the line. Remaining outside intervention capabilities of a deposit insurance agency by certain banks seem inevitable, for concentration processes will most probably not experience diversion. Therefore, in the above situation, it is crucial to find an answer to the question on what must be done in order for deposit insurance agencies to work more effectively, and for countries to be able to eliminate the biggest banks from their market without the loss of depositor funds. It seems that deposit guarantee mechanisms will have to be supported by alternative actions, based on a procedure alternative to payout.

4.4.5 Guarantee Level

Guarantee level has a direct impact on potential effectiveness of the deposit guarantee scheme and is key information for the depositor. Thematic literature underlines that deposits of high value should be treated differently than those belonging to small depositors (Kennickell et al. 1995). Yet, the boundary between a depositor who owns a small fund in a bank and one who owns a deposit that does not qualify for full protection is vague. Natural persons and small business owners belong to the first group, as depositors who do not have sufficient knowledge on the financial situation of a given bank, and whose bank accounts are of low value (though, it was not, in fact, agreed what the amount should be). The second group are depositors who are professional participants of the market—financial institutions and individuals, who keep above average funds on their accounts (for example, according to current EU legislature, the amount would exceed €100,000, while in the United States, it would be above $250,000).

Due to the outburst of the global financial crisis, certain countries started to raise deposit protection coverage levels. Some have even decided to declare their guarantees unlimited (complete) (IADI 2012). Such possibilities were analyzed in earlier years—in the case of Japan, as early as in 1996 (DICJ 2005). In 2008, due to uncoordinated actions of several countries (among them Iceland, Ireland, and Great Britain), temporary full guarantee coverage was also introduced in the EU (see Table 4.9). These solutions had a significant influence on the effectiveness of deposit insurance agencies. As a result, multiple publications on unlimited guarantees have emerged (Schich 2009).

According to Core Principles for Effective Deposit Insurance Systems (BCBS and IADI 2009), guarantee level must be well defined, clear, and expressed in numerical terms. According to IADI, complete guarantee must not be offered, because it intensifies temptation of abuse on behalf of clients, who do not have any interest in monitoring the financial condition of the bank whose services they are beneficiaries of. What is more, protecting the biggest possible number of depositors should be the goal, as it provides financial stability. Still, if complete guarantee is introduced

Table 4.9 Changes in guarantee levels in EU member states

	Guarantee level (expressed in euros)		
Country	Precrisis*	During the crisis**	Postcrisis***
Austria	20,000 (10% deductible for companies)	complete + 50,000 (10% deductible)	100,000 (for natural persons) + 50,000 (for companies)
Belgium	20,000	100,000	100,000
Bulgaria	20,452	51,129	51,129
Cyprus	22,222 (10% deductible)	22,222 (10% deductible)	100,000
Czech Republic	27,778 (10% deductible)	50,000	50,000
Denmark	40,229	40,306 + complete	complete
Estonia	22,222 (10% deductible)	50,000	50,000
Finland	25,000	50,000	50,000
France	70,000	70,000	70,000
Germany	22,222 (10% deductible)	22,222 (10% deductible)	50,000
Great Britain	44,083	64,329	56,092
Greece	20,000	100,000	100,000
Hungary	24,905 (10% deductible)	49,430	50,000
Ireland	22,222 (10% deductible)	22,222 (10% deductible)	100,000
Italy	103,291	103,291	103,291
Latvia	20,000	50,000	50,000
Lithuania	22,000 (10% deductible)	100,000	100,000
Luxembourg	20,000	100,000	100,000
Malta	22,222 (10% deductible)	22,222 (10% deductible)	100,000
Netherlands	40,000 (10% deductible)	100,000	100,000
Poland	22,500 (10% deductible)	50,000	50,000

Table 4.9 (continued)

	Guarantee level (expressed in euros)		
Country	Precrisis*	During the crisis**	Postcrisis***
Portugal	25,000	100,000	100,000
Romania	20,000	50,000	50,000
Slovakia	22,222 (10% deductible)	complete	complete
Slovenia	22,000	complete	complete
Spain	20,000	100,000	100,000
Sweden	26,173	50,474	50,000

Values expressed in country currencies have been calculated to euros (according to ECB rate). Precrisis period includes 15 September 2008. Crisis has been defined as the time between October and late December 2008, while postcrisis was expressed as guarantee levels of 4 January 2010

Source: Author's own formulation and Szeląg (2009), p. 60

(for example, as a way to stem the run on banks), limited guarantees must be reapplied as soon as it is possible.

Studies on the optimal guarantee value for depositors were pursued independently, yet researchers did not pay much attention to the meaning of financial coverage for the sake of insurance agency responsibilities. This negligence was a direct reason behind the weakening of deposit guarantee scheme importance.

An averaged value of guarantee for EU countries between the years 1994 and 2005 is presented in Fig. 4.8.

After crisis events in the EU, an abrupt rise in guarantee levels for depositors was noted. Still, it was not accompanied by a simultaneous rise in deposit insurance agency funds, thus escalating the problem of low credibility of fund coverage in the financial system (Iwanicz-Drozdowska and Lepczyński 2011).

Detailed information on the process of reaching raised coverage levels (€100,000) is shown in Table 4.9. Through such actions, governments obliged themselves, in practice, to support the deposit guarantee scheme financially in case of a cross-system crisis. Therefore, credibility toward a country's deposit guarantee scheme became reliant on belief in a given government's reliability. A weak public financial condition of a given

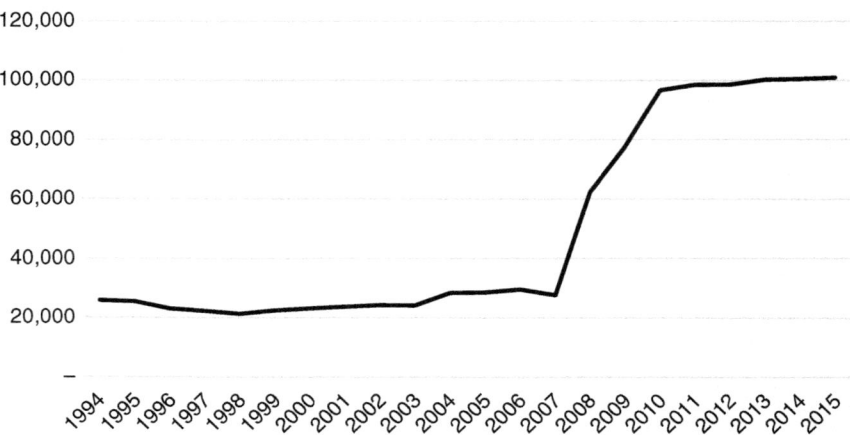

Fig. 4.8 Average guarantee level of current EU countries between the years 1994–2005 (expressed in euros)

Values expressed in country currencies have been calculated to euros (according to ECB rate)

Source: Author's own research

state (for example, in Greece or Cyprus) undermines the belief that, in such a situation, the deposit guarantee scheme will receive support from the government. This, in turn, may promote withdrawal of deposited funds and searching for alternative, more reliable places for their placement (despite unified EU regulations) (Smaga 2013).

In order to avoid the upkeep of value discrepancies of guarantee levels, the EU eventually harmonized the coverage level to €100,000. Therefore, as shown in Fig. 4.8, a situation takes place where the same, unified nominal protection amount granted for each country relates to varying values. Harmonization of the union creates a situation, where some countries receive a respectively higher security value, than others—namely, depending on a country's GDP *per capita*, €100,000 may correspond to different values. An extreme example is the comparison of Luxembourg (1.46) and Bulgaria (8.4), as shown in Fig. 4.9. Introducing a harmonized coverage level of €100,000 guarantee has different monetary worth in both countries.

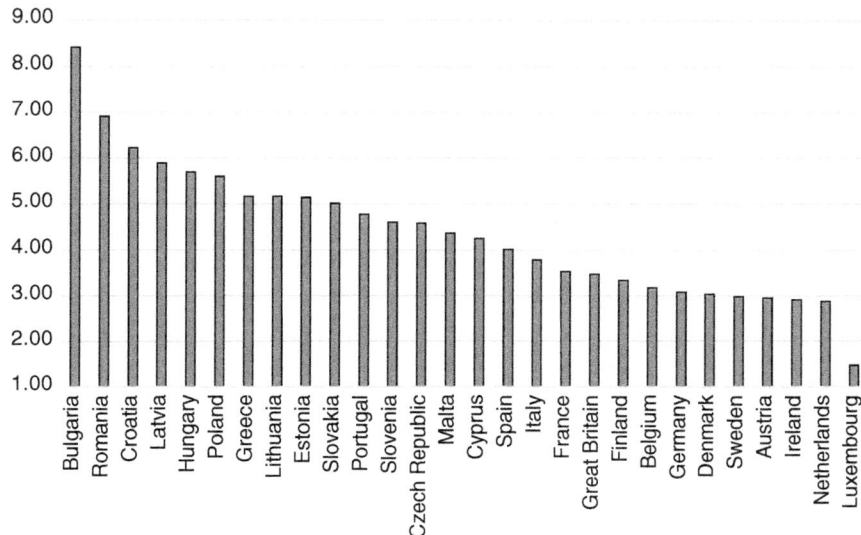

Fig. 4.9 Relation of nominal protection value to GDP per capita according to purchasing power parity in the given countries as of the end of 2013

Source: Author's own research and Eurostat (2015)

It is difficult to agree with the view that harmonizing guarantee levels will optimize depositor protection. Such a factitious harmonization triggers the desire for change of country guarantee levels during crises, which is proved by Table 4.9, where varying approaches of different countries toward crisis management is shown. It must be emphasized that rising coverage levels of guarantees resulted in burdening deposit guarantee schemes with additional responsibilities, while not providing them with proportionally higher contributions from financial institutions. Therefore, the value of protection was raised formally, but without the necessary funds required for new obligations.

4.4.6 Effectiveness of Insolvency Proceedings

The third direct factor negatively influencing intervention scope of EU deposit guarantee schemes is the low recovery rate of assets of an insolvent financial institution. It must be noticed that—as a rule—the guarantee scheme claims the rights of depositors, for whom it had returned deposited funds. Being thus, the scheme files a claim to the liquidator for the return of means it had paid out on behalf of the insolvent institution. In a favorable situation, the role of the deposit guarantee fund would be to assure temporary deposit payout financing, for as long as insolvency assets are not provided by the liquidator. Due to high recovery rates of assets of insolvent banks, means provided to depositors would be returned to the insurance agency, thus refilling its fund. For example, a bank in the state of insolvency with assets worth €100 million could be sold through court insolvency proceedings for €70–80 million, and the guarantee fund would be reinforced with such financial resources.

Effective insolvency proceedings (with a 70–80 per cent return) would cause that the guarantee fund would be burdened for a limited time only. Means recovered from the liquidator would gradually restore the financial potential of depositors. Although rebuilding the initial financial potential would happen progressively, it would not be fueled by new contributions provided by banks, but through capitalized, bank liquidation funds. In such a situation, even temporary governmental support in paying out covered funds would not be problematic, because taxpayers could rely on the return of means, acquired as a result of liquidation procedures.

Still, the specificity of bank activities causes that insolvency proceedings are characterized by rapid value loss. Specific data on return rates from bank liquidation per country are not available and are often subject to unique circumstances. Nevertheless, data on Poland may be shown as an example, where the average return rate for BGF amounted to 14 per cent of paid out deposits only, while some insolvency proceedings lasted for over a decade (Ministerstwo Finansów 2016). In BGF financial resources, the amount of funds recovered from insolvency procedures accounted for only PLN 54 million, which—with a nearly PLN 10 billion worth of funds—is a scarce amount (BFG 2014). Under the circumstances, deposit insurance agencies cannot count on funds resultant from insolvency proceedings of a bank, for which the institution settled client debt.

Nevertheless, the situation of the deposit insurance agency may be different in the remaining countries, where insolvency proceedings are a better maintained, faster process. After the bankruptcy of the Icelandic Landsbanki bank, in the United Kingdom (where the institution had its branch), a high recovery rate was noted from liquidation procedures, accounting for 96 per cent of the total balance sheet. Such a result is highly advantageous, as it allows for the protection of financial means of the deposit insurance agency. The British FSCS initially paid out funds to depositors and then effectively regained its claims through a judicial process (LBI 2011).

Still, expansive data for the American market, collected by the FDIC in reference to a group of over a thousand bankrupt banks, reveal that the return rate for the deposit insurance agency from insolvency proceedings usually oscillates between 50 and 70 per cent. Being thus, each time the missing part must be covered by the deposit insurance agency, which may not count on retrieving the costs (Bennett and Unal 2014, p. 47).

As a conclusion, it must be stated that increasing the effectiveness of bank insolvency asset sales would certainly help rebuild financial potential of deposit insurance agencies. Still, multiple barriers stand in the way, such as difficulties in finding an acquirer of assets of an insolvent bank, rapid decline of asset value, competitive claims of other creditors, and protracted legal proceedings. Overcoming the above obstacles seems easier, if the position of the deposit guarantee scheme in the financial net is stronger, and its interventions toward banks are planned in advance and carried out in the fastest possible manner.

4.5   Conclusion

The above chapter compared the *status quo* of deposit guarantee scheme effectiveness as well and the situation, which will take place after the introduction of reforms (hence, the implementation of the DGS and BRR Directives). For this reason, the financial potential of deposit guarantee funds was analyzed, and the degree to which the deposit insurer was authorized to intervene in a given country (with market structure taken into account) was evaluated. Analyzing the scope of successful deposit guarantee scheme effectiveness indicates that by the end of 2012, the situation was not favorable. In the majority of EU countries, deposit insurers are incapable of fulfilling designated tasks. The analysis of the financial potential of deposit guarantee schemes as of the end of 2012 allows for the conclusion that EU member states may be divided into four basic groups, which vary in terms of their intervention capabilities. Despite the fact that the above-described situation ought to improve as a result of the introduction of DGS Directive reforms in 2014, most countries will only be capable of dealing with insolvency of one average-sized bank.

The effectiveness of deposit insurers has been diminishing for years for several reasons. These include, most importantly, the dynamic rise of the banking sector and its current size, big values of covered deposits, the rising concentration in the banking sector, as well as low effectiveness of bank insolvency procedures. Potential liabilities of guarantee funds toward the biggest EU banks are too big to enable undisturbed payout of deposits by a paybox-based deposit guarantee scheme. As revealed by the study, even after reforms introduced by the DGS Directive, as many as 516 of 8,500 EU banks will remain outside the scope of deposit guarantee scheme payouts. Hence, it is necessary that new solutions regarding deposit guarantee scheme effectiveness enhancement be sought for, or that institutions be supported by other tools that influence bank performance.

References

Bankscope. (2015). *World banking information source*. Bureau van Dijk, www.bvdinfo.com.

Bartkowiak, R. (2005). *Finansowanie działalności systemu gwarantowania depozytów. Wnioski dla Bankowego Funduszu Gwarancyjnego*, "Bezpieczny Bank", nr 3(28), BFG, Warszawa.

BCBS; IADI (2009). *Core Principles for Effective Deposit Insurance Systems*, Basel.

Bennett, R.L.; Unal, H. (2014). *Understanding the Components of Bank Failure Resolution Costs*, Working Paper Series, FDIC.

BFG (2014). *Raport Roczny 2014*, Warszawa.

Bhattacharya, K. (2003). *How Good Is the BankScope Database? A Cross-Validation Exercise with Correction Factors for Market Concentration Measures*, Monetary and Economic Department, BIS Working Papers, no. 133, September.

Cannas, G.; Cariboni, J.; Veisari, L.K.; Pagano, A. (2014). *Updated Estimates of EU Eligible and Covered Deposits*, JRC Technical Reports, Report EUR 26469 EN.

CNB (2015). *Standard Presentation Format*, 1st quarter.

DAB. (2015). *Deposit insurance, Numbers at a glance*. State Agency for Deposit Insurance and Bank Resolution, www.dab.hr.

Demirgüç-Kunt, A.; Kane, E.; Laeven, L. (2014). *Deposit Insurance Database*, IMF Working Paper, no. 14/118.

DICJ (2005). *A Guide to the Deposit Insurance System, Outline of the System and Q&A*, April.

EBF (2011). *International Comparison of Banking Sectors*.

EC (2011a). *JRC Report under Article 12 of Directive 94/19/EC as amended by Directive 2009/14/EC*, JRC, Unit G09, Ispra (Italy).

EC (2011b). *Final Report on Risk-Based Contributions*, Annex 2, JRC.

EC (2012). *Commission Staff Working Document, Impact Assessment. Accompanying Document to the Proposal for a Directive .../.../EU of the European Parliament and of the Council on Deposit Guarantee Schemes [Recast] and to the Report from the Commission to the European Parliament and to the Council Review of Directive 94/19/EC on Deposit Guarantee Schemes* {COM(2010) 368} {COM(2010) 369} {SEC(2010) 835}.

ECB. (2006). EU Banking Structures, October.

ECB. (2008). EU Banking Structures, October.

ECB. (2014). EU Banking Structures, October.

EP (2013). *Deposit Guarantee Schemes*, Policy Department A: Economic and Scientific Policy, IP/A/ECON/NT/2013-02, July.

ESRB (2014) *Is Europe Overbanked?* ASC Report, June.

Eurostat (2015). *GDP at Current Market Prices 2002–2013*.

FDIC (2010). *Public Awareness*, Washington.

FSB (2012). *Thematic Review on Deposit Insurance Systems. Peer Review Report*, Basel.

FSF (2000). *Working Group on Deposit Insurance, International Guidance on Deposit Insurance. A Consultative Process*, June.

IADI (2008). *Annual Survey*, BIS, Basel.

IADI (2012). *Transitioning from a Blanket Guarantee or Extended Coverage to a Limited Coverage System*, January.

IADI (2013). *Annual Survey*, BIS, Basel.

IADI (2014). *Annual Survey*, BIS, Basel.

IBP (2012). *Cyprus Country Study Guide Strategic Information and Developments*, Intl Business Pubns, USA.

Iwanicz-Drozdowska, M. (2016). *Restrukturyzacja banków w Unii Europejskiej w czasie globalnego kryzysu finansowego*. Oficyna Wydawnicza, Szkoła Główna Handlowa w Warszawie, Warszawa.

Iwanicz-Drozdowska, M. (2011a). *Deposit Insurance Systems – Lessons from the Crisis for CESEE Banking Systems*. The Future of Banking in CESEE After The Financial Crisis, SUERF Studies, Vienna.

Iwanicz-Drozdowska, M.; Lepczyński, B. (2011). *Znaczenie regulacji i instytucji sieci bezpieczeństwa finansowego dla stabilności finansowej*, Część Edukacyjna „Stabilność finansowa od A do Z", „Bank i Kredyt", nr 5.

Iwanicz-Drozdowska, M.; Kerlin, J.; Smaga, P.; Tomasik, M. (2015). *EU Guarantee Schemes: Status Quo and Policy Implications*, "Journal of Banking Regulation", vol. 16, no. 3.

Kennickell, A.B.; Kwast, M.; Starr-McCluer, M. (1995). *Households Deposit Insurance Coverage: Evidence and Analysis of Potential Reforms*, "Journal of Money, Credit and Banking", 28 (August, pt. 1).

Laeven, L.; Valencia, F. (2012). *Resolution of Banking Crisis: The Good, the Bad, and the Ugly*, IMF, August.

LBI (2011). *Financial Information 2010*, Landsbanki receivership, 2 March.

Ministerstwo Finansów (2016). Ocena skutków regulacji projektu z dnia 23 października 2015 r. ustawy o Bankowym Funduszu Gwarancyjnym, systemie gwarantowania depozytów oraz przymusowej restrukturyzacji, Komisja Prawnicza, RCL, 19.01.

Schich, S. (2009). *Challenges Associated with the Expansion of Deposit Insurance Coverage During Fall 2008*, Economics Discussion Paper no. 2009–16.

Shin, H.S. (2008). *Reflections on Modern Bank Runs: A Case Study of Northern Rock*, Princeton University, August.

Smaga, P. (2013). *Paneuropejski system gwarantowania depozytów – część 1 (wnioski z kryzysu)*, "Bezpieczny Bank", nr 2–3(51–52), BFG, Warszawa.

Szeląg, K. (2009). *Recent Reforms of the Deposit Insurance System in the United States*: Reasons, Results, *and Recommendations for the European Union*, National Bank of Poland Working Paper, no. 59, Warsaw.

Ungureanu, M.; Cocriş, V. (2008). *Northern Rock: The Crisis of A UK Mortgage Lender*, Ştiinne Economice.

World Bank (2014). *Global Financial Development*.

5

The Concept of Resolution of Financial Institutions

5.1 Introduction

This chapter introduces the theoretical basis of resolution—a new EU procedure which, among others, is the answer to deposit guarantee scheme weaknesses described in the previous chapter. Here, basic goals and provisions of the procedure are introduced along with a description of administrative tools designed for the elimination of big financial institutions from the market. Due to the fact that resolution is financed from financial sector resources (which are not public), the procedure is presented with special attention. The chapter also describes the role of the deposit guarantee scheme in the above procedures, with emphasis on the level of flexibility in institutional shaping of the EU financial safety net after the crisis.

© The Author(s) 2017   **137**
J. Kerlin, *The Role of Deposit Guarantee Schemes as a Financial Safety Net in the European Union*, Palgrave Macmillan Studies in Banking and Financial Institutions, DOI 10.1007/978-3-319-54163-1_5

5.2   Reasons to Introduce New Solutions

The financial crisis revealed multiple flaws of regulatory instruments on various tiers of crisis management (not only in reference to specific institutions or countries, but also on a supranational level) (Marcinkowska 2009). First and foremost, legal instruments that would enable effective public authority actions in regard to struggles of financial institutions were lacking. As a result, public help for banks that are at risk of insolvency was imposed by legal and economical conditions and the weaknesses of regulations (Szczepańska et al. 2015, p. 18).

During the global financial crisis, ineffectiveness of deposit guarantee schemes was also noticed, which is described in Chapter 4. In many countries, decision makers were put in the situation where payout of most deposits was impossible due to lack of funds on behalf of respective insurance agencies. Thus, insolvency proceedings were either impossible to carry out, or an approval on behalf of the budget was needed in order to burden it significantly. What is more, regulators came to the conclusion that standard insolvency proceedings or reparative actions applied toward financial institutions were ineffective. The reason behind such inefficiency was, most often, the perseverant judicial control of insolvency proceedings, as well as the abrupt decline of the value of assets of the insolvent institution—a process nearly impossible to stop in the midst of court proceedings. The nature of lawsuits is an additional factor, characterized by the lack of quick intervention and intricate possibilities of appealing from decisions, as well as the delaying of proceedings as a form of postponing on behalf of owners and creditors. Standard judicial procedure does not promote the liquidity of critical functions of a failing financial institution and potentiates market instabilities (Iwanicz-Drozdowska et al. 2016, p. 120).

Furthermore, attempts at restructuring the EU banking sector were weakened by the discrepancies in national recovery legislatures, as well as the lack of a unified, decisive procedure regarding insolvency or the liquidation of supranational financial institutions. Difficulties in dividing costs among member states also took place (Pisani-Ferry and Sapir 2010, pp. 354–355). As for Directive 2001/24/EC on the reorganization and winding up of cross-border credit institutions in the EU, it did not provide administrative measures for orderly liquidation of given institutions, and it only shaped coordinative procedures and basic code of conduct.

The persistence of such a situation strengthened the lack of trust of market participants, as well as its instabilities. Country legislature and—as an effect of its absence—political decisions were made *ad hoc*, without foreseeing the potential success of resolution of a bank or the potential consequences of its bankruptcy. Still, it was known that insolvency of a large financial institution would most often signify grave consequences for the country budget, which would be, in turn, forced to pay out the value of lost covered deposits. Therefore, in order to prevent the fulfillment of guarantee requirements, various attempts at restructuring endangered financial institutions have been made (Iwanicz-Drozdowska et al. 2016).

With the above in mind, working out a new approach that would enable efficient elimination of financial institutions from the market—regardless of their size or connections with other entities—became necessary. As a result of crisis events, regulators decided that the time has come for implementing a set of versatile, quick administrative instruments enabling various interventions toward endangered financial institutions—also in a cross-border perspective. As a result, new solutions for the financial safety net that would enable applying innovative instruments in the place of unplanned, standard restructuring and insolvency proceedings of financial institutions were sought for.

5.3   Law Sources on Resolution

Regulatory deficits revealed in the years 2007–13 and their catastrophic effects on national budgets triggered the desire of the change of current *status quo* in many countries. For this reason, regulators started proposing the formulation of new tools that would prevent financial institutions' insolvency, regardless of their size and activity scope, or—if bankruptcy were to happen—minimizing its repercussions. For instance, working out a method enabling maintenance of all vital systemic functions of a given institution (for example, customer service, payment, and settlements of accounts), while not burdening the country budget, was the goal.

Resolution, worked out as a global effort (mainly by G-20 countries), is the answer to the necessity. As the deadline of the BRR Directive provision fulfillment terminated by the end of 2014, procedures of resolution and liquidation of financial institutions have been in force in EU member states since 1 January 2015.

As an effect of G-20 works in 2011, a document was formulated regarding the basic terms of effective functioning of a liquidation regime dedicated to financial institutions (FSB 2011). Working out a common document by FDIC and the Bank of England, concerning possible methods of liquidating big financial institutions, was also a true milestone (FDIC and BoE 2012). Formulations of various task forces, as well as reports of financial safety net institutions, preceded the time of creation of the legally binding, financial architecture legislative framework, and provided solid theoretical grounds. At a rough estimate, it may be assumed that since 2010, innovative (postcrisis) resolution and orderly liquidation frameworks were being introduced to country legal orders. Among the most important regulations are the following:

- enactment of the Dodd-Frank Act in the United States,
- amendment of bank law in Great Britain,
- enactment of the BRR Directive in the EU, foreseeing consistent resolution, and orderly liquidation procedures for financial institutions (Iwanicz-Drozdowska et al. 2016).

Detailed data on the formulation of respective introductory resolution legal acts are presented in Table 5.1.

Data presented in Table 5.1 prove that the necessity of a consistent resolution procedure in country legislature materialized mainly around the time of the crisis, despite official declarations of certain countries (Mexico, Argentina, or Indonesia, among others) that some extraordinary liquidation measures of financial institutions were already existent. As an effect of the vague definition of resolution and its diversified understanding, difficulties may be encountered while trying to establish

Table 5.1 Introducing resolution procedures in chosen countries of the world

Country	Entry of resolution provisions (or their significant amendment) into force	Country	Entry of resolution provisions (or their significant amendment) into force
Argentina	1997, 2003	Italy	2008, 2009
Australia	2008, 2010	Japan	2013, 2014
Brazil	2010	Mexico	2006, 2013, 2014
Canada	2012	Netherlands	2012
China	2012, 2014	Republic of South Africa	2012
Denmark	2010	Russia	2010, 2011
France	2013	Singapore	2013
Germany	2011, 2013	South Korea	2013
Great Britain	2009, 2012, 2014	Spain	2009, 2012
Hong Kong	2012	Switzerland	2011, 2012
India	2013	Turkey	2005, 2007
Indonesia	2008, 2009	United States	2010

Source: Author's own formulation based on Iwanicz-Drozdowska et al. (2016)

the exact date of introducing resolution in a given country. If we adopt a broad understanding, it may be assumed that even a minimal authority instrument set for public entities (for instance, supervisors or central bank) granting intervention capabilities in the form of receivership, or the possibility to enact a sale order of part of its banking activities, is often interpreted as resolution itself. In the United States, some solutions similar to the BRR Directive have been existent since the introduction of the bridge bank instrument in the 1980s. Therefore, indicating the time of the introduction of resolution is difficult. Most often, the most decisive moment is pinpointed—hence, when public authority in regard to bank restructuring is broadened. As far as instruments are concerned, they are subject to individual choices of each country, despite their unification in the EU in 2015.

Countries with the best-developed banking sectors (mainly Europe, United States, and chosen Asian countries) witnessed the most prominent advancements in regard to resolution implementation. EU member states, which have willingly introduced resolution even prior to the enactment of the BRR Directive, include Denmark, France, Spain, the Netherlands, Germany, and Great Britain. What distinguishes them is that their financial sectors all fell victim to the financial crisis (Iwanicz-Drozdowska et al. (2016).

As mentioned earlier, the union legislator was engaged in formulating world standards, established in October 2011, concerning resolution proceedings of financial institutions (FSB 2011). G-20 works (held within FSB) were carried out simultaneously to those in the EU. As a result, multiple general provisions, proved effective worldwide, were introduced into EU legislature, though not without significant differences (Gracie 2015). These concern, among others, the determination of minimal loss absorption capabilities of banks. The FSB worked out a general, unified indicator for financial institutions in the form of TLAC (total loss absorbing capacity), whereas in the EU, the indicator, arranged individually, is known as MREL (minimum requirement for own funds and eligible liabilities).

Eventually, key regulations regarding resolution in the EU were included in two legislative acts, where unified terms, as well as resolution and financial institution liquidation procedures, were established. Both acts differ mainly in regard to their ratione personae scopes, as shown in detail in Table 5.2.

The first document is Regulation 806/2014, which established unified resolution conditions for the biggest financial institutions within a banking union, as well as a common financing mechanism for their restructuring. The second act is the BRR Directive, designed for the use of all other entities. Therefore, it may be said that resolution in the EU is a two-level procedure, because a single organ was set up for the biggest entities —regardless of the country where their headquarters are registered.

An important difference between solutions implemented by the BRR Directive and Regulation 806/2014 is the varying organs responsible for proceedings. In the banking union, the organ will be a separate union entity (Single Resolution Board), responsible for carrying out procedures in its own right, on a supranational level. Meanwhile, in the EU, organs will be designated on a national level, and their number will correspond to the number of member states. This is further described in Section 5.7.

Table 5.2 Differences between Regulation 806/2014 and the BRR Directive

Criterion	Regulation 806/2014	BRR Directive
Resolution authority	SRB (a single organ for the entire EU)	Organ designated by member states (28 organs across the EU)
Subjective scope	As a rule, the biggest financial entities of the banking union	Small- and middle-sized financial institutions in EU countries (not covered by EBC consolidated supervision)
Number of entities covered by the act	Approximately 120 biggest Eurozone banking groups	Approximately 8,000 credit institutions and 3,800 investment firms
Financing source	Contributions from country financing mechanisms	*Ex ante* contributions collected from financial institutions
Application method	Regulations are applied directly	Regulations are applied after they had been implemented by country legal orders
Enforcement	20 August 2014	1 January 2015 (*bail-in* regulations since 1 January 2016)
Countries covered	Banking union	All EU countries

Source: Author's own formulation

Regulation 806/2014 is applied directly and regulates resolution proceedings of all entities located in countries of the banking union (Eurozone states and countries that have established a close cooperation), as specified in Article 2 of Council Regulation No 1024/2013 of 15 October 2013 conferring specific tasks on the European Central Bank concerning policies relating to the prudential supervision of credit institutions. Nevertheless, as in the case of consolidated supervision of EBC, approximately 120 banking groups are of interest to the SRB, which altogether control 82 per cent of bank assets in the EU (as of 2015), whereas resolution of smaller entities will take place with a dominant role of country organs. As for the BRR Directive, it is applicable only after its regulations had been implemented in country legislature and formally covers much more than 10,000 financial entities (mainly banks and investing companies). Still, it must be noted that organs will not intervene in every case, and resolution procedures will be launched only after several requirements, including the most important—public interest protection—had been met. Thus, it may be anticipated that proceedings will be carried out in part of the cases, while remaining financial institutions will declare standard insolvency. Nevertheless, due to the size of entities involved, the SRB will be authorized to expect a more common fulfillment of the public interest requirement.

A thorough description of financing proceedings may be found in the further part of the book, in Section 5.6. While carrying out comparisons, it must be noted that the cross-border, European mechanism (established by Regulation 806/2014) will be financed on the basis of contributions collected by country mechanisms. A system of country financial mechanisms, responsible for calculating and receiving contributions from entities that lie within its scope, was thus created. In the next phase, country mechanisms will transfer part of their collected contributions to the European mechanism, responsible for intervening in case of the biggest banking groups.

The reason behind establishing national and supranational solutions simultaneously is that—despite harmonization of regulations in the BRR Directive—country practices and resolution attempts would only remain in the domain of member states. Regulators worried that country organs would put their national interests first and minimize effects of bank crises primarily in their own economies, without much regard to the impact such an action would have abroad. In case of big banks, confinement to the country level of resolution management would create a moral hazard for states to implement one-sided actions, which would solely protect their own interests. Therefore, as far as big financial entities (most often, with a developed cross-border net) are concerned, the decisiveness level has been moved up to a union entity—Single Resolution Board of banking union states. Its establishment allowed for the centralization of decision making processes, as well as providing proper financing on a supranational level. Centralizing resolution proceedings has its advantages and allows for partial elimination of problems in the likes of those that occurred during the restructuring of Fortis and Dexia banks (Wiggins et al. 2015). The goal of the SRB is the establishment of an *ex ante* resolution plan for big entities, as well as agreeing on its various potential forms, even prior to a crisis event. As a rule, planned operations will be calculated for the sake of intervention in the parent company (for example, absorption of loss on the highest level of the banking group), thus avoiding actions in multiple countries. Absence of the SRB would create the threat of separate, uncoordinated, often contradictory actions of member states in regard to resolution of cross-border subsidiaries based in a given country. Harmonizing financing mechanisms and creating a unified system may positively affect total costs of a financial institution's resolution on the banking union level. It shall also facilitate coordination of actions after resolution procedures had already started, though voices of criticism, stating that SRB proceedings are time consuming, may also be heard (Junevičius and Puidokas 2014, pp. 84–87).

Apart from the two legal acts that are the basis of resolution procedures, other legal norms, formulated by the EBA, may also be named. Under the terms of the BRR Directive, it is obliged to publish implementation acts—either regulatory technical standards, or guidelines and recommendations for those cases, which require a more detailed analysis. Specifications and recommendations are not formally binding, but regulatory technical standards worked out during EBA forums are implemented through delegated regulations of the European Council. While their detailed analysis lies outside the scope of the following book, they certainly have an impact on resolution due to their elaboration on the topic of proceedings. These include, among others, conditions of disclosing group support agreements (EBA 2015d), MREL (EBA 2014c), functioning terms of resolution colleges, as well as decision-making methods and the approach toward contractual clause acceptance in regard to write down of debt (EBA 2014b).

Concluding the topic of legal basis of resolution, the scope of its existence must be hereby mentioned. Until the end of works on the shape of the BRR Directive, the case of its subjective scope remained unresolved (EC 2012). On the one hand, initial solutions were prepared primarily for the sake of banks (credit institutions), taking into account their operational specificity and the higher risk of insolvency procedural prolixity. In time, a broader scope of BRR Directive authority was considered, inclining other entities, which may also potentially severely destabilize the market and put customers at risk of big financial loss. Among them were investment companies (as defined by European legislature) and insurers, who have not been covered by the regulation due to the distinct nature of activity and a lower risk of bankruptcy (still, holdings and conglomerates with insurers in their structure are entirely covered the BRR Directive). Ultimately, it has been decided that the BRR Directive will apply to institutions that lie within the scope of prudential requirements, as well as financial holdings of various configurations (detailed subjective scope is regulated by Article 1 of the BRR Directive). Such an understanding of the case may be perceived as cautionary, for it concerns the subject of proceedings not only toward credit institutions, but also various financial groups that are often linked to banks (for example, mixed-activity holding companies) and influence financial stability.

5.4   Characteristics of New Procedures

5.4.1 Limitations of State Aid

Low social acceptance for the extensive use of public funds for the sake of resolving banks during the global financial crisis triggered the response on behalf of policy makers. As an effect, the use of public funds in such a manner was prohibited. According to the BRR Directive, when the entity reports financial problems, it is preferable that any alternative private sector measures, along with possible write-down or conversion of relevant capital instruments, which could prevent the failure of the institution, are searched for. The so-called private solution shall not engage any special powers of national resolution authorities. If such a situation takes place, other safety net members are authorized to take action. For instance, the competent authority (supervisor) may assist in the takeover transaction of the bank in bad financial condition by any interested, healthy entity (for example, through the prompt issue of authorization for such a transaction, or by seeking for a counterparty eager to purchase the problematic bank).

Although preferable, such a solution most often does not take place, because no banks are eager to engage in such a transaction—especially in times of unfavorable market conditions and uncertainty, when making decisions under pressure hinders the right assessment and valuation.

Anticipating the lack of any private solution, the BRR Directive provides multiple resolution tools (described in Section 5.5), which may be used in such circumstances. They may be applied in a twofold approach: either without any capital injections, or with the use of public funds (potential state aid), but under strict conditions and resolution authority control. Putting resolution tools to use seems rather impossible, if financial support is not provided; however, it is perceived as possible. It may be done through the so-called open bank bail-in process, when appropriate write-down of capital instruments is sufficient to maintain entity operations, or via the sale of part of the business on market conditions (asset separation), and the declaration of bankruptcy for the remaining residual entity. Because previous cases clearly showed that proper funding is needed when resolution actions take place, from 2015 onward, the industry is obliged to pay *ex ante* contributions for the sake of the purpose to the Single Resolution Fund.

In order to establish national resolution funds in each member state, the BRRD provides the collection of funds from financial institutions. Additionally, the Single Resolution Fund mutualizes part of the contributions on the EU banking union level. The same is provided by the DGS Directive, which states that financial means (paybox fund) may be used either for reimbursements, or as an alternative to payout measures (supporting resolution). Both funds are collected from the industry and are perceived as public money. Despite being financed by participating credit institutions, their resources are of public nature, as the fund is completely under public control. Thus, its resources are considered as state financial means. Altogether, all participating member states of the banking union account for approximately €100 billion. The last potential opportunity to resolve a bank under the BRR Directive from public resources is the use of government financial stabilization tools, which have no special funds established for the purpose. This instrument may consist of public equity support or a temporary public ownership tool only and is an extraordinary, *ad hoc* measure.

Accessing any facilities (resolution, paybox fund, or funding for government financial stabilization tools) is subject to the state aid framework (which is under authorization by DG Competition). While state aid and use of public money are legally permitted, it is only possible when several conditions described in the BRR Directive are met. First and foremost, the funds need to be utilized in accordance with state aid rules, laid down in Article 107 of the Treaty on the Functioning of the EU. In general, the aid cannot be incompatible with the internal market. Resolving a bank may be considered compatible with the internal market, when aid provided is remedy to a serious disturbance in the economy of a given member state. Other conditions apply only once the above general condition has been met. State aid aiming at resolving a bank ought to be connected with other EU and national measures. These include, among others, requirements of the Restructuring Communication, as adapted by the 2013 Banking Communication, as well as specific provisions of the Impaired Assets Communication, as adapted by the 2013 Banking Communication. Secondly, in order to assess whether state aid is legal, it is appropriate the state aid measure is examined on the basis of specific provisions of the BRR Directive, which need to be transposed to the national law (EC 2015e, pp. 19–27). In general, resolution proceedings may be supported with public funds (accumulated by banks), once it is ensured that shareholders and creditors bear an appropriate share of losses. Resolution tools shall be applied before any public sector injection of capital, or equivalent extraordinary public financial support, is granted to an institution. The minimum loss absorption requirement contained in the BRRD corresponds to 8 per cent of own funds and liabilities. Moreover, the funding provided by the resolution fund is limited to the lower of 5 per cent of total liabilities including own funds or the means available to the resolution fund and the amount that can be raised through *ex post* contributions within three years. The use of public resources is restricted under the standard EU state aid framework, which requires that authorization is granted and conditions checked before they are granted by DG Competition (which, itself, is authorized to block the use of public money).

5.4.2 Objectives

Throughout the works on resolution procedures in the EU, objectives have been formulated, that are to be achieved through the resolution of financial institutions. These are described explicitly in Article 31 of the BRR Directive; still, the majority of goals is also listed in the preamble of the act and included in other articles. Most important objectives include (Iwanicz-Drozdowska et al. 2016):

– ensuring the continuity of essential financial activities on behalf of a given financial institution (so-called critical functions),
– avoiding adverse effects on the financial stability (for instance, through fighting the domino effect, as well as maintaining market discipline),
– public fund protection through minimizing reliance on public financial support,
– depositor protection (at least to the covered, guaranteed levels),
– protection of client funds and assets of a financial institution, endangered by insolvency.

First and foremost, resolution shall aim at providing continuity of critical functions of an endangered financial institution, thus stabilizing the market. The core of the goal is that critical functions of an entity under resolution remain active (FSB 2013b). They may, in fact, be executed by the acquiring entity or the so-called bridge bank, but clients should not encounter notable difficulties throughout the entity's restructuring process. Achieving such a goal will allow for maintaining key elements of bank activity. These include uninterrupted access to deposits, operation of all checking and saving accounts' functionalities, possibility of entering payments, monetary transfers, or regulating short-term obligations of a given bank—also toward other financial institutions (FSB 2013b, p. 14). As a result of maintaining critical functions, requirements for guarantee payout will not be fulfilled (unavailability of deposits), which conditions the necessity of carrying out fund payouts. Thus, using cheaper solutions than standard insolvency is permitted (such as partial takeover). Achieving the above goal not only allows to avoid costly payouts but also prevents events such as payment gridlocks between entrepreneurs. In the long term, maintaining critical functions of an entity through enabling bank debt management toward other financial institutions (including short-term payment obligations, for instance, on the interbank market) allows to avoid adverse effects on the financial stability.

Due to previous significant public sector burdening (public assistance provided to financial institutions on a big scale during the global crisis) it was decided (FSB 2011) that establishing in advance a hierarchy of individuals or entities that were to be burdened by loss was necessary. According to the new approach, those who were to be burdened by resolution proceedings in the first place were people or entities responsible for the bad condition of the respective financial institution. Thus, loss shall be incurred primarily by shareholders and contributors of endangered companies, and then by their creditors (hence, starting from professional participants of the market). Such an approach allows for communicating the planned division of loss *a priori*, for which preparations will be possible in advance, and whose details will be determined prior to intervention itself. The BRR Directive foresees the necessity of creating resolution execution plans for a financial institution even before conditions had been fulfilled. Therefore, prior to resolution commencement, categories of people primarily burdened with losses of a specific financial institution will be known. Determining and announcing clear resolution terms and code of conduct in advance will also allow for the protection of public funds through minimizing the need for extraordinary financial support for institutions on the brink of bankruptcy.

Despite the lack of standard payout procedures for depositors, the aim of resolution is to provide special protection for depositors, amounting to the sum of guarantee levels. Protection of other creditors is of lesser importance, yet, through the initiation of a more financially efficient resolution procedure, limiting asset value loss (in comparison to declaring a bank's bankruptcy) may be expected. This, in turn, also coincides with the interest of other creditors.

5.4.3 Principles

After determining the objectives of resolution proceedings toward financial institutions, it was decided that cataloging its basic principles was also necessary. Due to the establishment of a new administrative path in the form of resolution, which leads to arbitrary decisions on important changes (or even a total halt of a financial institution's activities), it was crucial that basic, general principles that would regulate such actions be determined, and their use justified. These are specified in Article 34 of the BRR Directive. The following may be classified as basic terms and code of conduct, worked out during EU legislative works (Iwanicz-Drozdowska et al. 2016):

1) maintaining a strict hierarchy of loss absorption and costs of proceedings; under this principle, shareholders of the institution under resolution shall bear losses first, and then its creditors (according to the reverse order of claim settlements, as in a standard insolvency procedure),
2) necessity of dismissing previous and appointing new board members and senior management,
3) support on behalf of board and senior management,
4) "no creditor worse off" procedure (also referred to as NCWO)—preventing creditors from bearing costs higher than those they would be burdened with if a given financial institution was liquidated through a standard procedure,
5) superior protection of covered deposits,
6) caution and limiting the influence of intervention on other types of entities,
7) maintaining financial stability.

As far as most of the principles listed above do not raise doubt, three—listed as 1, 4, and 5—require a broader explanation.

Firstly, due to the fact that resolution actions are final and irreversible, and possibilities of appeal are much more limited, than in other administrative proceedings (appealing from a resolution initiation decision may only result positively in case of compensation claims), a protection principle for creditors and shareholders, oriented at preventing the worsening of a given situation, has been introduced (Iwanicz-Drozdowska et al. 2016). In fact, two principles (1 and 4) are combined during a resolution event.

It is assumed that—as an effect of an ongoing resolution procedure—owners and creditors shall not bear loss greater than in the case of a standard insolvency event. It is one of the most important guarantees provided by the procedure (Davies and Dobler 2013). In order to classify the situation of creditors, comparison of settling their claims in case of resolution and a hypothetical standard insolvency procedure was performed. Establishing the creditor situation is possible through evaluation (for instance, as presented in Article 36 of the BRR Directive regarding the mode and financial simulation criteria). Applying general provisions of insolvency law, which define the hierarchy of claim settlement up front, is crucial for the efficiency of the procedure above.

The resolution-introducing BRR Directive does not indicate directly the hierarchy of settling creditor claims, nor does it do so in regard to loss. Only Article 34 inclines that it is creditors of a resolution-covered company that are burdened immediately after shareholders, in accordance with standard, national insolvency procedures. Meanwhile, Article 108 of the BRR Directive indicates the privilege level of deposit categories during insolvency proceedings.

As a rule, the higher the category, the better the situation of creditors in regard to claim settling. Still, it must be kept in mind that a general rule of settling liabilities of higher categories gradually, as relevant sums appear on insolvency administration accounts, applies. Respectively, lower categories are settled only after the preceding category had already been entirely settled. Therefore, with the resolution loss absorption rule in mind, creditors of further categories are first to be burdened with institutional losses. This is important, because the NCWO rule is an argument used to legitimize resolution instruments such as expropriating shareholders. Resolution instruments significantly intervene in the right of ownership and implementation of agreements between entities; still—as pointed out by regulators—creditor situation in the midst of resolution will be better than it in case of a standard insolvency procedure (if such was inevitable). This, in turn, legitimizes the application of even the gravest regulatory instruments. Furthermore, the privileged legal position of deposit insurance agencies deserves special attention while evaluating the level of creditor debt settlements. In all cases, where payouts from deposit guarantee schemes may be encountered—regardless of whether they take place in an *in lieu* or standard payout mode—a special privilege of debt settlement priority will be applied for the claims of the guarantee fund. This will take form in recourse of the insurance agency to the liquidator (or bank in resolution). Usually, the claim is so prominent that funds of shareholders and creditors of other categories will not be returned even in the smallest part.

The implementation of depositor preference, and—in consequence— the deposit guarantee scheme (which claims depositor rights once it carries out payouts), is another important rule. The concept of instating such a principle lies in the fact that deposits are remitted last during resolution (depositors are at the top of creditor hierarchy). As a result, after guarantee requirements are fulfilled and deposits paid out, the deposit guarantee fund gains privileged depositor rights and recovers its funds as one of the first creditors.

During construction works on global G-20 standards, the above rule triggered further debate; nevertheless, it was entered into the BRR Directive to a certain extent. The principle is regulated in Article 108 of the act; still, derogations in favor of certain depositor categories (for example, deposits of other financial institutions) have been included. It may be noticed that introducing the rule might bring multiple effects for the banking sector. The rule deserves a detailed analysis, for there are concerns that its implementation may bring a result contradictory to the intentions of the regulator.

It must be noted that four legal regimes may be singled out in regard to the hierarchy of depositor preferences:

1) lack of depositor preference and equal treatment of all creditors of a financial institution,
2) giving privilege to all depositors, regardless of the size of their deposits,

3) giving privilege to depositors up to the level of guarantee, while anything above that level is treated equally with the remaining creditor interests,
4) a two-level system, where liabilities of depositors worth less than €100,000 are given top priority, subsequently, deposits above guarantee levels (eligible), and lastly, other categories of liabilities.

Each of the above regimes (different concepts of giving privilege to depositors) influences the financial situation of the deposit insurer differently. The key argument in favor of applying the rule of depositor privilege was the conviction that depositors, as a dispersed customer group, deserve special protection, because they have marginal possibilities of influencing politics of a bank (for example, they do not take responsibility for its financial malfunctioning) and have the smallest capabilities of monitoring such an entity. Furthermore, it is an important creditor category—most significant for the financing of a bank—and, being more distributed, requires more interest protection (Hardy 2013, pp. 6–9).

Still, voices of objection were heard throughout conversations on the validity of such a solution. Opponents (Meguro 2014) pinpointed that analyses performed were based on wrong presumptions. This is due to the premise that financial structure of banks will remain unaltered after introducing the depositor privilege rule. Meanwhile, after the global financial crisis, the process of asset encumbrance on behalf of bank creditors, based on their demands toward banks regarding the demonstration of additional obligation fulfillment guarantees (for instance, bondholder expectations of presenting bank obligation purchase guarantees), may also be noticed (BoE 2012, p. 9). Protected assets are not included in any category throughout insolvency proceedings, and covered creditors are paid off first, as in a standard procedure, before any other creditors (including depositors). The occurrence of asset insurance as an answer to depositor situation privilege has a twofold effect.

Firstly, introducing depositor protection may increase bank financing costs. Part of capital acquired by a bank for the sake of its activities is burdened with higher costs, because it must either pay creditors for risk or demonstrate its security measures. As an effect, the hierarchy structure of meeting creditor claims is changed. Introducing depositor protection priority may be accompanied by the rise in secured liabilities in the bank balance sheet, which will lie outside the scope of claim settlement hierarchy (namely, funds will be paid out even before those of depositors, thus depleting future bankruptcy resources).

In effect, due to asset encumbrance existence, legal depositor privilege may become ostensible. If half of subordinated liabilities were changed into secured debt (settled primarily from its protection systems), it may, in fact, mean a bigger participation in losses on behalf of deposit insurers, even despite the rule of depositor protection. Due to the decrease in subordinate (unsecured) debts, losses are moved into further categories. The situation of seemingly protected depositors (with deposits above €100,000) has been deteriorating, because it is them who strongly experience the burden of insolvent bank losses. Without the depositor privilege rule, the deposit guarantee scheme with acquired depositor rights would be burdened with lower costs.

Due to lack of empirical data, as well as the period of adjusting financial institutions to new regulations, it is difficult at the time of implementing new regulations to clearly evaluate the scale of asset encumbrance in the EU, as well as the true influence of BRR Directive depositor privileges on current bank financing methods and deposit guarantee scheme costs. Still, it is a process necessary from the regulator monitoring point of view.

In conclusion, it may be said that through the BRR Directive, EU regulators introduce and communicate universal terms and conditions of resolution, which have been worked out with the inclusion of various courses of events and hypothetical circumstances, ahead of time. Still, certain rules are of theoretical nature only and have not, as of yet, been tested in practice. Only after resolution had been implemented, will the true situation of an insolvent bank's owners and creditors be constituted. Nevertheless, it must be restricted that the depositor privilege rule may, in certain cases, bring an effect contradictory to expectations, thus weakening the deposit guarantee scheme position within the financial safety net.

5.4.4 Phases and Mode of Action

The directive introduces several activity phases of bank intervention, including the use of instruments provided by the BRR Directive. First and foremost, prudential procedures (including caution in running a banking business), supported by supervisory activities, ought to help in avoiding banking activity threats (first phase). Regardless, once worsening of the financial condition of a given institution takes place, public authorities shall take on coordinated, reparatory actions and start the process of early intervention (second phase). Sound cooperation of financial safety net organs is needed in a way that prevents the worsening of an entity's situation to the point, where there are no other options but carrying out its liquidation. In case no effects are achieved, are insufficient, or the right moment to initiate early intervention is overlooked, carrying on to the next (third) phase will be required—deciding on the form of market elimination of the given institution (resolution or standard insolvency). Examples of possible actions in further phases are presented in Table 5.3.

According to the provisions of the BRR Directive, the third phase takes place only if the previous two had not resulted in the desired event. Detailed BRR Directive requirements state that the decision on initiating liquidation procedures in resolution may take place once the resolution organ decides that:

- the institution is endangered or on the verge of bankruptcy,
- it is highly unlikely that any alternative private sector activities would be able to salvage the endangered institution in a way that would save it from bankruptcy,
- the action is crucial for public interest.

After the first two conditions had been met, resolution organs ought to take on appropriate, coordinated actions immediately in order to protect public interest—the core goal of the action.

The attempt at determining the time of the third phase (initiating resolution), recommended by the BRR Directive, is cautious. While

Table 5.3 Phases of resolution procedure activities

Phase 1	Phase 2	Phase 3
Sound operation	Early intervention	Resolution
Supervision: • Capital and liquidity requirements • Periodic reports Preparatory instruments: • Supervisory programs • Individual recovery plans • Scenario-based stress tests Preventive instruments: • Individual resolution plans • Activity scope limitation orders	Measures undertaken by the supervisor: • Own capital raise order • Change of board members • Recovery plan provisions' implementation order • Introducing receivership	Decision on the form of procedure: • Decision on initiating resolution or standard insolvency Resolution: • Choice of adequate instruments • Remission and conversion of debt • Sale of bank institution • Bridge institution • Distinguishing assets Standard insolvency: • Informing appropriate organs about the initiation of a standard procedure • Liquidation of institution

Source: Author's own formulation and Iwanicz-Drozdowska et al. (2016)

actions should be commenced without undue delay, they should take place prior to an institution's insolvency, within the meaning of accounting policies, and before its own funds run out (as stated literally in point 41 of BRR Directive Preamble—before accounts of the given financial institution reveal insolvency). Prerequisites of acknowledging an institution's endangerment, or being at the brink of bankruptcy, are vague. In order to recognize the first condition, it is sufficient that the resolution organ is convinced a given institution has or will, most likely, infringe conditions crucial for maintaining their respective licenses (for example, bank or brokerage house permissions). Activities of an institution on the verge of bankruptcy shall be maintained with the employment of resolution instruments, while using the highest possible financial potential of private funds.

To launch resolution procedures, the second condition of finding private sector financial support must be exhausted. In order to prove the case, it must be shown that no entities are willing to increase a given institution's capital to a degree that would, at least, allow for restoring profitability of its future, cautious activity.

Thirdly, in order to initiate resolution, it is necessary to prove that such a procedure is more beneficial for the public interest than standard insolvency. This is due to the fact that before resolution instruments are applied, standard insolvency proceedings must be considered as the first resort. If it is proved that such action may endanger financial stability, interrupt sound work of critical functions, or significantly influence depositor protection, resolution must be chosen. Public interest, which may be expressed in the form of minimizing procedure costs or guaranteeing the value of financial assets of the institution, should be scrutinized (EBA 2014a). It is the superiority of public interest protection that makes limiting shareholder and creditor rights possible, while maintaining the guarantee of actions such as the mentioned NCWO rule.

5.5   Resolution Planning

In order to increase the probability of successful resolution, actions were planned, which aim at preparing for crisis events, corresponding to phases 2 and 3 shown in Table 5.3. Respectively, it is necessary that each financial institution is presented with two independent plans, namely, recovery and resolution. Although they both concern dealing with bank struggle events, they must be treated separately. Therefore, it may be said that planning is a two-tier process, and recovery and resolution procedures differ in terms of their goals, possible instruments, and organs responsible for the creation and potential execution of actions.

Preparing *ex ante* action strategies for the sake of bankruptcy threat of a financial institution is the crucial element of both planning types. It allows for the timely recognition of the adequate action method and choice of instruments that best suit the given situation and financial institution. The desired effect is the advantageous position of supervisors (responsible for recovery plans) and resolution organs (responsible for resolution actions), as well as the ability of facing up to extreme circumstances (Szczepańska et al. 2015, p. 59).

5.5.1 Recovery Plans

Recovery plans are regulated by Articles 5–9 of the BRR Directive. Each financial institution is responsible for their creation, maintenance, and timely amendments. A prepared plan is supposed to be a signpost of reform of a given institution in case its financial situation worsens and shall result in the unassisted recovery of an entity's financial condition.

Plans must also meet regulatory requirements in regard to compulsory information. Those include, among others, indicating critical functions of a given bank, a detailed description of the process of evaluation and transferability of main lines of business, as well as the description of means that allow for minimizing risks and leverage (EBA 2015c). An important plan requirement is that the bank covered by the procedure does not have access to extraordinary public financial support. It is also crucial that it includes an analysis of capabilities and terms of using standard instruments of the central bank. Recovery actions shall include several scenarios related to changes in macroeconomic conditions— including such, which foresee events that have an influence on the entire financial system and all other entities connected to the bank.

Parent units in the EU prepare group recovery plans that cover subsidiaries. While they are subject to the same regime as isolated plans, they oversee the implementation of funds equal to the combined levels of parent and subsidiary units. An additional goal of the group recovery plan is to stabilize a whole group, or one of its institutions, in case they find themselves in a difficult situation. This would also include the appropriate coordination and acquired fund consistency agreements.

Although responsibility for preparing the plan rests with the bank, it is the supervisor who plays the role of the inspector. After the submission of recovery plans to the supervisor, a review and evaluation are prepared. The supervising body examines the scale to which plan implementation will maintain or restore profitability of a bank through enhancing its financial situation, as well as checks whether plan provisions may be introduced effectively during times of financial turmoil. The supervisor also analyzes the degree to which complexity of the bank, market relationships, and critical functions are all taken into consideration (Hamilton 2015). If introducing recovery plan provisions does not bring expected results and the situation of the bank is not improved, the second plan—resolution—is implemented.

5.5.2   Resolution Plans

After the unsuccessful attempt at salvaging an entity or implementing recovery plans at an early stage of intervention, the resolution plan is executed. In order to enable the process, Articles 10–8 of the BRR Directive implement the obligation of preparing individual, separate resolution plans for each financial institution. Contrary to recovery plans, it is the resolution organ that is obliged to prepare a plan (previously consulted with the supervisor), and, subsequently, carries out its resolvability assessment.

The resolution plan oversees all actions that may be carried out by the responsible organ once an institution fulfills the requirements of the procedure. In order to achieve this, the resolution organ is obliged, first and foremost, to identify any possible obstacles that may be encountered on the way to implementing the procedure and indicate how to eliminate them. After the phase above, the resolution organ shall assume various scenarios, which oversee that a given bank's insolvency may be of individual nature, as well as that it may take place due to a general financial instability situation or events that influence the whole financial sector, thus resulting in unfavorable asset valuation of a bank on the brink of bankruptcy.

Similarly to recovery plans, certain subsidiary instruments may not be applied throughout resolution. Among forbidden instruments are the use of extraordinary public financial support, emergency liquidity support from the central bank, or non-standard central bank support in regard to securing the date and level of interest rate.

It must be brought to attention that the plan includes a prearranged set of information, such as specifying the ways critical functions and main business lines may be separated from others in order to maintain continuity, a detailed description of resolution strategy, and critical correlations (EBA 2015a).

As in the case of group recovery plans, planning resolution also includes procedures for the whole group, which is supervised by a resolution organ from the country of the parent unit. The plan indicates solutions for both the whole group and single subsidiaries. It also includes the analysis of coordinating the use of multiple instruments in various units, as well as defines the conditions for executing authority in regard to resolution of linked entities. An important restriction is the fact that group resolution plans may not influence disproportionately any member state.

The BRR Directive also introduces basic rules of applying group resolution plans, which are enacted by the resolution college in the form of a joint decision. Plan acceptance is an extensive formal process and exceeds the scope of this book (EBA 2015b). Determining the approach toward resolution in regard to cross-border activities is one of the biggest decisions to be made in regard to banking groups. Two approaches are possible: single point of entry (SPE) and multiple point of entry (MPE) (FSB 2013a, pp. 12–13).

"Single point of entry" means that authority to use resolution instruments and carry out the whole process belongs entirely to the resolution authority of the home country, which intervenes in the case of the parent unit of a given group, as well as its subsidiaries (influencing indirectly the parent company only). This strategy is based on taking on actions high in group hierarchy, thus absorbing losses on the level of the parent unit. It is the parent entity that bail-in instruments are applied to, whose debt is either remitted or converted into capital. This may take place if it is assumed that capital and debt eligible for conversion are sufficient on the level of the parent (dominant) entity. The SPE approach additionally postulates that resolution organs of hosting countries should carry out activities that support restructuring efforts staged from the home country.

MPE is a different path, which grants restructuring capabilities directly to subsidiaries of a given group through respective resolution organs of the hosting countries. With such a strategy, each entity of the group must own an appropriate level of capital and debt eligible for conversion, so that the bail-in instrument may be applied directly. Such a strategy requires high-level coordination works on behalf of respective EU member states' resolution organs, because their actions must be cohesive and supportive of one another, if intervention is applied simultaneously toward several subsidiaries of the same group. These coordination processes are within the authority of resolution organs of the home country.

While both strategies lead to the same objective, they may be distinguished by the varying ways of its achievement. They also differ in regard to the role of the deposit guarantee scheme engaged in resolution procedures. Strengths and weaknesses of both strategies are presented in Table 5.4.

The analysis of advantages and threats presented in Table 5.4 does not provide a clear answer as to which strategy should dominate in the EU. It seems that countries where banking groups are based in will opt for the SPE strategy, because it grants them control over all resolution processes within the group. From their perspective, choosing the MPE strategy will deprive them of control capabilities in regard to subsidiaries in hosting countries. A contrasting perspective will be encountered in hosting countries, which are not interested in restructuring the group on the highest tier, and simply care for protection on the country level. Furthermore, negligence of home country resolution authorities, or their delayed intervention in choosing the SPE strategy, may cause commotion in hosting countries.

Choice of strategy is not limited to selecting either SPE or MPE, because a combination of both solutions is also possible. In the previously mentioned document prepared jointly by FDIC and the Bank of England (2012), both institutions declared that they will consistently apply SPE strategy toward groups within their authority. The intention of creating predictability of resolution organs on a given market

Table 5.4   Comparison of SPE and MPE strategies

Strategy	Potential advantages	Potential threats
SPE	• Maintaining sound operation of subsidiaries • Encouragement for country resolution organs to abstain from individual efforts in favor of a consistent group strategy • No changes in the structure of subsidiary shareholding • Lower cost of emission of bail in-eligible debt (issued by a big parent company) • A more simple function mechanism	• Complicated process of transferring capital and liquidity (may encounter tax and accounting barriers) • Complicated way of determining an appropriate capital level and liabilities eligible for remission, corresponding to the structure of the group • Risk of limiting ring fencing of assets by country authority
MPE	• Solving the problem in the place of occurrence • No legal risk resultant from regulatory differences between countries	• Moral hazard of protecting national interest on behalf of local authorities • Possibility of altering the ownership structure of an entity, or even separating it from the group • Necessity of acquiring support in case loss absorption is not sufficient • More expensive for banking group functioning

Source: Author's own research and Pruski (2014a) and Szczepańska et al. (2015), p. 67

motivated such an approach. Among key arguments that legitimized such a standpoint were certain G-SIFI characteristics, such as size and a complicated organizational structure, which are easier to manage during an SPE strategy resolution process.

Due to the fact that resolution plans in the EU are still in their formulation phase, empirical data allowing for the evaluation of SPE and MPE strategies, and their effectiveness for resolution (should they be chosen), are missing. First and foremost, the sole fact that bank restructuring plans are implemented is a positive sign, as such procedures were missing during the recent global financial crisis. Secondly, granting the right to choose between SPE and MPE strategies to the resolution group college in the provisions of the BRR Directive also deserves recognition. Effectively, countries where subsidiaries are based will actively participate in the decision making process in regard to the preferable resolution form. If compromise is not achieved, they will also be authorized to apply for a legally binding mediation of the EBA, or single-handedly work out a plan for their dependent unit (such rights are granted by Article 13 of the BRR Directive).

5.6   Resolution Tools

Works on new bank restructuring solutions created the need to formulate operative procedures that should be taken on in order to ensure sound functioning of the new resolution procedure. In order for it to be effective, a set of instruments that allow for successful intervention toward financially troubled or bankrupt institutions had to be introduced.

If a financial institution fulfills requirements for such a procedure, resolution organs ought to make an individual decision regarding the type and scope of planned instruments that have been, for the most part, determined in the previously accepted resolution plan. Enforcement instruments have been specified in the BRR Directive, and their use is subject to common rules for the entire union. They include:

– sale of business tool,
– bridge institution,
– asset separation,
– bail-in.

Resolution proceedings with the use of all of the above instruments will, as a rule, aim at terminating activities of an entity through the liquidation of its resources (for example, by the sale of part or all assets) and the liquidation of the residual entity (part left for insolvency).

Resolution instruments are described below according to a unified analytical scheme, spanning, as follows: the legal basis for application of the instrument, its characteristic, and chosen examples of practical use. Table 5.5 demonstrates the comparison of flaws and advantages of resolution instruments, presented in this chapter.

5.6.1   Sale of Business Tool

The sale of business tool, also known as the form of purchase and assumption agreement (as referred to by the FDIC in the United States), is regulated by Articles 38–9 of the BRR Directive.

The tool allows the resolution organ to perform a complete or partial sale of an institution to an interested private acquirer. Application of the company takeover instrument (sale of business) allows for a full or partial transfer of a given entity's activities to a private acquirer, who continues the operation. This enables avoiding repercussions that might be felt by clients of a liquidated entity in case they are no longer provided services (FSB 2013, pp. 50–52). Nevertheless, this strictly relates to an important requirement regarding the possession of an operational license, granted by the supervisor, which will be taken over (for example, bank activity rights). In order to open up to a broader group of entities that may be interested in taking over a troubled institution, a promise on behalf of the supervisor that such a license will be granted to the acquiring party should it fulfill the requirements is sufficient.

The use of such a tool requires introducing to the legal order the right of carrying out transfer procedures on behalf of the resolution organ. Such a transfer would include, for instance, passing shares and other instruments at the disposal of owners, as well as assets, rights, and liabilities, to the new acquirer (Szczepańska et al. 2015, pp. 29–33). In the case of Poland, according to the implementation act of the BRR Directive, the BGF will be capable of using the tool to enact a transfer decision of the following to the acquirer:

- companies of the entity under resolution,
- chosen or all property rights or liabilities of the entity under resolution,
- shareholding rights of the entity under resolution.

Table 5.5 Comparison simulation of flaws and advantages of resolution tools

Tool	Advantages	Flaws
Sale of business	• One of the least legally complicated elimination methods on the financial market • Low instrument application costs • Possibility of complete acquisition of the insolvent bank and its shutdown in a single transaction	• Low demand for business acquisition is expected • Limited number of entities capable of purchasing the company (weak negotiating position of the resolution organ) • Difficulty in proper asset and liability valuation as of the day of company acquisition • Limited time for transaction • Method hardly applicable in times of systemic
Bridge institution	• Longer company sale period • Consolidation of financial difficulties in one entity (of even several banks) • Capability of proper valuation of assets and liabilities of the institution	• Difficulties with operational continuity of a bank in a bridge institution (for example, troubles with providing customer retail account management) • Potentially higher administrative procedure costs (necessity of sustaining the bridge institution) • Necessity of liquidating the residual entity in a standard insolvency procedure
Asset separation	• Lower operational costs of the company and their asset management, than in the case of bridge institution • Longer company operation time • Possibility of staggering asset profits and profitability assessments • Ease of asset sale in packages	• Necessity of carrying out proper asset valuation as of the day of acquisition • Necessity of long-term acquired assets' management
Bail-in	• Supports market discipline • Primarily burdens creditors with costs • Lowers resolution costs	• Causes strong interference in bank owners' acquired rights • Often causes appeal from remission decisions • High administrative costs

Table 5.5 (continued)

Tool	Advantages	Flaws
		• Possible change in bank owner structure as an effect of conversion and remission
		• Rise in bank financing costs

Source: Author's own formulation

Takeover of the above type may take place even without the consent of owners, debtors, or creditors of the given entity. The rule was introduced, because crises experiences proved that withholding the acquisition decision destabilizes the financial market, whereas shareholders are mostly reluctant toward resolution and do not permit acquisition if the alternative of capitalizing the given bank from public resources exists (Iwanicz-Drozdowska et al. 2016).

The acquiring entity, using the rights granted by resolution provisions, is obliged to pay a specific price for the overtaken bank (or its part); still, payment usually takes form in the acquisition of a given entity's liabilities, correspondent to the market value of the acquired property rights, as valuated on the day acquisition takes place.

The BRR Directive foresees that—through the application of the above-mentioned instrument—attention to detail will be needed throughout the entire resolution process. Therefore, it is crucial that while the choice of entity acquirer is being made, transparency, openness, equal treatment, and lack of conflict of interest, along with providing the most profitable choice of entity (from the perspective of procedure provisions), are all delivered in the fastest possible mode. Hence, not only does the tool aim at finding an acquirer of the institution at the highest possible price, but also maintaining the financial stability and cautionary action warranty.

Applying the instrument of company takeover makes possible the protection of interest of clients of an endangered institution, but, as an effect of halting value loss, it should also be beneficial to other groups of creditors.

From the perspective of the resolution tool, financing takeover of the entire company is a more advantageous solution. Such acquisition results not only in the takeover of an entity's assets, but also all or a major part of its liabilities. Such a procedure is permitted even with the financial support of the resolution organ, in the form of grants or long-term guarantee of preserving acquired assets (through loss-sharing agreements), provided for the sake of settling loss arising from discrepancies between liabilities resulting from covered funds and acquired property rights. This allows for avoiding difficulties related to the insolvency of part of the entity (namely, the residual part) and limiting administrative costs. Financing for such a transaction ought to be provided by the resolution organ from its own resources and may, in part, be supported by grants from the deposit guarantee fund (in return for acquisition of covered deposits).

Such a solution was applied for the sake of EU bank resolution during the current crisis (for example, Denmark and Belgium) (Iwanicz-Drozdowska et al. 2016) and is commonly used in the United States (FDIC 1997, pp. 193–209). Total takeovers in the Polish financial sector, which took place four times within recent years due to the resolution of cooperative savings and credit unions in the years 2014–5, may be named as examples of successful entity resolution, performed with the use of the sale of business tool.

5.6.2   Establishment of the Bridge Institution

Establishment, functioning, and the shutdown of a bridge institution are all procedures regulated by Articles 40–1 of the BRR Directive. Due to the more complex nature of the tool (in comparison to the sale of business instrument described above), it is characterized precisely in the directive, for instance, in reference to its establishment, functioning, and termination conditions, including the liquidation of the resultant residual entity.

In terms of economical practice, the public authority struggles to sell big financial institutions due to lack of interest—especially in times of systemic market instability. Market participants are also aware that a limited number of potential entities that are capable of purchasing a struggling institution allows for them to offer a low price for the entity taken over. Because the sale of an entire insolvent bank institution is not always possible, a different tool, bridge institution, was also designed (FSB 2013, pp. 52–55).

The above-mentioned instrument is a mechanism that foresees the creation of a special-purpose vehicle (SPV)—most often, a bank or a different joint-stock company for an investment firm. Such a company must either belong to or, at least, be under public control. As a result, the bank remains public property, and the state delegates its board members and, indirectly, shapes the operational method. A bridge institution is created for the sake of two elementary goals. The first is the management of acquired (transferred) share rights, and the second is the operational continuity and its reorganization prior to the final sale to a private investor. Bridge institution does not aim at developing new financial activities, but merely continues the operational basis of a financially troubled bank (Szczepańska et al. 2015, pp. 33–34).

The sole transition of activities from one entity to another resembles an entire transfer procedure. Similarly, the process does not require approval of all owners or creditors of an endangered institution. The possibility of consolidating problems of several entities of the banking sector under one resolution institution during times of systemic turmoil is an advantage of establishing a temporary, public entity. In such a case, the bridge institution is responsible only for managing transferred means of each institution under resolution separately, or preparing activity records in a way that allows for the separation of the estate, as well as indicating its liabilities and their management effects.

Bridge bank controlled by the state provides warranty of cautionary activity, aimed at maintaining financial stability. It also gives stronger trust to the potential rise of own capital delivered by country authorities. Acquiring an operational license by the bridge institution on behalf of the supervisor, authorizing the acquired entity's form of activity, is also a crucial condition. Additionally, the institution is subject to regular banking law regulations, including requirements of maintaining adequate capital levels.

The duration of bridge institution activities ought to be limited. The indicated time shall allow for waiting out systemic crises, as well as provide an appropriate asset and liability valuation of the entity under resolution. It is also required that sufficient time be granted so that search for the entity acquirer—either partial or complete—is performed without time pressure. The period most often lasts two years, but it may be prolonged in certain circumstances. After the provided time expires, the company (bridge bank) shall be either sold or liquidated. Such a time horizon is described by Article 41(5) of the BRR Directive, stating that "the resolution authority shall terminate the operation of a bridge institution as soon as possible and in any event two years after the date on which the last transfer from an institution under resolution pursuant to the bridge institution tool was made".

Financing such a resolution tool consists mainly of granting financial aid to the bridge institution through its recapitalization, providing starting capital, and liquidity.

The solution had limited application to EU bank resolution after the global crisis breakout, but was used significantly in the United States at the beginning of the 1990s, as well as in Asian countries (Japan, Taiwan, South Korea), where it became a popular procedure after futile company sale transaction attempts. At the time, the FDIS created 32 bridge institutions in the United States, where 114 banks, with a total value of approximately $90 billion, were transferred (FDIC 1997, pp. 171–191).

5.6.3 Asset Separation Tool

The asset separation tool, which often leads to the establishment of an SPV, is regulated in Article 42 of the BRR Directive. It is similar in shape to previously described tools, nevertheless, as a rule, it is not used separately and is usually combined with a different resolution instrument.

It is applied in specific situations—mainly, when the resolution organ decides that transferring property rights to the asset management entity will raise income resulting from their possession, thus making use of bridge institution solution pointless.

Such a tool allows the resolution organ to transfer chosen assets or rights and liabilities of a financial institution to a different entity—a special company referred to as the "special purpose vehicle" or "asset management company". The goal of the entity is to manage its acquired property rights and liabilities from one or several entities during resolution, and—if possible—their gradual sale. The SPV is obliged to manage its acquired assets in a mode that their maximum value is maintained until the company is sold or liquidated.

The so-called bad bank transfer process for low-quality assets is the basic approach toward transferring company rights to the SPV. The asset separation tool increases the changes of sale of a restructured bank (namely, the remaining, properly functioning part), because toxic assets are exempt from the bank balance sheet and are transferred, for a fee, to the SPV. In turn, the asset managing company attempts to maintain its value. Such a company may also exist in a long time horizon.

As for financing costs, a bank isolates part of its assets, which are then passed on to the SPV. Next, the institution valuates the market worth of assets and finalizes the transaction with the bank in the process of resolution. Remuneration for toxic assets is, in fact, paid by the resolution organ, which utilizes means from the resolution fund. The organ also contributes initial capital to the asset management company in the form of resolution funds. Furthermore, expenses of the SPV also qualify as costs of the instrument, as long as the institution does not achieve sufficient income resulting from asset management.

Such a solution was applied during resolution of EU country banks during the current crisis (for instance, Ireland, Great Britain, Slovenia, and Spain—in the case of cooperative funds). An example of a successful use of the asset separation tool is the establishment of the UK Asset Resolution company in Great Britain. Created in order to manage bad bank assets isolated from the Northern Rock and Bradford & Bingley banks, the company initially noted loss in 2009, but quickly began generating profits and successfully sells acquired assets (Iwanicz-Drozdowska et al., 2016).

5.6.4 Bail-In

The most controversial instrument provided by Articles 43–4 of the BRR Directive is the bail-in tool, which deeply intervenes in ownership rights (IMF 2012). It is not an exception in global postcrisis regulations, because the solution is already being applied in G-20 countries (FSB 2014). The instrument is based on the rule that shareholders and certain creditor categories (the biggest) shall be the first to be burdened with bank loss. Nevertheless, not only is bail-in considered a resolution tool, but also a self-reliant financing source for resolution. Therefore, it is described at the end of the chapter and directly precedes the analysis of resolution funding methods. The book presents a mixed concept, because, as a procedure tool, bail-in has various functions, including its self-reliant financing (Kerlin and Maksymiuk 2015, pp. 97–107).

The fact that bail-in is used in order to restore a capital level of a bank, which will enable its continuity (the concept of going concern—open bank bail-in), is one of its most prominent functions. The aim of such an action is lowering bank liabilities and loss absorption by creditors, as well as restoring trust toward the entity through rehabilitating its situation with radical measures. Another concept (gone concern—closed bank bail-in) is that bank operation may not be continued, while write-down allows for the decrease in bank liabilities, thus facilitating its closing and liquidation—a process that, as a rule, requires more assets than insolvency. It is possible that this may take place through the use of other resolution instruments, namely, bridge institution and asset separation (FSB 2013, pp. 55–60).

Applying bail-in may be a multilevel process. In its first phase, entity shareholders are the first category eligible for write-down. First, the share capital (CET1) is remitted. If it does not cover all losses, capital instruments of the first (Additional Tier I) and second (Tier II) categories are also remitted (Szczepańska et al. 2015, p. 36). Shareholder capital and liabilities of other capital instrument owners are also repealed. During the second phase, conversion of bank liabilities to capital takes place. Potential debt (for instance, of big bank creditors) is transformed into newly emitted assets, thus causing the expiration of the main liability.

As a rule, all liability categories mentioned in the BRR Directive may undergo conversion, but some, as shown in Fig. 5.1, have been excluded from such a possibility. Covered deposits and secured liabilities, which mostly concern bonds and financial instruments that are the basis of securing other transactions, are considered most prominent and worthy of absolute protection. The third category is other liabilities, protected by the insolvency law of the given state.

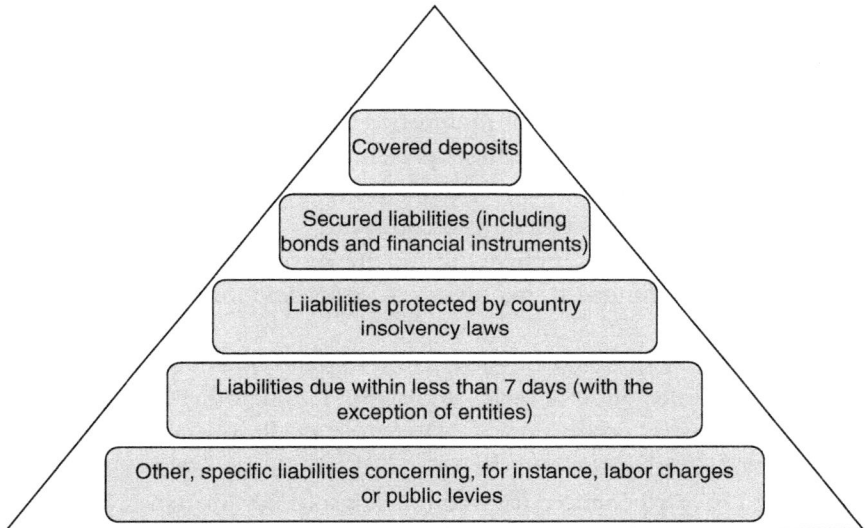

Fig. 5.1   Liabilities exempt from bail-in scope
Source: Author's own formulation based on Article 44(2) of the BRR Directive

Such a solution is a form of compromise, because—depending on the country—categories exempt from the insolvency regime may vary to a certain degree. For example, the majority of insurance company reserves, pension company receipts, and receipts related to trust funds of property management operations may all be included in this group. As a rule, liabilities due in a time shorter than seven days may not be subject to write down, unless they are charges of a different entity of the group. Lastly, the possibility of remitting debt on the base of its social significance was also excluded. This concerns labor charges, commercial and trade liabilities (for instance, payment for telecommunications services, electricity, etc.), public levies—namely, income tax and social security—as well as, importantly, contributions for the participation in the deposit guarantee scheme.

The rule of participation in losses has several specific exemptions. It was assumed that, in return for excluding depositors from bail-in, the deposit insurance agency shall participate in financing resolution through the financial coverage of part of resolution costs, up to the amount corresponding to net losses the guarantee institution would need to experience if standard insolvency payouts for depositors had been carried out (Dübel 2013). The rule is specified in Article 109 of the BRR Directive and is of crucial importance for monitoring the deposit insurer's influence on resolution, as well as the analyses presented in Chapter 6. Examples of practical application of the rule are lacking, and the experiences come from Denmark, the United States, and Kazakhstan.

Such a solution was applied during the restructuring of EU banks during the current crisis, mainly in Cyprus and Slovenia (Iwanicz-Drozdowska et al. 2016).

There are also additional limitations to the application of the bail-in tool. The potential integration of ownership rights, among other basic acquired privileges, must be proportionate. Therefore, creditors and shareholders covered by resolution shall not be burdened with losses higher than those they would have experienced if a traditional insolvency procedure had been applied (the previously mentioned NCWO rule of Section 5.4.3). For this purpose, all creditors are assigned to groups according to their claim settling hierarchy during insolvency. Next, conversion ratios of specific creditor groups are calculated in accordance with each category's liabilities. A general rule is that liabilities of higher hierarchy within claim settlement categories will have a more favorable conversion ratio. Through this, the owner and creditor situation during resolution is similar to that the institution would have experienced during standard insolvency. It must be emphasized that it is crucial to maintain proportions during works on establishing the conversion ratio. A liability write-down exceeding its necessary level, in return for assets, may trigger ownership structure changes of the entity. As an effect, the bank's biggest creditor or group of creditors, who cannot grant warranty of cautious maintenance of the troublesome entity, may become the bank's owners. For instance, the application of the bail-in instrument in Cyprus in 2013, and the conversion of deposits worth more than €100,000 into Laiki bank assets, changed the ownership structure of the bank significantly. Also, as an effect, the majority is currently in the hands of minority shareholders from non-EU countries.

Introducing bail-in posed a threat to the change in bank behavior. Regulators anticipated that the instrument would not be suitable in all cases due to the undesired changes in the liability structure of the bank (from the perspective of its supervisor). After new solutions have been introduced, the catalogue of conversion-applicable bank liabilities decreased significantly, thus the loss absorption capabilities of the bank also dropped. Therefore, as a part of the bail-in tool, MREL was introduced (Illmer 2013). According to the BRR Directive, banks shall ensure that bail-in is applied. This shall be achieved by maintaining MREL on a specific ratio level, equivalent to the quotient of own funds and liabilities of a given bank. The ratio is not preset and is to be determined individually by the resolution organ for each bank separately, after its risk profile, financing structures, and activity type had been considered. By the end of 2016, EBA will have had performed an overview of solutions applied in specific EU member states.

Bail-in is a multidimensional tool, which is hard to evaluate unequivocally. Its advantages include, among others, the rise in share capital, loss settling directly by owners, elimination and limitation of public help costs, as well as the increase of market discipline due to bail-in's additional, preventive function. The risk of burdening the above-mentioned groups with significant loss would encourage shareholders and creditors to monitor the financial situation of the entity more thoroughly in ordinary circumstances, thus improving the market discipline.

Simultaneously, the introduction of the tool creates a series of risks. The necessity of maintaining MREL will cause changes in bank financing structures. Hence, it also means that certain banks, which are mostly financed from deposits, will have to change their activity profile—often, to a much riskier mode. Furthermore, rise in bank financing is also expected due to the necessity of maintaining an envelope of liabilities eligible for conversion (thus, more costly due to the higher investment risk).

5.7   Resolution Funding

Introducing resolution entails the necessity of providing proper financing. It is crucial for the execution of two key functions:

- providing operational actions of the resolution organ (including planning resolution, maintaining information systems, or evaluating the enforceability of plans),

- ensuring the possibility of using supportive tools during resolution, such as providing grants, loss coverage guarantee, or providing share capital for bridge institutions.

In fact, ensuring the proper financing of the resolution organ will allow for withholding from using public resources for the sake of financial institutions' salvation.

5.7.1 Resolution Financing Mechanism

Member states shall provide adequate financing for resolution procedures. A set of norms aimed at providing resolution financing is known as the European System of Financing Arrangements. Each resolution intervention is financed on the basis of country financing mechanisms. Articles 99–109 of the BRR Directive specify financial sources of the procedure, as well as its basic rules.

Several resolution financing possibilities may be indicated. The basic methods include (FSB 2011, p. 12):

- collecting *ex ante* and *ex post* contributions from entities covered by resolution (mainly banks and investment companies),
- specifying minimal liability requirement levels in financial institutions that will absorb losses in case of procedure initiation (TLAC or MREL),
- legal capability of remitting capital instruments of a financial institution prior to resolution—in contrary to the method presented above, this source aims at expropriating owners, while maintaining MREL applies mostly to creditors of credit institutions,
- receivables acquired by the resolution organ as a result of applying resolution tools (for example, revenue from the asset management company),
- regaining receivables by the resolution organ from bankruptcy funds, as an effect of insolvency procedures,
- participation of the deposit insurance agency in costs of procedures, if depositor protection was provided,

– arranging agreements regarding obtaining loans and other forms of support (in case conventional financing sources are exhausted).

Furthermore, in countries of the so-called banking union, mutualization of country financing mechanisms took place for the sake of increasing overall restructuring resources, as well as for the better effect of resolution of a given entity. Rules of fund's mutualization are specified in the Intergovernmental Agreement on the Single Resolution Fund, which is under the SRB's remit.

Although there are not many practical experiences in the field, it may be anticipated that resolution will be supported through several financial streams, the majority of which may be classified as *ex ante* contributions of financial institutions, loss absorption capabilities of single entities, as well as the supportive participation of the deposit insurance agency.

Summarizing the topic of resolution financing mechanism, its multi-tier construction, foreseen by the BRR Directive, must be indicated. Bail-in, the tool for write-down of capital instruments and the conversion of liabilities into capital, will be applied first. This is an effect of the implementation of big creditor and shareholder participation in a given financial institution's resolution costs. Only after eight per cent of liability and own funds' value of a bank is remitted, will the use of further procedure financial tools be possible. Utilizing the accumulated *ex ante* resolution funds will also be then permitted.

In case of their exhaustion, it is additionally possible to acquire *ex post* contributions from financial institutions. If they, as well, prove to be insufficient, acquiring funds from alternative streams will be possible, including loans (from third parties and financing mechanisms of other member states).

Further on, the possibility of utilizing deposit guarantee schemes was foreseen. It was assumed that in order to strengthen the financial potential, deposit guarantee schemes shall be capable of supporting resolution funds with capital. This may only be achieved under the condition that, through this support, access to covered deposits will be maintained. In such circumstances, funds will be obliged to contribute with an amount of not less than the value of losses they would be burdened with should the given institution be liquidated in a standard insolvency procedure. Conditions regarding the participation of deposit insurance agencies in resolution may be found in Article 109 of the BRR Directive.

Despite the transparency of hierarchy of obtaining financing for resolution tools, the BRR Directive foresees one extraordinary measure in the form of government financial stability instruments. According to their provisions, countries may grant public financial support of extraordinary character (compliant with union frameworks regarding state aid), including direct intervention in case such actions will not serve the goals of the procedure. Although state intervention tools are a measure of last resort, such provisions may create an obstacle for the firm respect of resolution principles.

Responsibility for providing appropriate resolution financial resources rests with the resolution organ. It is obliged not only to provide the required financial levels, but also use them only for the sake of resolution procedures.

Solutions applied in regard to financing resolution in the EU, complaint with the BRR Directive, are convergent with global standards (FSB 2013c). Nevertheless, they are characterized by varying specificity and, often, a casuistic approach toward regulating certain matters. For example, union specificity includes specifying detailed conditions regarding, for instance, the obligatory participation of the deposit insurance agency in resolution costs, maintaining individually assigned MREL levels by banks, and the harmonization of minimal country benchmarks of the resolution fund.

The fact that member states may use the same administrative structure of the resolution financial mechanism for the sake of deposit guarantee is an important element of the BRR Directive (Article 100). This means that the union legislator predicted that the resolution organ and the deposit guarantee scheme managing authority are close to one another, and their administrative scope overlaps so significantly that certain mechanisms may be mutualized. At the same time, other members of the financial safety net were not indicated. This has grave implications for the future financial architecture, and—despite many practical experiences—it may be expected that the deposit insurance agency and the institution responsible for carrying out resolution will cooperate closely in the financial safety net environment.

5.7.2 Target Levels and Contributions

Throughout works on the BRR Directive, legislators attempted to accordingly calibrate European resolution funds' target levels (Marcinkowska 2011, pp. 100–127). On the one hand, they needed to be sufficient for the sake of restructuring a number of financial institutions, but on the other, it could have created an excessive burden for banks. Various concepts regarding the target and level of resolution fund exhaustion, as well as the possibility of supporting these actions from the resources of deposit guarantee schemes (DGS—paybox fund) collided throughout the works. The majority of member states claimed that both funds did, in fact, protect similar interests and the synergy may not remain unused. Representatives of the financial industry represented the same point of view (EC 2012). Eventually, it has been decided that the fund of resolution financing mechanism shall be between one and four per cent of covered deposits' value in the bank sector—with the assumption that ten per cent of a given bank's liabilities will qualify for write-down. Finally, the lower limit of the range—one per cent of covered deposits' value for a given country—was accepted by the BRR Directive. Meanwhile, the obligatory write-down threshold was set to at least eight per cent of capital instruments or liabilities of a given financial institution, in order to permit the process of resolution fund expenditure. While it was also noticed that the sole fact of remitting assets of financial institutions' owners was an act allowing for the takeover of control over a financial institution, new capital was still required. It is the resolution fund's role to provide such financing (EC 2012). Still, it is difficult to find the answer to the question on whether such a calibrated fund (equal to one per cent of covered deposits of a given country) would be sufficient in case an intervention in a specific state was needed. This mostly depends on the intervention scale and a given country's market structure, whereas analyses of the European Commission did not research the area thoroughly in this regard (EC 2012).

In order to harmonize the target level of resolution funds in the EU, it was decided that states ensure that—until 31 December 2024—country financial mechanisms have at their disposal funds equal to at least one per cent of covered deposits of all financial institutions that are licensed on the market and are potential subjects of the procedure. It is the minimal level, because member states may set target levels exceeding this threshold. Regardless, it is worth mentioning that including a minimal target level in the BRR Directive equal to one percent was not a common precrisis practice. Target levels of accumulated funds usually provoked debate among member states, because they directly burdened their respective banking sectors.

Table 5.6 presents the target levels that are required in the EU by 2024. The second and fifth columns express overall values of deposits gathered in EU banks as of the end of 2012, expressed in millions of euros. The third and sixth columns present resolution fund target levels assumed by the directive, equivalent to one per cent of covered deposits' value in the sector (data as of the end of 2012).

Due to the size of their banking sectors, Germany, France, and Great Britain will need to collect the biggest amounts. Assuming that the trend of covered deposit value increase will persist, due to the indexing of minimal accumulation of resolution fund to covered deposits' level, the target amount is expected to rise year after year. While calculations from 2009 expressed a value of 57 billion euros, studies carried out in 2012 witnessed a rise to 65 billion euros.

It was decided that in the early stage, contributions acquired from banks and investment companies will be spread out in time evenly, until the target level is achieved. The time period until the end of 2024 may be prolonged by four years at most, if—as part of financing mechanism activities—payouts exceeding a total of 0.5 per cent of all covered deposits were to be carried out. If the level of available financial means after 2024 decreased below the target level of one percent, regular contribution collection would be resumed until the target level was once again achieved. The BRR Directive also specifies that during the assessment of contributions, business cycle phases should be taken into account, as well as the negative effects that a procyclical form of activity may bring in regard to adjusting increased yearly contributions at a time of economic downturn. The European Commission evaluated that establishing a budget equal to one percent of covered deposits' value will be reflected on the annual GNP of the EU by 0.04 per cent (EC 2012, p. 69).

The resolution fund ought to be financed by private institutions (covered by the scope of the directive application), whereas the case of

Table 5.6 Data on the overall value of deposits of the EU banking sector as of the end of 2012 (expressed in millions of euros), and with the assumed target levels of resolution funds (one per cent of covered deposits)

Country	Overall deposit value	1% of covered deposits	Country	Overall deposit value	1% of covered deposits
Austria	324,900	1,734	Ireland	194,000	800
Belgium	529,000	2,291	Italy	1,511,600	4,905
Bulgaria	28,972	184	Latvia	17,765	60
Croatia	37,496	375*	Lithuania	13,400	67
Cyprus	104,392	519	Luxembourg	215,900	304
Czech Republic	123,620	653	Malta	28,004	70
Denmark	166,900	1,055	Netherlands	863,684	4,470
Estonia	10,825	53	Poland	278,563	1,032
Finland	136,538	778	Portugal	221,500	1,102
France	1,577,301	11,035	Romania	64,295	274
Germany	3,171,800	15,752	Slovakia	45,940	242
Great Britain	2,922,200	12,188	Slovenia	23,512	149
Greece	175,000	1,048	Spain	1,568,800	6,749
Hungary	60,048	303	Sweden	267,100	1,409

*Data on Croatia demonstrate value as of 2010. Data presented in the third column concern one per cent of overall deposits
Source: Cannas et al. (2014)

setting the contribution assessment basis was not yet resolved. According to the BRR Directive, EBA shall submit to the Commission a report with recommendations on the appropriate reference point for setting the target level for resolution financing arrangements—and, in particular, whether total liabilities constitute a more appropriate basis than covered deposits—until 31 October 2016. As a general rule, contributions shall be collected before any resolution works are commenced, whereas the fund shall be accumulated in an *ex ante* mode.

5.7.3 Use of Financial Resources

A key provision of new bank intervention solutions is that financing mechanisms instated by the BRR Directive may be used solely in regard to the scope necessary for the proper use of resolution instruments. The EU legislator intervenes deeply in the possibility of using aggregated funds for procedure execution, as well as what the funds may be used for —without exceptions to the catalogue. According to Article 101(1) of the BRR Directive, resources may be thus used only to:

- guarantee the assets or the liabilities of the institution under resolution (its subsidiaries, a bridge institution or an asset management vehicle),
- make loans to the institution under resolution (its subsidiaries, a bridge institution or an asset management vehicle),
- purchase assets of the institution under resolution,
- make contributions to a bridge institution and an asset management vehicle,
- pay compensation to shareholders or creditors in accordance with the NCWO rule,
- make a contribution to the institution under resolution in lieu of the write-down or conversion of liabilities of certain creditors, when the bail-in tool is applied (when the resolution authority decided to exclude certain creditors from the scope of bail-in),
- to lend to other financing arrangements (on a voluntary basis).

Using financial resources for the sake of settling losses of financial institutions or their direct recapitalization was also banned. Still, it is troublesome to understand the ban on direct assistance granted toward an institution on the point of bankruptcy. It seems that the union legislator aimed at implementing a ban on covering financial institutions' losses through their recapitalization. As for direct loss coverage, the method will be, for instance, the payment of share capital of the bridge institution, of which potential losses (already after the assets had been moved to the bridge institution) will be allowed to be paid for. Questions on covering loss of a company by a fundamentally sound bank in case the acquisition tool is used also remain unanswered. In order to encourage transactions, the resolution organ does, in fact, cover losses of the entity under resolution, in order to sell it subsequently to another financial institution. Nevertheless, it seems that such assistance is possible thanks to the legal construction, which oversees that the beneficiary of the aid (for example, granted guarantee of loss coverage of acquired assets) is a sound acquiring entity, and not the insolvent bank.

5.8 Institutional Architecture of the Financial Safety Net

Before the analysis of the postcrisis landscape seen through the prism of the institutional safety net is presented, it is worth noting that, as time passed, not only did deposit guarantee schemes evolve throughout the years (as described in Section 3.2), but also the entire financial safety net. In the mid-1960s, the entry model of the net, initially consisting of the central bank as a lender of the last resort, entity supervisor on the financial market, as well as financial regulations (including prudential), created by the government or the minister of finance, was enhanced with the formulation of the deposit insurance agency (Pawłowicz and Wierzba 2007, p. 15). It may thus be acknowledged that the deposit insurer was created as the fourth independent institutional element, besides supervisors, central banks, and the government (Szczepańska et al. 2015, p. 29). The evolution of the financial safety net is presented in Fig. 5.2.

In the transition model, which functioned until the end of 2007, two additional nodal points of the financial safety net were developed and

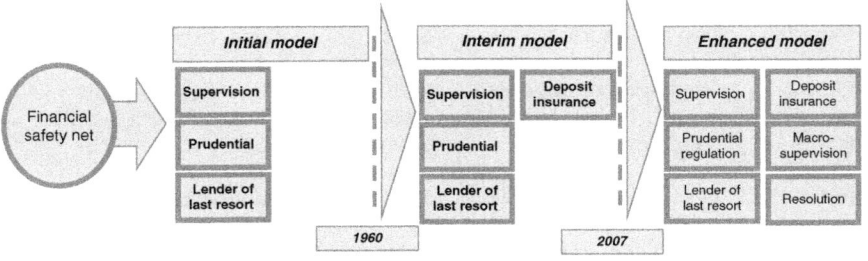

Fig. 5.2 Evolution of the financial safety net
Source: Pruski J. (2014b)

introduced in the EU. The two new elements are macro-prudential oversight and resolution. Until the year 2007, as a rule, one of the functions of the financial safety net was performed by a separate institution, instated for the sole purpose of dealing with specific tasks. For example, the deposit guarantee scheme was operated by the guarantee fund, macro-prudential oversight by the supervisor, and the lender of last resort by the central bank (although, the latter often also performed a supervisory role). After the global financial crisis, attempts were made at developing the net institutionally. As far as macro-prudential oversight was preferably assigned to central banks, the allocation of resolution proceedings in the financial safety net was a more complicated matter.

Introducing new instruments and legal frameworks regarding the elimination of financial institutions from the market deserves, first and foremost, a proper institutional preparation. This, in turn, made necessary the designation of an entity responsible for resolution procedures in the financial safety net. Detailed information on institutional solutions in chosen countries of the world is presented in Table 5.7.

Table 5.7 Entities responsible for resolution procedures in chosen countries of the world

Country	Entity responsible for resolution procedures	Country	Entity responsible for resolution procedures
Argentina	Central bank, supervisor	Japan	Deposit insurer
Australia	Supervisor	Mexico	Deposit insurer
Brazil	Central bank, supervisor	Russia	Central bank, supervisor, deposit insurer
Canada	Deposit insurer	South Africa	Supervisor
China	Central bank, supervisor	South Korea	Supervisor, deposit insurer
Hong Kong	Supervisor	Switzerland	Supervisor
India	Central bank, supervisor	Turkey	Supervisor, deposit insurer
Indonesia	Orderly liquidation organ	United States	Deposit insurer

Source: Iwanicz-Drozdowska et al. (2016)

Choosing the entity responsible for resolution procedures in a global perspective is a diversified subject matter. Outside Europe, the role is often entrusted to the deposit guarantee scheme or remains a shared task of the central bank and supervisor.

The BRR Directive requires that member states designate public authority organs, which will be authorized to perform functions and tasks related to the resolution of financial institutions (Article 3). Due to complicated legal authority incarnations, as well as the protection of many participants of the process, the harmonized, EU-wide decision as to who shall exercise the function has not yet been made. On the one hand, harmonization of the aspect above would facilitate work coordination, and overall improve the resolution procedure, especially in its cross-border form (for instance, due to the functioning of working classes and the exchange of information). Nevertheless, the degree of required intervention in the legal protection order of creditors in particular countries could, in such circumstances, be too bold, thus blocking the possibility of rapid transposing into national legal solutions. For this reason, the case was resolved in a non-invasive mode, with the assumption that an appropriate coordination scope may also be achieved through a requirement with a lower level of intervention. In accordance with the BRR Directive, "resolution and orderly liquidation authorities may be national central banks, competent ministries or other public administrative authorities". Despite the listed entity catalogue not being of enumerative nature, regulators underline that organs of country rulership shall be designated (namely, such that have been granted public administration rights). In other thematic publications, recommendations addressed to rulers present a similar catalogue of entities capable of carrying out resolution procedures (FSB 2012; Pollner 2012).

Further detailed resolution regulations additionally indicate several objections. First and foremost, member states may designate supervisory authorities as resolution organs only as an exception to the general separation rule of supervisory and resolution roles. This is due to risk of forbearance, which is highest in the case of supervisors (ESRB 2012). For the sake of such a possibility, additional conditions, based on the fact that appropriate measures must be taken in case one entity performs both supervisory and resolution roles, have been foreseen. Their aim is to guarantee the operative autonomy of both functions, which shall be performed in a way that prevents conflict of interest. The BRR Directive also introduces the clear requirement of participating in resolution on behalf of the government or minister of finances, if granting public aid were necessary.

As a result of limiting allocation functions of resolution, the catalogue of entities capable of receiving such authority, includes, as follows:

- the central bank,
- financial market entity supervisor,
- autonomous resolution organ,
- minister of finance,
- deposit insurance agency.

Member states, through indicating the entity responsible for resolution execution, ought to take into account the regulatory environment and functioning conditions of the country financial market. For this reason, the potential decision shall be preceded by an analysis of possible solutions in regard to the institutional setup in resolution and crisis management. Among key issues supporting the proper choice of authority are:

- experience of the authority (for example, in assistance activity or performing the role of forced administrator),
- financial resources of the organ (for example, acquiring contributions from banks through the respective deposit guarantee scheme),
- competences to perform specific authoritative functions (for example, license to carry out inspections),
- autonomy and a well-established structural position in jurisdiction.

The delegated resolution organ shall be equipped in indispensable authority (tools) foreseen by the BRR Directive and be responsible for maintaining the proper sequence of course of events, as well as aggregating financial resources for resolution. The directive also brings to attention that resolution organs ought to possess a wide influence authority scope of public administrative character. These include, among others, a one-sided transfer of shares or assets of an institution on the brink of bankruptcy from one entity to another, the right to deprive third parties (for instance owners) of certain rights, as well as the right to one-sidedly terminate a contract or remit chosen liabilities of an endangered institution. Therefore, resolution organ characteristics such as independence and strong structural position are crucial and allow the application of broad authoritative powers.

At the current stage of BRR Directive development works (as of 30 September 2015), all EU member states had already decided on locating their resolution rights in country financial safety nets (even despite the lack implementation of the BRR Directive). A detailed overview of the topic is presented in Table 5.8.

The analysis of data presented in Table 5.8 shows that the central bank was chosen as the resolution organ in 12 countries and is thus dominant in the EU. Six states have chosen to divide resolution organ functions among various financial safety net participants, including the deposit guarantee scheme (Croatia, Finland, and Sweden). A less popular choice is the supervisor, nominated as the resolution authority in five countries. Four have chosen a separate public entity for the role. The deposit guarantee scheme will be responsible for resolution in Poland only (although it will, in fact, hold strong executive functions in Croatia, Finland, and Sweden).

Although it is difficult to generalize the reasons behind the choice of various financial safety net institutions in EU member states, it seems that the popular selection of central banks is caused by the high operational capabilities of the institutions and the wish to grant them additional operative rights, as a form of bridging the gap resultant from the precrisis supervisory authority migration to separate entities. It seems the precrisis depletion of central bank influence on the financial market was, in light of the global financial crisis, evaluated negatively, hence the compensation in the form of resolution authority (Masciandaro and Quintyn, 2009; Archer 2009).

Table 5.8 Country resolution organs in EU member states

Country	Designated resolution organ	Country	Designated resolution organ
Austria	Supervisor	**Ireland**	Central bank
Belgium	Central bank	**Italy**	Central bank
Bulgaria	• Central bank (for credit institutions) • Supervisor (for investment companies)	**Latvia**	Supervisor
Croatia	• Central bank (for credit institutions)—until resolution is initiated • Supervisor (for investment companies)—until resolution is initiated • Deposit guarantee scheme—applicable to all entities once resolution is initiated	**Lithuania**	Central bank
Cyprus	Central bank	**Luxembourg**	Central bank
Czech Republic	Central bank	**Malta**	Supervisor
Denmark	• Supervisor—until resolution requirements are fulfilled • Separate organ—applicable once resolution is initiated	**Netherlands**	Central bank
Estonia	Supervisor	**Poland**	Deposit guarantee scheme
Finland	Separate organ (with deposit guarantee scheme functions)	**Portugal**	Central bank
France	Supervisor	**Romania**	• Central bank—for credit institutions • Supervisor—for investment companies
Germany	Separate organ	**Slovakia**	Separate organ
Great Britain	Central bank	**Slovenia**	Central bank

Table 5.8 (continued)

Country	Designated resolution organ	Country	Designated resolution organ
Greece	• Central bank (for credit institutions) • Supervisor (for investment companies)	**Spain**	• Central bank—applicable once resolution is initiated • Separate organ—applicable throughout resolution
Hungary	Central bank	**Sweden**	Separate organ—Ministry of Finance agenda (with deposit guarantee scheme functions)

For those countries, where the BRR Directive has not been yet implemented, the assumed institution was named
Source: EBA (2015f), ISDA (2015), and websites of country institutions of financial safety nets

5.9 Criticism of the Resolution Concept

Practical experiences of postcrisis operations of the financial safety net are missing—not only in the EU, but also globally. Therefore, it is not known whether the proposed new shape will be lead to the strengthening of the financial stability. Thus, apart from the study of concepts and resolution theory presented earlier in the book, it is also necessary that arguments against the new concept of insolvency procedures (as improperly designed and prone to failure in changing market conditions) be analyzed.

Obstacles of political nature are an important factor, which may negatively influence the possibility of efficient resolution. Critics of BRR Directive solutions (Hellwig 2014b; Mazhenova 2014) rightly point out that national interest and protection of certain stakeholders (owners, bondholders) will always override restructuring carried out in accordance with the earlier agreed resolution plan. Therefore, it may be expected that rulers will not decide on the use of radical measures, such as the partial conversion of liabilities of an endangered bank to capital, or the write-down of capital. An example of such actions is the lack of binding law implementation, as well as not respecting such basic principles as the protection of covered deposits worth less than €100,000 (Cyprus), or the denial of paying out covered deposits to foreign clients (Iceland). The example of the SNS Reaal bank in the Netherlands, where bail-in law was not fully applied, may also be mentioned. Although supervisors remitted capital, thus expropriating owners (Government of the Netherlands 2013), they did not decide on limiting the costs of rescuing the bank through burdening uninsured owners, despite having the necessary authority (Bijlsma 2013). The action was later justified by the anticipation of an excessive influence on the Dutch banking sector, big systemic repercussions, and the increase of financing costs of the already weakened bank debt market. Similarly, participants of the financial safety net in Kazakhstan showed similar indifference in regard to consequences of applying resolution provisions. Attempts of saving local banks caused drainage of public resources and created ongoing expenses on behalf of deposit guarantee scheme funds, instead of the owners of BTA Bank and Alliance Bank (Mazhenova 2014). In light of the above, a standard use of public funds for partial support of resolution was an appropriate alternative (Szczepańska et al. 2015, pp. 41–42). Nevertheless, it is difficult to eliminate political risk, although—through the application of resolution tools—partial moral hazard may be very high. It is difficult to scientifically contest arguments of political nature, as well as those concerning informal protection of group interest. Therefore, for the sake of future analyses, it ought to be assumed that new union regulations will cause ruling parties to act consequently, and in compliance with the letter of the law.

It must be noted that the most important accusation of critics of BRR Directive resolution concepts (Hellwig 2014a) is that directive provisions will cause its unenforceability. This is attributed to three elementary reasons.

The first argument is the possibility of simultaneous intervention in several entities of the same group, which showcases the same difficulties (MPE approach). Hence, in theory, various resolution organs in different countries and under multiple jurisdictions will be capable of intervening in the case of entities belonging to the same group. The actions of the British supervisor in London toward the Lehman Brothers bank may be used as support of the claim. Analysis revealed that in case of the banking group above, liquid financial resources were transferred to the United States, whereas those remaining in London were insufficient for even a single day of basic, critical operations of the bank in Great Britain. According to critics, the problem will continue to grow, as financial group integration deepens. Even if resolution takes place within a given group, and actions are restricted to its biggest entity only (SPE approach), it will be difficult to reach compromise in regard to the division of costs for procedures carried out in multiple countries (Hellwig 2014a pp. 30–34).

As far as EU proceedings are concerned, the problem has been largely solved. One the one hand, all actions toward prominent financial groups functioning within the banking union will be handled by the SRB, whose scope covers mainly G-SIFIs entities. Therefore, the above resolution organ will not only solve the problem of carrying out cohesive intervention, but also select the desired action scenario. On the other hand, in the case of cross-border entities, group resolution organs were introduced, which are constituted by country organs, and jointly decide and plan actions. In case a clear decision cannot be made within a group organ, the EBA will be the resolving party.

Secondly, the BRR Directive brings too little attention to preserving the sources of financing of a troubled financial institution. If resolution procedures are initiated toward a bank, maintaining its financing on the market will be practically impossible. What is more, big participants of the market will withdraw their contributions from other institutions of similar profile in fear of consequences. The sole exemption of short-term financing from bail-in resources may prove insufficient, thus causing further events of bank panic—at least among prominent investors and depositor environments (Hellwig 2014a, pp. 30–34). The above statement is partially valid, nevertheless the same accusations toward financing problems and bank panic may be attributed to non-resolution circumstances. Still, new solutions undoubtedly lack instruments allowing for the prevention of bank panic among institutional investors. It seems that communicating to the market in advance what the terms of intervention toward a given financial institution will be is better from the point of market rules' preservation than *ad hoc* actions, which convey many uncertainties regarding the final result. As for cutoff from financing, the problem is to be partially resolved by the possibility of using resolution fund resources, for example, for the maintaining of critical functions.

Thirdly, the scale of financial losses and needs in common bail-in instrument use may prove to be much bigger than it is currently assumed. Costs of carrying out resolution may be higher than those accredited to granting capital support from the public budget; similarly, costs of operation and maintaining the sector will also be high. If funding of financial institutions will come from deposit resources, bail-in will cause the shift of the burden on the deposit guarantee scheme. Critics point out (Hellwig 2014a, pp. 30–34) that since 2008, a lobby in favor of not transferring the burden of losses by bank owners has been functioning. At the same time, resolution tools grant the possibility of burdening the state with restructuring costs, thus limiting bail-in use. Once again, it is an argument of political nature, either questioning the application of current law, or showcasing the risk of selective use, which may lead to the mere realization of chosen goals overseen by the BRR Directive. It seems that prior to the introduction of the reform and resolution provision, the risk was also existent. The creation of a politically autonomous resolution authority, which would not be prone to political impact, would be the answer to the above endangerment. Such a structure would function as a form of maintaining the autonomy of central bank organs. Nevertheless, conditionalities of the BRR Directive left the case open and at the authority of member states.

A more thorough financial analysis leads to the conclusion that rise in financing costs on behalf of banks shall be expected as a result of higher regulatory requirements, and new risk of converting liabilities to capital, which, in turn, will have to be compensated to the bank's funding party (Goodhart and Avgouleas 2014, p. 36). What is more, functioning of MREL will cause banks to enter agreements with creditors in such a way that part of its liabilities will be excluded from bail-in procedures and solely maintain minimal levels specified by regulations. Therefore, in order to meet MREL requirements, EU banks will find themselves under pressure of acquiring new covered liabilities, eligible for bail-in. This means the necessity of issuing debt securities that are part of Tier II capital, as well as other unsecured debentures. It shall be expected that liabilities of the above type will be costly, because uninsured owners will demand higher return rates (compensation of the loss of *implicite* governmental insurance). The above rules will have a negative influence, especially on banks with high capital ratio, which are financed by retail customer deposits. Thus, the introduction of MREL penalizes traditional banking based on financing credit shares with client deposits. The opinion of critics (Groendahl and Jennen 2015) that MREL functioning creates risk of conflict between prudential and resolution politics is justifiable. MREL will encourage traditional (deposit) banks to the issuing of debt, thus artificially and needlessly increasing their leverage. The problem will be especially severe in smaller countries outside the Eurozone with local, hermetic capital markets, with little place for issuance. This is especially true in the case of banks in Central and Eastern Europe (Borsuk 2015). Still, it seems that an individually setup MREL (at a level adjusted to a specific financial institution, with the assumption of a rational operative capability of the resolution organ) will cause the appeasement of potential conflict of prudential politics and resolution procedures by the low requirements for banks functioning in a traditional model.

The claim that the use of radical tools such as bail-in creates the risk of contagion effect in related institutions is a different category of arguments contesting the validity of the BRR Directive. What is more, some resolution tools will work in a procyclical mode, thus boosting negative effects in the postcrisis banking sector (this applies especially to bail-in, as well the low valuations of assets while bridge institution and rights' isolation take place) (Goodhart and Avgouleas 2014, p. 36). Nevertheless, it must be noted that several resolution tools will work in a countercyclical mode—for example, financing the resolution fund through the collection of *ex ante* contributions, notably intensified in times of prosperity (Marcinkowska 2010b, pp. 492–503; Smaga 2015). Furthermore, chosen resolution tools, such as bridge institution and asset separation, will allow for the application of temporary solutions, thus making possible the overcoming of systemic crises, and preparing ground for the sale of the insolvent bank once the market situation is salvaged.

Another group of arguments is related to the legal risk of resolution tool application. The BRR Directive introduces a specific procedure, which grants broad powers to resolution organs. These include, among others, the authorization to issue legally binding mandates—even prior to the fulfillment of resolution requirements—which concern basic bank activities. Such an action may also be based on the sole conviction of the institution on the presence of circumstances, which may hinder or make impossible future effective resolution procedures. What is more, failure to abide by the recommendations is subject to penalty. Another effect is the potential conflict of interest between the supervisor and resolution organ, if their roles are performed by separate institutions. Thus, it may also mean that two, often contradictory, supervisory actions are being performed simultaneously—for instance, in the form of prudential regulations and attempts at preserving MREL (RCL 2015, pp. 1–2). Furthermore, as inclined previously, the resolution procedure is itself authoritative and does not welcome any second-party contribution (hence, also on behalf of the problematic bank), at any stage. As an effect, the bank cannot protect its own interests and becomes a passive observer of resolution proceedings. Such a formulation of rights of sides participating in resolution breaches fundamental provisions of the rule of law (RCL 2015, pp. 1–2). The effect is additionally strengthened by the practical exclusion of the judicial channel from resolution. Judicial control is limited, because decisions made during the proceedings—even those enacted unlawfully—remain in power and legal circulation. In such a situation, the entity under resolution is left with the option of judicially proving illegality of resolution organ actions, thus paving the way to compensation procedures. Although resolution organ actions are of definitive character, and often decide directly on the existence or liquidation of a troubled bank, they are also exempt from judicial and administrative control, for instance, on behalf of the minister of finance (RCL 2015, pp. 1–2). What is more, the (multiple) goals of the procedure have been shaped vaguely, as was the hierarchy of their validity. It is not known, *per se*, whether resolution aims primarily at restructuring the entity and achieving long-term financial stability (liquidating it as a last resort), or the elimination from the market and liquidation is the goal itself.

Table 5.9 Chosen legal disputes on resolution

Country	Entity	Year	Dispute description
Great Britain	Bradford & Bingley	2008–2012	Shareholders of the bank challenged the decision of the Bank of England on their total expropriation. Their claims have been dropped after substantive study of the case, because, in a standard insolvency procedure, their situation would not have been more favorable (lack of NCWO rule infringement).
Netherlands	SNS Reaal	2013–2015	Shareholders, expropriated from the SNS Reaal bank by the Dutch government, filed a claim for the acknowledgement of the unlawfulness of the decision. The court confirmed the legality of governmental actions and the righteousness of action, nevertheless, a separate legal case—concerning, among others, granting and determining the compensation amount—is still ongoing and a topic of separate dispute.
Slovenia	Nova KBM	2012–2015	Shareholders of the bank were expropriated, and shares listed on Slovenian and Polish stocks were annulated. Shareholders filed a suit to the Slovenian Constitutional Court, demanding the regulations, on the basis of which the Bank of Slovenia was authorized to make the expropriation decision, be annulated. At the same time, a different, compensation proceeding is being held from the initiative of shareholders, who are trying to prove that their loss would have been lower, if restructuring actions were not commenced (infringement of the NCWO rule).

Source: Iwanicz-Drozdowska et al. (2016), ECHR (2015), Bankier (2015), and author's own research

Only several accusations drawn against the new resolution procedure have been described. Nevertheless, it must be noted that the few experiences of instrument application triggered the filing of claims for damages against owners and creditors of liquidated banks. An example of such a situation is Great Britain, the Netherlands, and Slovenia, whose cases are presented in Table 5.9.

Despite words of criticism of BRR Directive provisions, the prevailing number of advantages of its proposals must be underlined, as presented in Section 5.5 analyzing resolution instruments. These include limiting the risk of moral hazard on behalf of financial institutions, triggering the need of stricter control of ownership and creditor control of bank activities, securing public resources from their use for the sake of financing resolution of financial institutions, as well as placing emphasis on a more responsible bank management model (*ex ante*) and actions of the financial safety net at an early stage, as soon as troubles at a bank are detected.

A clear analysis of advantages and flaws of the new solutions is impossible at the current stage. It is not until practical experiences with empirical data are provided that the voices of critics and supporters of new resolutions will be properly evaluated. Nevertheless, it seems that both sides agree that the proposed solutions—hence, the attempt of institutional strengthening of the financial safety net and putting emphasis on complex crisis management—are heading in the right direction. As for the ways of achieving the goal itself, namely, the protection of public resources and the efficient, timely elimination of banks on the brink of bankruptcy from the market, they are very extensive. The choice of the right path and suitable course of action are crucial for the effectiveness of resolution proceedings.

5.10 Conclusion

This chapter describes the concept of resolution procedure introduction as a form of response to the global financial crisis. It also identifies and systematizes the possible functioning forms it may take, including the use of deposit guarantee scheme funds along with an indication of weaknesses and potential hazards of the procedure. The role of deposit insurance agencies in the institutional shaping of the financial safety net has been noticed by regulators, who acknowledged them as full-fledged members of the safety net. Provisions of new legislative solutions implementing resolution tools indicate that the application of public funds in the time of global financial crisis should not have happened and ought not to happen to such an extent in the future. This is caused by the fact that new regulations significantly limit the possibilities of such interventions toward financial institutions. Nevertheless, a detailed analysis of BRR Directive provisions reveals that certain regulations were worked out on a union level to a minimal degree only. These include, among others, the creation of the financing mechanism of the new procedure. It may be anticipated that the determination of a target level of one per cent of covered funds will be insufficient for successful resolution interventions. Still, gradual mutualization of country funds, supervised by the SRB, addresses the problem. In light of introduction of the new resolution procedure, a greater role of the deposit insurance agency in the entire process ought to be noticed, because goals of both participants of the financial safety net (the deposit guarantee scheme and resolution organ) are convergent and proceed in the same direction—bank functioning and customer service continuity, targeted mostly at depositors. The latter function also relates to the role of depositor preference, aimed at depositor protection. Still, its effects as of today remain uncertain. The analysis of BRR Directive provisions leads to the conclusion that new roles, which may be successfully performed by the deposit insurer, have been singled out in the financial safety net. Thus, a new functioning model and subsequent evolution stadium may also be anticipated.

References

Archer, D. (2009). *Roles and Objectives of Modern Central Banks, Issues in the Governance of Central Banks*, BIS, Basel, May.

Bankier. (2015). *Są szanse na odszkodowania za akcje banku Nova KBM*, www.bankier.pl, 21 January 2015 (access 15.09.2015).

Bijlsma, M. (2013). *Six Lessons for Europe from the Nationalization of SNS Reaal*, www.bruegel.org, (access 19.01.2016).

BoE. (2012) *Financial Stability Report*, June.

Borsuk, M. (2015). *Banki będą bardziej bezpieczne, ale i agresywne*, www. obserwatorfinansowy.pl, sierpień 2015 (access 19.01.2016).

Cannas, G.; Cariboni, J.; Veisari, L.K.; Pagano, A. (2014). *Updated Estimates of EU Eligible and Covered Deposits*, JRC Technical Reports, Report EUR 26469 EN.

Davies, G.; Dobler, M. (2013). *Bank Resolution and Safeguarding the Creditors Left Behind*, Research and Analysis, Bank of England.

Dübel, H.J. (2013). *The Capital Structure of Banks and Practice of Bank Restructuring. Eight Case Studies on Current Bank Restructurings in Europe*, CFS Working Paper, Berlin, 8 October.

EBA. (2014a). *Final Draft Regulatory Technical Standards on the Content of Resolution Plans and the Assessment of Resolvability*, 19 December, EBA/RTS/ 2014/15.

EBA. (2014b). *Regulatory Technical Standards on Contractual Recognition of Bail in*, EBA/CP/2014/33.

EBA. (2014c). *Regulatory Technical Standards on Minimum Requirement for Own Funds and Eligible Liabilities (MREL)*, EBA/CP/2014/41.

EBA. (2015a). *Draft Implementing Technical Standards on Procedures, Forms and Templates for the Provision of Information for Resolution Plans under Article 11 (3) of Directive 2014/59/EU of the European Parliament and the Council*, EBA/ITS/2015/06, 7 July.

EBA. (2015b). *Final Draft Regulatory Technical Standards on Resolution Colleges under Article 88 (7) of Directive 2014/59/EU*, EBA/RTS/2015/ 03, 3 July.

EBA. (2015c). *Guidelines on the Minimum List of Qualitative and Quantitative Recovery Plan Indicators*, Final report, EBA-GL-2015–02, 6 May.

EBA. (2015d). *Implementing Technical Standards on the Disclosure of Group Financial Support Agreements*, EBA-ITS-2015-07.

EBA. (2015f). *Status Quo, BRRD Transposition*, London, 30 September.

EC. (2012). *Commission Staff Working Document, Impact Assessment. Accompanying Document to the Proposal for a Directive . . . / . . . /EU of the European Parliament and of the Council on Deposit Guarantee Schemes [Recast] and to the Report from the Commission to the European Parliament and to the Council Review of Directive 94/19/EC on Deposit Guarantee Schemes* {COM(2010) 368} {COM(2010) 369} {SEC(2010) 835}.

EC. (2015e). State aid SA.40441 (2015/N) – Hungary Restructuring of Magyar Kereskedelmi Bank Zrt, Brussels, 16.12., C(2015) 9349 final.

ECHR. (2015). *Judicial Procedures Designed for Expropriation of Shares and Bonds Were Not Unfair*, Press Release, 9 April.

ESRB. (2012). *Forbearance, Resolution and Deposit Insurance*, Reports of the Advisory Scientific Committee, no. 1, July.

FDIC. (1997). *Managing the Crisis: The FDIC and RTC Experience*, Washington.

FDIC; BoE. (2012). *Resolving Globally Active, Systemically Important, Financial Institutions. A Joint Paper by the Federal Deposit Insurance Corporation and the Bank of England*, Washington – London, 10 December.

FSB. (2011). *Key Attributes of Effective Resolution Regimes for Financial Institutions*, Basel, October.

FSB. (2012). *Thematic Review on Deposit Insurance Systems. Peer Review Report*, Basel.

FSB. (2013). *Assessment Methodology for Key Attributes of Effective Resolution Regimes for Financial Institutions*, Basel, 28 August.

FSB. (2013a). *Recovery and Resolution Planning for Systemically Important Financial Institutions: Guidance on Developing Effective Resolution Strategies*, July.

FSB. (2013b). *Recovery and Resolution Planning for Systemically Important Financial Institutions: Guidance on Identification of Critical Functions and Critical Shared Services*, 16 July.

FSB. (2013c). *Thematic Review on Resolution Regimes. Peer Review Report*, April.

FSB. (2014), *Towards Full Implementation of the FSB Key Attributes of Effective Resolution Regimes for Financial Institutions*. Report to the G20 on Progress in Reform of Resolution Regimes and Resolution Planning for Global Systemically Important Financial Institutions *(G-SIFIs)*, 12 November.

Goodhart, C.; Avgouleas, E. (2014). *A Critical Evaluation of Bail-ins as Bank Recapitalisation Mechanisms*, Centre for Economic Policy Research, Discussion Paper 10065, July.

Government of the Netherlands. (2013). *Decree by the Minister of Finance Regarding the Expropriation of Securities and Capital Components of SNS REAAL NV and SNS Bank NV*, 1 February.

Gracie, A. (2015). *TLAC and MREL: From Design to Implementation*, Bank of England, 23 July.

Groendahl, B.; Jennen, B. (2015). *ECB Touts German Bond Bill as Blueprint for FSB's TLAC*, Bloomberg Business, www.bloomberg.com, 2.06.2015 (access 21.10.2015).

Hamilton, J. (2015). *HSBC, BNP and RBS Faulted on Living Wills by U.S. Regulators*, Bloomberg Business, www.bloomberg.com, 23.03.2015 (access 23.10.2015).

Hardy, D.C. (2013). *Bank Resolution Costs, Depositor Preference, and Asset Encumbrance*, WP/13/172, IMF, July.

Hellwig, M. (2014a). *Financial Stability, Monetary Policy, Banking Supervision, and Central Banking*, Preprints of the Max Planck Institute for Research on Collective Goods, Bonn 2014/9.

Hellwig, M. (2014b). *Yes, Virginia, There Is a Banking Union! But it May Not Make Your Wishes Come True*, Max Planck Institute, 42nd Economics Conference of the Austrian National Bank, May.

Illmer, A. (2013). *Russia's Rich Dominate Cyprus' Largest Bank*, Deutsche Welle, www.dw.com, 18.10.2013 (access 23.10.2015).

IMF. (2012). *From Bail-out to Bail-in: Mandatory Debt Restructuring of Systemic Financial Institutions*, 24 April.

ISDA. (2015). *BRRD Implementation Monitor*, 17 June.

Iwanicz-Drozdowska, M. (ed.); Kerlin, J.; Kozłowska, A.; Malinowska-Misiąg, E.; Nowak, A.; Smaga, P.; Wisniewski, P.; Witkowski, B. (2016). *European Bank Restructuring During the Global Financial Crisis*, Palgrave Macmillan.

Junevièius, A.; Puidokas, M. (2014). *The Single Resolution Mechanism of the European Banking Union: Its Structure and Functioning*, International Business and Global Economy, University of Gdansk, no. 33.

Kerlin, J.; Maksymiuk, A. (2015). *Comparative Analysis of the Bail-in Tool*, "Copernican Journal of Finance & Accounting", vol. 4, no. 1.

Marcinkowska, M. (2009). *Regulacje w dobie kryzysu: nadzór, normy ostrożnościowe i rachunkowość*, "Zeszyty Naukowe Uniwersytetu Szczecińskiego. Finanse. Rynki finansowe. Ubezpieczenia", nr 17.

Marcinkowska, M. (2010b). *Procykliczność i antycykliczność regulacji bankowych*, "Zeszyty Naukowe Uniwersytetu Ekonomicznego w Poznaniu", nr 140.

Marcinkowska, M. (2011). *Dodatkowe podatki i opłaty od banków - potrzeby praktyki i dylematy teorii finansów*, "Prace Naukowe Uniwersytetu Ekonomicznego we Wrocławiu", nr 170.

Masciandaro, D.; Quintyn, M. (2009). *Reforming Financial Supervision and the Role of Central Banks: a Review of Global Trends, Causes and Effects (1998–2008)*, Policy Insight, no. 30, CEPR, February.

Mazhenova, B. (2014). *The Basic Challenges for DIS in Bail in Application. Kazakhstani Bail In Experience*, Kazakhstan Deposit Insurance Fund, 25–26 June, Warsaw.

Meguro, K. (2014). *Implications of Depositor Preference for Deposit Insurers*, Informal Staff note from the DICJ, DICJ, 20 March.

Pawłowicz, L.; Wierzba, R. (2007). *Sieć bezpieczeństwa a integracja rynków finansowych w Unii Europejskiej, Integracja Rynków Finansowych w UE od A do Z*, "Bank i Kredyt", nr 8–9, NBP, Warszawa, sierpień–wrzesień.

Pisani-Ferry, J.; Sapir, A. (2010). *Banking Crisis Management in the EU: an Early Assessment*, [w:] *Economic Policy*, G. de Menil, R. Portes, H.W. Sinn (ed.), CEPR, Blackwell Publishing, no. 62, April.

Pollner, J. (2012). *Issues and Assumption Paper for the Design of an Upgraded Bank Resolution Framework*, World Bank, June.

Pruski, J. (2014a). *Evolving Role of Deposit Insurer in Cross Border Resolution*, Kuala Lumpur, May.

Pruski, J. (2014b). *Ewolucja światowego systemu ochrony depozytów oraz systemu recovery i resolution*, BFG, Warszawa.

RCL. (2015). *Zestawienie uwag do projektu z dnia 23 października 2015 r. ustawy z dnia ... 2015 r. o Bankowym Funduszu Gwarancyjnym, systemie gwarantowania depozytów oraz przymusowej restrukturyzacji*, Ministerstwo Finansów, Komisja Prawnicza, Warszawa.

Smaga, P. (2015) *Procykliczność – przyczyny i sposoby zapobiegania*, [w:] *O nowy ład finansowy w Polsce. Rekomendacje dla animatorów życia gospodarczego*, red. J. Ostaszewski, Oficyna Wydawnicza SGH, Warszawa.

Szczepańska, O.; Dobrzańska, A.; Zdanowicz, B. (2015). *Resolution, czyli nowe podejście do banków zagrożonych upadłością*, NBP, Departament Stabilności Finansowej, Warszawa.

Wiggins, R.Z.; Tente, N.; Metrick, A. (2015). *European Banking Union: Cross-Border Resolution-Fortis Group*, NBER, Yale Program on Financial Stability, 12 March.

6

The Impact of Deposit Guarantee Schemes on the Effectiveness of Resolution

6.1 Introduction

This chapter presents studies focused on the effectiveness of resolution procedures. Several favorable and unfavorable scenarios are analyzed with multiple variants of financial institution restructuring. This, in turn, directly corresponds to the guarantee of access to deposits by bank customers. Effectiveness of resolution is hereby tested, both with the assumed participation and absence of the deposit insurer in the procedure. It also serves as a quantitative measure of public administration efforts' effectiveness toward banks, resulting from the inclusion of the deposit insurer in the process. The analysis was carried out in order to define the extent to which deposit guarantee scheme participation in resolution increases the effectiveness of intervention toward banks, as well as the preparations required on behalf of deposit insurers.

© The Author(s) 2017   **203**
J. Kerlin, *The Role of Deposit Guarantee Schemes as a Financial Safety Net in the European Union*, Palgrave Macmillan Studies in Banking and Financial Institutions, DOI 10.1007/978-3-319-54163-1_6

6.2   Background and Purpose of the Study

Studies on EU resolution procedures focused mainly on the justification of the need of carrying out crucial reforms in the financial safety net (EC 2012; BoE 2014). It is a natural direction of studies, inextricably linked to the legislative process, where the need for change and implementation of new, more effective provisions is justified. EU bodies have mainly analyzed the topic of how implementing resolution would influence the financial safety net and participants of the financial market on a macroeconomic scale. Various options of implementing new solutions and their influence on the financial market were among the most studied issues.

Other analyses (Fonteyne et al. 2010; Schich and Kim 2010; Bolzico et al. 2007) indicated that, next to providing administrative tools for governmental impact on financial market entities, resources, which finance their activity, are key. Thus, while legal circumstances were to provide legitimization of public authority, financial means were designed to ensure the applicability of actions. In the pre-crisis period, EU member states virtually did not create separate resolution funds, accumulated through the collection of *ex ante* contributions from market participants. Therefore, even if public authorities possessed a sufficient intervention toolkit, financial resources that would enable administrative instrument support during resolution of financial institutions were missing.

Financial intervention capabilities during the pre-crisis period were of binary nature. Resources for the sake of resolution of big financial entities could either come directly from the country budget (public resources) or a financial safety net institution (central bank or deposit guarantee scheme's aggregated funds). In the financial safety net, liquidity support granted by the central bank acting as the creditor of last resort or the recapitalization on behalf of the deposit insurer, who—depending on its mandate—could either pay out lost deposits or support resolution tasks otherwise, thus preceding bank insolvency, could have both been expected. For example, the liquidity support in Great Britain took place throughout attempts at restructuring the Northern Rock bank, whereas in Spain and Denmark it was outlined that the deposit insurance agency would support the restructuring of the whole banking sector.

As shown in Section 4.3, even despite the introduction of deposit guarantee scheme reform in the EU (enacted by the DGS Directive), approximately 500 EU entities remain outside the scope of potential deposit guarantee scheme intervention in the case of insolvency and covered deposits' payout obligation. The situation is more favorable than before the DGS Directive was introduced, because more entities were outside deposit insurance agency's scope prior to reform. It means that in some EU countries (for example, France or Italy), funds aggregated by deposit guarantee schemes will be insufficient for the execution of payouts toward even medium-sized entities. Hence, utilization of public funds for resolution of a financial institution or for the sake of deposit payouts from the insolvent bank would once again be required.

The introduction of the BRR Directive and the involvement of the deposit guarantee scheme in resolution procedures was supposed to salvage the above-described problem of public fund use, as well support the too big to fail institutional status, through preparing countries for systemic crises and the single events of prominent financial institutions' insolvencies (Recital 6 of the Preamble to the BRR Directive). It is possible only through the assurance of appropriate resources to resolution organs, which directly include resolution funds (1 per cent of the value of covered deposits of a given country), and, indirectly, deposit insurance agency resources (0.8 per cent of covered funds of a given country) (Recital 15 of Preamble to the BRR Directive).

The goal of the study was the verification of effectiveness (scope of successful intervention) of new resolution tools introduced by the BRR Directive, with the inclusion of the supportive role of the deposit insurance agency. The scope is expressed in numeric value. For instance, the result of 12 for Poland indicates that successful intervention with the use of resolution tools is possible for the twelfth biggest financial institution in the country (in terms of its own capital size), and 11 institutions with higher results do not fall into the successful intervention scope due to the insufficient amount of funds at the disposal of the resolution organ.

As a result of the introduction of BRR and DGS Directives' provisions and the participation of the deposit insurance agency in resolution of financial institutions, it is justifiable to verify the scope of successful interventions of such a procedure in the aftermath of post-crisis reform implementation.

Improvement of the scope of public authority toward financial institutions was expected in comparison to the pre-crisis state, which is presented in Section 4.3 on the scope of successful deposit insurance agency participation (as a result of lack of resolution funds). A key issue was the definition of the range of successful intervention capabilities of new resolution tools in specific EU countries, the evaluation of the impact of deposit guarantee scheme support on resolution, and whether the designed solutions would, in fact, prove themselves applicable to public administration realm, with all of the financial institutions within its authority.

6.3   Method Description

The attempt of the study was to evaluate whether target levels of financial resources of the resolution organ, proposed in the BRR and DGS Directives, were sufficient for the effective elimination of a given financial institution from the market. The study proposed deviation from pan-European considerations, which took place during the enactment of the BRR Directive (EC 2012). An approach of acquiring the perspective of respective countries, in which the procedure will be performed, and where the financial market asset structure of individual entities were crucial factors, was also recommended.

Due to the fact that costs of carrying out successful resolution procedures directly influence the scope of potential, effective intervention, they are the most important factor that requires determining. Nevertheless, the assessment of bank resolution expenses is difficult and measured in various ways.

A popular measure of price evaluation of a bank's intervention is the cost of its restructuring, compared to the GDP of a given country. Such a method is often adopted by the IMF (Zoli 2001; Laeven and Valencia

2013) and the World Bank (Klingebiel and Laeven 2002). Still, the results achieved through the above methodology differ greatly among specific countries. An example of high fiscal bank restructuring costs are the nearly 57 per cent of GDP of Indonesia in the years 1997–2001, or 44 per cent in Thailand in the years 1997–2000 (Laeven and Valencia 2013, p. 26). Much lower costs were noted in the above-mentioned studies in the case of the United States (4.5 per cent of GDP) and Germany (2.8 per cent). Still, such a cost perspective would not be not useful for the study, because the referral to restructuring costs of specific banks (units) in a given country is needed—not their entire, respective sectors.

The evaluation of costliness of resolution in the case of specific banks, carried out by the FDIC in the United States, is another form of measure. It is there that bank restructuring experiences are most numerous, and instruments applied—similar to those specified in the BRR Directive. Costs of resolution (that is, financial means dedicated for resolution, received from public authorities) were expressed as a percentage of the balance sheet of the restructured institution. Recalling chosen FDIC studies: the average restructuring cost for a bank was nearly 15.8 per cent, and its median, nearly 30 per cent of its balance sheet value (Bennett and Unal 2014, p. 40). FDIC analyses in the above topic covered a group of 1,208 banks that were under restructuring procedures between the years 1986 and 2007. It must be noted that recapitalizing the bank (open bank assistance), which was a—currently obsolete—resolution method applied mostly in the 1980s and 1990s by the FDIC in the United States, on average cost, between the years 1980 and 1994, from 0 to nearly 41 per cent of the balance sheet value of selected, evaluated institutions (FDIC 1997, pp. 167–169). Other experiences come from the application of the bridge institution tool within the years 1987–94, which cost the FDIC from 0 to nearly 23 per cent of the total balance sheet value—depending on the given institution (FDIC 1997, pp. 167–169).

It must be underlined that tools applied by the FDIC are similar to those foreseen by the BRR Directive. Thus, in this case, it was possible to apply a resembling study methodology. Nevertheless, with BRR Directive solutions in mind, it was proposed that a personalized costliness evaluation of resolution proceedings of specific EU banks, inclusive of the new union approach, be applied. It was decided that resolution procedure costs ought to be referenced to the value of own capital of a given financial institution prior to intervention. The choice is justifiable for several reasons.

According to the BRR Directive, two types of entities are compulsorily burdened with costs of resolution of a given financial institution:

- owners (due to the write down of capital)—for the sake of loss coverage,
- creditors (due to the write down of capital or conversion of liabilities) and the country resolution authority, financed from the resources of financial institutions (or, alternatively, supported by the funds of the SRB)—for the sake of loss coverage and recovery of capital.

Thus, own capital is a basic financial institution balance sheet element, which the BRR Directive refers to due to its crucial significance for resolution procedures. It is a form of capital, which—first and foremost—must be utilized for the sake of loss of a given institution and must be rebuilt. It is the above capital that bail in will be used for the sake of covering loss of a given financial institution. Whereas, write down of actions of owners of a financial institution is a procedure that allows for the acquisition of control over a given financial entity, nevertheless, rebuilding own capital is necessary in order to restore the sound functioning of the troubled financial institution. Hence, the initial task of the resolution organ is to provide the continuity of critical functions of an institution, which shall be achieved through the restoration of missing own capital (regardless of the chosen procedure tool). Moreover, according to the BRR Directive, the financial institution is obliged to maintain a certain amount of eligible liabilities (MREL) that allow for loss absorption, while resolution actions shall encourage the restoration of the institution's own capital.

After determining the category to which own capital belongs, it was important to evaluate the possible cost scenarios for the sake of resolution effectiveness tests, which would assume varying levels of financial burden needed to either salvage the entity or eliminate it from the market. In order to ensure that the study's scenario concepts were precise and realistic, practical, historical experiences of bank resolution in the EU were referred to during their formulation.

On the basis of data acquired from previous studies on the costs of resolution of EU banks (Iwanicz-Drozdowska et al. 2016), presented in detail in Table A.8 Annex VI, it was calculated for a sample of banks under resolution that:

- the year that aid was granted, costs of resolution of a sample of 53 banks, evaluated by the relation of granted public aid to bank's own capital value was, on average, 43 per cent, and its median—53 per cent,
- the year before aid was granted, costs of resolution of a sample of 35 banks, evaluated by the relation of public aid to the value of bank's own capital value (one year before aid was granted) was, on average, 24 per cent, and its median—48 per cent.

Nevertheless, the amount of public aid often exceeded the value of own capital of a given financial institution. Such a situation took place in 27 of the 76 studied banks.

Taking the above into consideration, the analysis adopted two basic cost scenarios, referring to own capital of financial institutions—a favorable (optimistic) and unfavorable (pessimistic):

- the favorable scenario assumed that the cost of resolution of a single financial institution was worth half the value of its own capital (prior to intervention),
- the unfavorable scenario assumed that the cost of resolution of a single financial institution was equal to the entire value of its own capital (prior to intervention).

Several restrictions must be made to the premises above. First and foremost, the 50 and 100 per cent of own capital cost thresholds are discretionary. The assumption of the favorable (optimistic) scenario for public organs, regarding the obligation of engaging half of their own capital, is an effect of average costs, which public authorities would be burdened with during EU bank resolutions. The concept is legitimate especially in the case, where authorities plan future operations of an entity on the market, while its losses are sufficiently low and will not rule out its continuity. Assuming the unfavorable (pessimistic) scenario for public organs, regarding the necessity of engaging resolution fund resources corresponding to the value of own capitals, does not derive from average historic records, but from the attempt at testing extraordinary circumstances, in which resolution will be strongly hindered. Interestingly, such an event did, in fact, take place in the EU in the years 2007–14 in the case of 27 banks. The assumption is probable in the situation, where ruling bodies decide on terminating operation and liquidating a big financial institution once coverage of most of its liabilities is needed.

Secondly, the restructuring costs presented in the study refer solely to gross costs the resolution authority is burdened with, without the inclusion of potential recovery rate or the return of granted aid. What is more, costs of bank restructuring will be covered not only by the resolution authority, but also owners and creditors of the given bank. Moreover, certain additional restrictions of the BRR Directive that concern the value of funds that may be used for the sake of resolution of one institution were not applied in the following study for the sake of its clarity and simplicity. This discloses a limitation of the above study, because, while owners and creditors partially cover the losses of a given entity (as a resolution cost), it is not taken into account by the study, which focuses on evaluating the restructuring possibilities of using resolution funds.

Thirdly, practical EU experiences of the years 2007–14 may not be a valid point of reference. The most important reason is the fact that European restructuring experiences do not resemble those presented in the BRR Directive and were not applied in EU countries at the time. Still, *ad hoc* forms of aid were dominant—most often, in the form of governmental loans or the issuance of covered securities by the country (Iwanicz-Drozdowska et al. 2016).

Fourth, while evaluating the study's provisions, it was stated that individual experiences of countries in financial institution restructuring differ on many levels. It is clearly visible in the case of the United States, where, depending on the entity, resolution costs vary greatly. It is difficult to evaluate resolution costs among institutions under resolution, because each insolvency event has its own reasons and specificity. What is more, financial institutions differ in terms of their asset structure. While part is easy to sell on the market, others are not considered an attractive purchase. In addition, the financial market of a given country and its regional specificity also influence restructuring costs (for example, it is easier to find an acquirer of an insolvent bank's assets on the big, experienced American market, than it is in certain small economies of the EU). The influence of a chosen resolution instrument on costs of the entire procedure, as well as providing a proper diagnosis at its very beginning (choice of restructuring method), is a separate issue.

Despite certain limitations of the method, it is favorable that the study results must be easily comparable among EU member states. Similarly, the role and influence of the deposit guarantee scheme during resolution shall also be transparent.

During the collection of data, the following approach was adopted: financial institutions, which are covered by the BRR Directive scope of entities, were sorted separately for each member state, from the biggest to the smallest in regard to their own capital. Resolution fund resources were also taken into consideration, and determined upfront at the level of 1 per cent of covered deposits of a given country.

Figure 6.1 presents the approach on verifying both scenarios. For instance, in the case of Poland, the first institution was the PKO BP SA bank, which—by the end of 2012—reported nearly €6 billion of own capital. The study assumes that in the unfavorable scenario, this is the exact sum that will be required for the entity's resolution. As for the favorable scenario, problems may be overcome with half of the above value, namely, €3 billion.

Next, each of the above scenarios was allocated to two possible financing procedure variants, which are:

– limited variant—also referred to as resolution fund variant (RF variant), which assumes the hypothetical BRR Directive resolution fund budget (1 per cent of the value of covered deposits) on the level

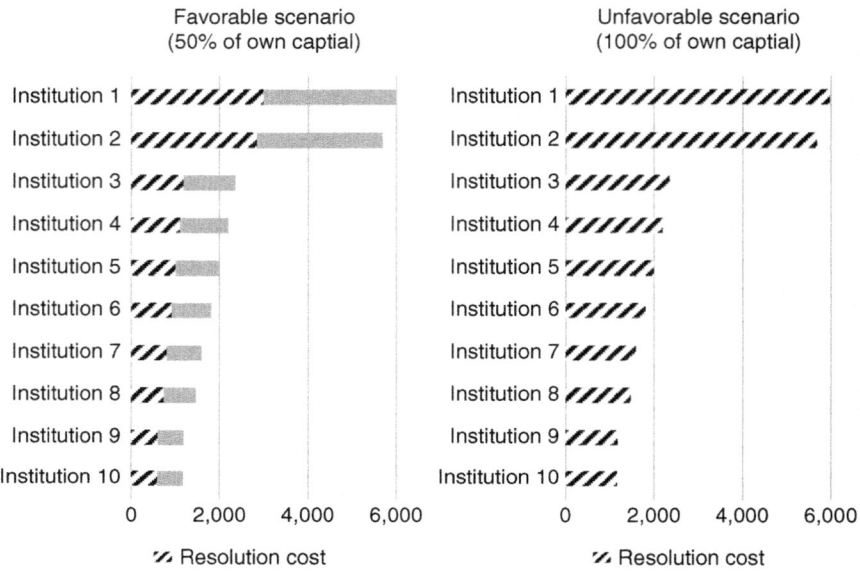

Fig. 6.1 Comparison of scenarios applied in the study on the example of Poland, with the assessment of individual resolution costs for each financial institution (data in millions of euros)

Value of own capital of institutions as of the end of 2012 (expressed in millions of euros)

Source: Author's own formulation

of half (optimistically) or all own capital of all financial institutions based in the given country;

– extended variant—also referred to as resolution fund and deposit guarantee scheme variant (RF+DGS variant), which assumes the hypothetical BRR Directive resolution fund budget (1 per cent of the value of covered deposits) with capital participation of the deposit insurer (assumed by the BRR and DGS Directives) on the level of all own capital (or its half, in the favorable scenario) of all financial institutions based in the given country.

It must be noted that financing applied in the extended variant (RF+DGS) is possible, as long as there are covered deposits present in the entity under resolution. In such a case, the capital participation of the deposit guarantee scheme is limited to 50 per cent of its target level of 0.8 per cent of covered deposits of the given country, which has been included in the study (a detailed scope of the participation of the deposit insurance agency in resolution is specified in Article 109 of the BRR Directive).

After the comparison, an evaluation was performed, which indicated the number of institutions, which—in assumed variants and scenarios—would have either found themselves within the scope of successful intervention of resolution in a given country, or would have "evaded" the procedure and required alternative measures (most often, financing from public funds).

In order to ensure better clarity of the applied methodology, the course of the study on effective intervention, with two variants and their respective scenarios, was graphically expressed on the example of Poland in Fig. 6.2. The figure presents 15 leading financial institutions in scope of the BRR Directive in terms of their own capital value in Poland, as of the end of 2012 (expressed in millions of euros), which were subject to the resolution regime. On the chart, the scope of successful interventions of the resolution authority was marked with black arrows, both for the limited (RF) and extended (RF+DGS) scenarios.

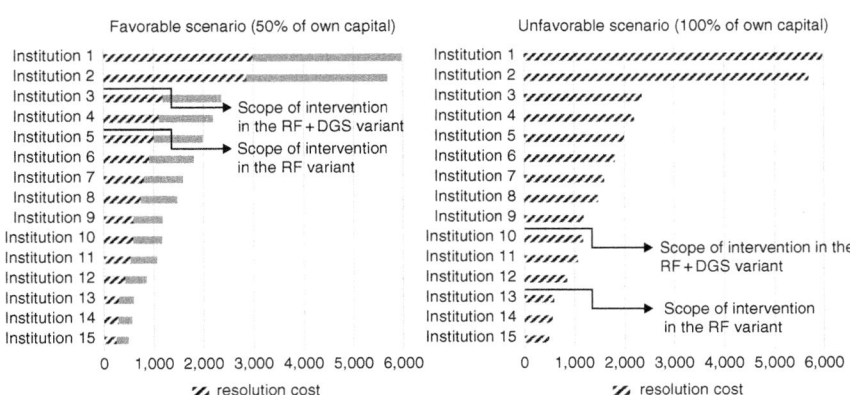

Fig. 6.2 Comparison of variants (RF and RF+DGS) in two scenarios on the example of Poland, in case one of the financial institutions becomes insolvent

Value of own capital as of the end of 2012 (expressed in millions of euros)
Source: Author's own formulation

In comparison to the value of own funds of specific financial institutions, the analysis of available resolution resources reveals that in the favorable scenario (where half of own capital value of a given institution needs to be engaged for the sake of successful intervention), the Polish resolution organ would be capable of intervening effectively toward the fifth (RF variant) and third (RF+DGS variant) largest institutions. These would be, respectively, ING Bank Śląski and mBank.

Still, the analysis of the unfavorable scenario reveals worse results. It assumes that the Polish resolution organ would be capable of intervening in regard to the tenth and twelfth institutions (Bank Millennium and BGŻ, respectively).

Thus far, the presented scenarios and variants referred to one situation only—intervening toward a failing financial institution. In order to extent the analysis scope, a second situation was added—the simultaneous insolvency of two financial institutions of similar size in the same country, toward which the resolution organ ought to intervene.

The above situation was analyzed with the same scenarios and variants. Conditions, which justify the conviction that resolution of two financial institutions is needed, are presented in Section 6.6.

Additionally, Fig. 6.3 demonstrates the described situation (the necessity of commencing concurrent action toward two financial institutions in Poland). It must be noted that the chart does not include the biggest institutions, because they are outside the intervention scope, and the scale starts from the sixth position onward. The figure presents top financial institutions in Poland as of the end of 2012, in terms of own capital (positions 6–20), which are under the scope of the resolution regime (expressed in millions of euros). The scope of successful intervention of the resolution authority toward two adjacent institutions with similar own capital value, shown on the chart, was marked with black arrows, both for the limited (RF) and extended (RF+DGS) scenarios.

The analysis of available resolution resources in regard to own capital of specific financial institutions, in case intervention toward two banks is necessary, leads to several conclusions. In the favorable scenario (assuming the need to engage half of own capital value of a given institution for the sake of its restructuring), the Polish resolution authority will be

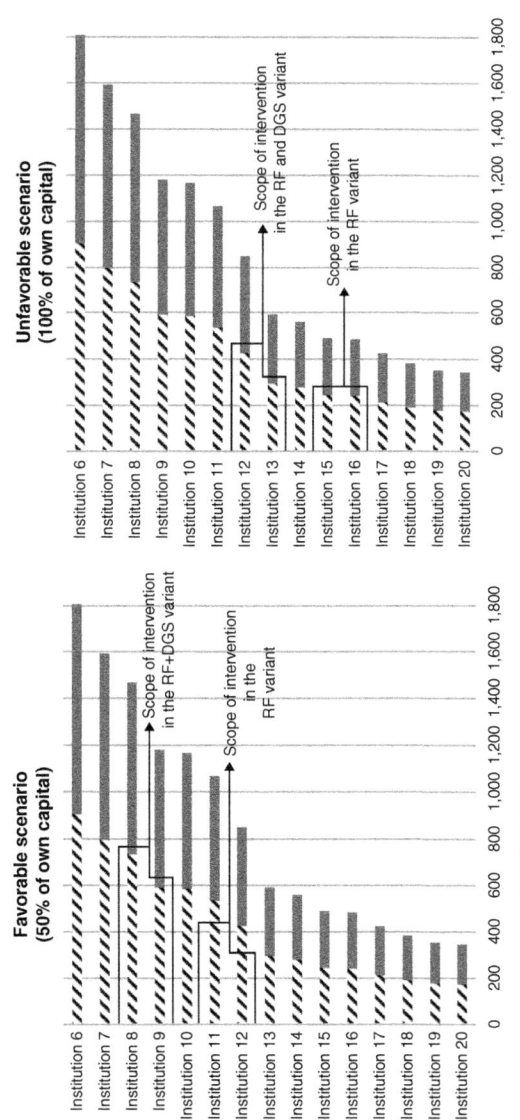

Fig. 6.3 Comparison of variants (RF, RF+DGS) in two scenarios on the example of Poland, in case intervention is needed simultaneously toward two financial institutions

Value of own capital as of the end of 2012 (expressed in millions of euros)

Source: Author's own formulation

capable of intervening effectively toward two financial institutions from ranks 11 to 12 (RF variant) and 8 to 9 (RF+DGS variant).

The analysis of the unfavorable scenario presents relatively worse results. With the assumptions adopted in the unfavorable scenario, as well as the need to simultaneously take action toward two institutions of similar size, the Polish resolution authority would be capable of effectively intervening in case of banks with numbers 15–16 (RF variant) and 12–13 (RF+DGS variant), at most.

In conclusion, during the study of all 28 EU member states:

1) **two situations** were analyzed:

– necessity of intervening toward one financial institution by the resolution fund,
– necessity of intervening toward two financial institutions, similar in size in terms of their own capital;

2) each of the above situations was subsequently verified in **two variants:**

– limited variant—assuming that only resolution fund resources would be required (RF variant),
– extended variant—assuming that resolution fund resources would need to be subsidized by the deposit guarantee scheme (RF+DGS variant);

3) furthermore, each variant was tested in **two varying scenarios:**

– favorable scenario, assuming that the cost of resolution of a single financial institution is equivalent to half of its own capital value,
– unfavorable scenario, assuming that the cost of resolution of a single financial institution is equivalent to all of its own capital.

Hence, the outcome of the study, in terms of successful intervention of resolution, is comprised of several, partial results for each EU member state. Altogether, there are eight results that describe the intervention scope for each country (two situations, each with a set of two variants with two scenarios). Results of studies for all EU member states, supplemented by the interpretation and calculation method of specific results, may be found in the tables of Annex VII. It must be noted that the most important results are those presented in the fourth and sixth columns of Tables A.9 and Tables A.10 of Annex VII. The fourth column indicates the true effectiveness of the procedure introduced to the union by the BRR Directive, whereas column six presents the influence of the deposit guarantee scheme on the effectiveness of actions executed toward separate entities.

6.4   Data Sources

Data on deposits, used for the sake of the study described in the following chapter, come from the same sources indicated in Chapter 4. Detailed supplementary information on EU countries, applied in the research, may be found in Table 6.1.

The first column of Table 6.1 presents the names of EU member states as of the end of 2012, nevertheless, in order to complete the study, Croatia was also included, despite its accession to the union in 2013.

In the second column, it was assumed that the available resolution fund levels, as in the BRR Directive, are equal to one per cent of covered deposits' value of a given country's financial sector. It must be highlighted that the study assumes that countries already had such values at their disposal by the end of 2012, while the BRR Directive requires the accumulation of funds in a much broader perspective. For the sake of simplicity, the existence of a European mechanism (the sharing of resolution funds) and the functioning of the SRB, which performs the role of coordinator and does not increase the size of available resolution funds (Recital 113 of the BRR Preamble), were also omitted.

In the third column, through the evaluation of the extent of possible deposit insurance agency participation in resolution, the maximum responsibility of the deposit guarantee scheme was included—hence, half of the minimal target level of 0.8 per cent of the value of covered deposits, described in the DGS Directive (thus, 0.4 per cent). In each of the countries, the

Table 6.1 Data used for the evaluation of resolution effectiveness in specific countries

1.	2.	3.	4.	5.
Country name	Size of the resolution fund (in millions of euros)	Potential subsidiary aid of the deposit guarantee scheme (in millions of euros)	Number of evaluated entities	Deposit correction ratio (%)
Austria	1,734	693	278	72
Belgium	2,291	917	67	67
Bulgaria	184	74	27	70
Croatia	383	88	34	67
Cyprus	519	208	17	67
Czech Republic	653	261	36	67
Denmark	1,055	422	95	85
Estonia	53	21	9	61
Finland	778	311	41	61
France	11,035	4,414	383	72
Germany	15,752	6,301	1,790	67
Great Britain	12,188	4,875	356	56
Greece	1,048	419	14	75
Hungary	303	121	32	69
Ireland	800	320	32	57
Italy	4,905	1,962	592	68
Latvia	60	24	19	41
Lithuania	67	27	10	67
Luxembourg	304	122	84	19
Malta	70	28	13	74
Netherlands	4,470	1,788	70	78
Poland	1,032	413	43	59
Portugal	1,102	441	38	67
Romania	274	110	26	83
Slovakia	242	97	16	90
Slovenia	149	60	21	85
Spain	6,749	2,700	155	72
Sweden	1,409	563	101	71

Data on Croatia as of the end of 2013; an average correction ratio for the EU was hereby applied

Source: Iwanicz-Drozdowska et al. (2015), EC (2011a), FSB (2012), IADI (2008a, 2013), Cannas et al. (2014, pp. 9, 12) and DAB (2015)

deposit guarantee scheme may support the resolution fund, as long as the failing institution has covered deposits at its disposal, to which access is uninterrupted throughout the whole procedure. Similarly, as in the previous example, levels of covered funds as of the end of 2012 were adapted. It was also assumed that the target levels specified in the DGS Directive have already been achieved.

The fourth column includes financial institutions based in EU countries, which all fall into the scope of resolution. Hence, the scope of the analysis is broader than in the case of deposit guarantee scheme fund use, as shown in Section 4.2, because the authority of the latter includes financial institutions with aggregated covered deposits only. Hence, it is believed possible that an entity without covered deposits will be subject to resolution. An example is investment firms (the participation of the deposit guarantee scheme as a subsidiary funder is, in this case, omitted, which was also included in the study). The size of the group of evaluated entities was confined to the Bankscope database, with information as of the end of 2012. The sample included all financial institutions apart from central banks of respective countries, which have been excluded from the analysis. Bankscope contains information on majority of European financial institutions (Bureau van Dijk 2015). Hence, if certain entities were omitted in the study and outside the main interest area, it was most probably caused by their small size, because the line separating entities under resolution and outside its scope (due to the excessive financial burden size) does not pass through the above group. Altogether, 4,399 institutions were evaluated in the study. Estonia represented the smallest (nine), and Germany—the biggest (1,790) number of entities.

The fifth column of Table 6.1 includes the deposit correction ratio, which allows to achieve precise data on the value of covered deposits of each financial institution. The calculation method for each entity is presented broadly in Section 4.2.

Data that have not been included in Table 6.1, but were used in the study, concern the value of own capital of specific financial institutions in the EU. Similarly to the previously mentioned number of entities (fourth column), the information was also derived from Bankscope. In terms of validity of data on own capital, the above database was also evaluated positively and enjoys good reputation in the scientific community. An especially high note—with benefit for the study—was granted to data on European and American institutions (Bhattacharya 2003).

6.5 Analysis of Carrying Out Resolution of a Single Institution

Section 6.5 presents results of the study on the insolvency of a single financial institution. Results of the limited (RF) and extended (RF+DGS) variants are demonstrated for both scenarios (favorable and unfavorable). Results of the unfavorable scenario in both variants may be found in Table A.9 of Annex VII, whereas favorable scenario results are available in Table A.10 of Annex VII. The lower the number in the second and fourth columns of both tables, the more favorable the situation of a given country. This is because the number expresses the hierarchy of effective resolution toward a certain institution, as well as those that do not fall into restructuring altogether. For example, a result of five means that the fifth biggest institution (in terms of own capital) may be restructured, whereas the remaining four do not fall into successful intervention scope. Hence, the lower the number, the bigger the potential number of institutions that may be restructured in the given country. Interpretation of sample study results is provided in Table A.12 of Annex VII.

Due to the transparency of later comparisons of resolution organ situation in case it acts independently, and when it is supported by the deposit guarantee scheme, the study results have been divided according to applicable variants.

6.5.1 Effectiveness of Resolution in the RF Variant

Depending on the evaluation of the scope of successful resolution interventions with the sole use of resolution fund resources, EU states may be divided into three basic groups. A detailed division of countries is presented in Table 6.2.

Table 6.2 Division of EU countries based on the evaluation of their resolution scope in case only resolution funds are used

The evaluation of restructuring capabilities	High	Moderate	Low
Which institutions may be covered by resolution (in terms of their own capital size)?	1–5	6–10	Above 10
Unfavorable scenario	Finland, Greece, Lithuania	Belgium, Croatia, Czech Republic, Estonia, Spain, Netherlands, Latvia, Malta, Germany, Portugal, Romania, Slovakia, Hungary, Italy	Austria, Bulgaria, Denmark, France, Ireland, Luxembourg, Poland, Slovenia, Sweden, Great Britain
Number of countries	3	15	10
Favorable scenario	Croatia, Cyprus, Estonia, Finland, Greece, Spain, Lithuania, Germany, Poland, Romania, Slovenia	Austria, Belgium, Bulgaria, Czech Republic, Denmark, France, Netherlands, Ireland, Latvia, Malta, Portugal, Slovakia, Sweden, Hungary, Italy	Luxembourg, Great Britain
Number of countries	11	15	2

Source: Author's own formulation based on the evaluations presented in Tables A.9 and A.10 of Annex VII

Unfavorable Scenario

The analysis of the variant, which considers the use of resolution fund resources in an unfavorable scenario, leads to the conclusion that only a small group of EU countries (three—Finland, Greece, and Lithuania) is capable of carrying out effective resolution of big financial institutions. The fact that they are all small EU economies with a relatively modest number of banks (respectively, 41, 14, and 10) deserves recognition. High results of the above countries are an effect of their small banking sectors, which—though concentrated—are insufficient to make carrying out resolution of even the biggest entities possible. It is also worth noticing that the group of countries with a moderate resolution effectiveness rating is quite numerous (15 countries). The fact that the group is comprised of countries with big banking sectors, such as the Netherlands, Spain, and Germany, whose stability is important to the entire union, is especially favorable. Germany deserves special attention, because—despite its big banking sector—the German resolution organ (FMSA) will be capable of restructuring the tenth biggest entity (Bayerische Landesbank) in the unfavorable scenario.

The group of countries with low banking sector resolution capabilities is numerous in the unfavorable scenario (ten states). It is disadvantageous that countries with big financial sectors—namely, France and Great Britain—are only capable of restructuring the 13th (France) and 18th (Great Britain) banks. Countries with average-sized banking sectors, such as Austria and Sweden, also did not achieve good results and are characterized by a big number of financial institutions outside the scope of potential intervention.

The analysis of the first part of Table 6.2 leads to the conclusion that—despite the introduction of post-crisis reforms in the EU—268 financial institutions are still outside the scope of effective resolution procedures.

Favorable Scenario

To avoid the accusation of an exceedingly strict approach toward the costs of resolution of financial institutions, the favorable scenario was also included in the study. The results of the evaluation may be found in the second part of Table 6.2. The analysis indicates that, if a less severe course of events during insolvency of a financial institution is assumed, the group with a high resolution scope increases dramatically to as many as 11 countries, including Germany, Spain, and Poland, hence, countries with big and average-sized EU banking sectors. In both scenarios, Greece is at the forefront of the highest pointed group, which requires a more detailed explanation. In the given country, extensive financial sector restructuring efforts had already been previously started. Thus, even the biggest financial institutions such as Marfin Investment Group are characterized by relatively low own capital value and achieve more favorable results.

The group with moderate results is nearly as numerous as that of the unfavorable scenario. Nevertheless, countries, which previously achieved low results, have moved here. The high positions of France, Austria, and Sweden (countries with prominent EU banking sectors and a high overall asset value) deserve special recognition.

The last group in the favorable scenario is comprised of only two countries: Great Britain and Luxembourg. The second last place of Great Britain has a simple explanation—the country has a big financial sector, which is capable of carrying out resolution for the 12th biggest entity with the use of one per cent of covered deposits. Nevertheless, the explanation in the case of Luxembourg, which, yet again, took the last place, is different and a result of the specificity of the local financial sector. The size of the resolution budget was imposed by the EU and was based on the value of covered deposits of the entire sector of the given country. Numerous investment companies, which fall into the resolution-covered group, are based in Luxembourg, yet many of them do not accept deposits. Hence the big number of formally eligible entities, with a relatively modest resolution budget caused by their categorization to covered deposits, which are, as a fact, missing on the Luxembourg market.

Unfortunately, from the perspective of the effectiveness of the procedure, even the favorable scenario leaves 160 of the biggest EU financial institutions (in terms of own capital) out of the scope of successful resolution organ intervention.

Summary

The analysis of study results for the RF variant in both scenarios, described in Table 6.2, leads to the conclusion that EU countries, due to the distinctiveness of the financial sector structure, vary greatly from one another in terms of financial institution resolution capabilities. While Greece may cover its biggest entity with resolution procedures in the favorable scenario, Luxembourg, given the same provisions, may only do so for the 12th entity. Still, it is most disturbing that countries with big financial sectors, such as France, Germany, Great Britain, and Spain, have unsatisfactory sector resolution capability results. It must be evaluated positively that, with the application of the BRR Directive, a great majority of EU entities are under the scope of resolution. Over 4,000 entities have been hereby tested, and only 160 or 268 (in the favorable and unfavorable scenarios, respectively) are outside intervention capabilities. Nevertheless, it may be noticed that at the current level of research, the restructuring of many entities, under given conditions of the following study, remains impossible in both scenarios. It must be hereby emphasized that the optimistic study assumes that countries have already achieved the levels required for resolution. It is also worth noticing that resolution intervention must always be justified by public interest. Such a goal, most often, materializes in the case of the biggest financing institutions—hence, precisely those, which remain outside effective intervention scope of EU resolution authorities, despite reform. Thus, it may be hereby stated that due to the existence of a big group of financial institutions that will not be covered by effective resolution intervention due to lack of funds, resolution with the application of the RF variant only will not solve the too big to fail problem for the EU. This, in turn, may reflect poorly on certain proposed post-crisis reforms.

6.5.2 Effectiveness of Resolution in the RF+DGS Variant

In order to provide a more through analysis and a complete evaluation of BRR Directive solutions, the analysis of the effectiveness of the procedure was performed not only in the case of use of resolution funds (RF variant), but also deposit guarantee scheme resources. The study of such an option (RF+DGS variant), with the capital participation of the deposit insurance agency, is presented in Table 6.3. As stipulated, the inclusion of the deposit guarantee scheme in resolution procedures causes the rise of restructuring

Table 6.3 Division of EU countries based on the evaluation of their resolution scope in the RF+DGS variant

The evaluation of restructuring capabilities	High	Moderate	Low
Which institutions may be covered by resolution (in terms of their own capital size)?	1–5	6–10	Above 10
Unfavorable scenario	Cyprus, Estonia, Finland, Greece, Lithuania	Belgium, Bulgaria, Croatia, Czech Republic, Spain, Netherlands, Latvia, Malta, Germany, Poland, Portugal, Romania, Slovakia, Slovenia, Hungary, Italy	Austria, Denmark, France, Ireland, Luxembourg, Sweden, Great Britain
Number of countries	5	16	7
Favorable scenario	Bulgaria, Croatia, Cyprus, Czech Republic, Estonia, Finland, Greece, Spain, Lithuania, Latvia, Germany, Poland, Portugal, Romania, Slovenia, Hungary, Italy	Austria, Belgium, Denmark, France, Netherlands, Ireland, Malta, Slovakia, Sweden, Great Britain	Luxembourg
Number of countries	17	10	1

Source: Author's own formulation based on the evaluations presented in Tables A.9 and A.10 of Annex VII

capabilities of the financial sector in EU countries—as long as the institution achieved the target level of 0.8 per cent of covered deposits' value.

Unfavorable Scenario

In the unfavorable scenario, Cyprus and Estonia were acknowledged to the first group with the highest score. Despite the small size of the countries' banking sectors, they have improved their position in regard to the scope of intervention. The size of the group with average intervention capabilities rose by one, and includes Bulgaria, Poland, and Slovenia (in the place of Cyprus and Estonia). With the participation of the deposit guarantee scheme in the unfavorable scenario, the above countries are capable of intervening in regard to entities of the group from five to ten, measured by their own capital. Despite the input on behalf of the deposit guarantee schemes, the group with low evaluations remains numerous. It is comprised of seven EU countries, among them, once again, France and Great Britain. Such an outcome has a negative effect on the evaluation of the countries' respective financial safety nets. Hence, in the unfavorable scenario, and in the variant, where the resolution fund is supported financially by the deposit guarantee scheme, 226 financial institutions still remain outside intervention capabilities.

Favorable Scenario

The favorable scenario of the above variant provides more optimistic effects. Here, the group with high results is comprised of 17 countries, including those that are characterized by a big banking sector in terms of asset value. These include Spain, Germany, and Italy, which ought to be evaluated positively. The group with an average result is made of remaining EU countries, with the exception of Luxembourg. The advancement of Great Britain deserves special recognition and a positive evaluation, whose banking sector's stability is of crucial relevance to the entire union. In the analyzed variant (RF+DGS) and favorable scenario, 126 financial institutions remain outside the scope of intervention.

Evaluation of the Influence of the Deposit Insurance Agency on Resolution

The analysis of the RF+DGS variant leads to the conclusion that the participation of the deposit guarantee scheme in resolution triggers the increase of possible intervention scope by 34 institutions in the favorable scenario, and 42 in the unfavorable scenario. Detailed changes concerning the inclusion of the deposit guarantee scheme in resolution are presented in Table 6.4.

Table 6.4 Division of EU countries based on the evaluation of changes in the resolution scope after the deposit guarantee is introduced as a co-financing side

	Significant rise of intervention scope	Moderate rise of intervention scope	No influence on intervention scope
Scale of rise of success-ful inter-vention scope	3–7	1–2	0
Unfavorable scenario	Bulgaria, Denmark, Germany, Poland, Romania, Slovenia, Italy	Austria, Cyprus, Czech Republic, Estonia, Spain, Netherlands, Ireland, Lithuania, Luxembourg, Latvia, Malta, Slovakia, Sweden, Hungary, Great Britain	Belgium, Croatia, Finland, France, Greece, Portugal
Number of countries	7	15	6
Favorable scenario	Luxembourg, Hungary	Austria, Belgium, Bulgaria, Czech Republic, France, Ireland, Latvia, Poland, Portugal, Romania, Slovakia, Slovenia, Italy, Great Britain	Croatia, Cyprus, Denmark, Estonia, Finland, Greece, Spain, Netherlands, Lithuania, Malta, Germany, Sweden
Number of countries	2	14	12

Source: Author's own formulation based on the evaluations presented in Annex VII

In the unfavorable scenario, the resolution financing scope increases significantly in seven EU countries after the introduction of the deposit insurance agency to the procedure. Although the change concerns three or four institutions only, they are the biggest players on the financial sector of the respective countries. Hence, it may be said that the influence of the deposit guarantee scheme on the effectiveness of the procedure is significant. Its capital support may be especially crucial in the case of the more costly interventions toward smaller entities. In the unfavorable scenario, countries, where the intervention scope will enhance by one or two institutions, constitute the biggest group. Lack of influence of the deposit guarantee scheme on the procedure may be, in the unfavorable scenario, justified either by the achievement of the maximum scope even prior to resolution (Greece), or the specificity of the financial sector structure, in which subsequent institutions with bigger capital do not accept covered deposits (investment firms), or the capital of the next institution is so big, that the modest participation of the deposit insurance agency (in some countries) is insufficient even for a slight improvement in result. Portugal is a good example, where an approximately €500 million difference in terms of own capital between the seventh and eight entities is existent, and the input of €441 million on behalf of the deposit insurance agency is incapable of its covering. A similar situation may be encountered in Croatia, where the €88 million of potential deposit guarantee scheme participation is too little to successfully support resolution proceedings on the highest intervention tiers.

What may startle in the favorable scenario is the lack of influence of the change of variant in the case of as many as 12 countries. Most often, it is caused by the structure of the local financial sectors, as well as the fact that institutions that do not accept deposits altogether (thus excluding deposit guarantee scheme participation in resolution) are among the leading entities with the biggest own capital. Belgium is an example of such a situation, where the potential intervention of the deposit guarantee scheme would be an important financial support of nearly €1 billion. Nevertheless, in the above country, the tenth position marks the limit of intervention capabilities. Among financial institutions with the biggest own capital is the Euroclear company, which is a financial institution specializing in transaction services for financial markets, but does not accept covered deposits. Therefore, there are no possibilities of financial participation of the Belgian deposit insurance agency in resolution. Nevertheless, Euroclear is a holding financial group. In the case of one of its subsidiary companies, the Euroclear Bank, which holds the 13th place in terms of size in Belgium, such an intervention with the deposit guarantee scheme would be possible, because it includes directly allocated covered deposits. This is reflected in the results of the study, because the Euroclear Bank, as a subsidiary, is fully eligible for resolution, because the analysis reveals that the 13th biggest institution in Belgium in terms of capital size may be successfully restructured. Finland is also an interesting case, as it is characterized with its five-point intervention scope—regardless of the chosen scenario and whether the deposit insurance agency participates in resolution or is omitted in the process. This is due to the fact that between the fourth financial entity in terms of own capital (Danske Bank Plc), and two consecutive (Finnvera Plc and Akatia Bank Plc), which hold the fifth and sixth places, there is a enormous own capital gap. Hence, even the changes in levels of support or scenarios have no influence on the indicator.

Summarizing, it is revealed that the introduction of nearly € 27.8 billion of deposit guarantee scheme resources from EU member states to the resolution procedure increases the effectiveness of intervention by 34–42 country financial entities, which is a good result. The importance of deposit guarantee scheme funds and their inclusion in resolution procedures also reveals the scale of the evolution of deposit insurance agencies, as well as outlines new directions of their actions. Detailed information on entities remaining outside the scope of successful intervention is presented in Table 6.5.

Table 6.5 Number of EU financial institutions that remain outside the scope of resolution

Scenario/variant	Favorable	Unfavorable
RF variant	160	268
RF+DGS variant	126	226

Source: Author's own formulation based on results of the study presented in Annex VII

The fact that 226 entities in the EU (in the RF+DGS variant) remain outside the scope of successful intervention in the unfavorable, and 126 in the favorable scenario—despite the introduction of resolution through the BRR Directive—deserves special recognition. Assuming that the costs of potential resolution will be lower than those assumed by the author, and part of obligations will be taken over by the SRB and its financial mechanism (which is unified, to a certain extent), it still leads to the conclusion that part of entities will remain outside the scope of successful intervention.

Results of the study question the core concepts of the reform concerning the target levels of resolution and deposit guarantee funds, because—as seen in the outcome—the situation, where other public resources are needed for the sake of financial institutions' resolution, is still likely. A potential solution to the problem is the calibration of resolution and deposit guarantee schemes funds, so that their levels correspond to the structure of the country financial sector, as well as acknowledging the indicators instated by the BRR Directive at the least necessary levels. A decision of authorities on country calibration would, on the one hand, trigger the rise in liabilities of the banking sector, but on the other, it would support the increase in intervention scope toward banks and investment companies, as well as allow maintaining financial stability.

6.5.3 Supplementary Study Results

It was previously inclined that the most important results from the study's point of view are those presented in columns two, three, and six of Tables A.9 and A.10 of Annex VII. Nevertheless, two other supplementary components are also worth mentioning. The third, fifth, and seventh columns of the mentioned tables present the results of less informative value, but—although comparison is not easy—they deliver valuable conclusions.

The first component is the evaluation of the percentage of financial institutions that stay outside the scope of successful intervention in relation to the number of all financial institutions of a given country that are covered by the resolution scope. The results are shown in columns three and five of Tables A.9 and A.10 of Annex VII.

t seems that the valuation of assets of the banking sector that remain outside intervention scope would have been a more valuable indicator—and also easier to interpret. Nevertheless, with the previously adopted methodology, division of capital groups into units becomes a challenging task. This is due to the fact that as far as the mother company is concerned, intervention may deem impossible, while effective restructuring of the subsidiary unit is still possible. With such a method, controlled assets would have been duplicated (acknowledged twice to the mother and subsidiary units). Such an eventuality is the result of specificity of reporting, the core of which lies in the fact that assets controlled by the subsidiary (individually) are also controlled by the parent entity (on a consolidated level). Hence the decision to remain only with the sample evaluation of entities outside the scope. Also, potential assistance on behalf of the mother company has not been included in the study, because such aid may only be granted during early intervention and recovery phases. If resolution is initiated, it may be expected that, in accordance with the BRR Directive, help on behalf of the mother entity had already been granted, but did not bring desired results.

Due to the reasons presented above, the study has a less informative value, because assets are key—not the number of entities. Still, even such a calculation leads to the formulation of initial conclusions. Detailed information on the topic is presented in Table 6.6, which includes the analysis of the sample of financial institutions that remain outside the scope of effective intervention in the crucial variant (in both scenarios) with the use of resolution and deposit guarantee funds.

Paradoxically, in the analysis of the percentage of institutions that were outside the scope of effective resolution intervention, countries with good results in previous studies perform worse, while countries that have, thus far, achieved poor results note a positive change (for example, Great Britain, France, or Germany).

If we look only at the percentage of entities outside intervention in both scenarios (favorable and unfavorable) in the RF+DGS variant, the first group with high intervention score is comprised of big

Table 6.6 Division of EU countries based on the percentage of entities remaining outside the resolution scope in the RF+DGS variant

Evaluation of intervention scope	High	Moderate	Low
Ranges of percentage of entities outside the scope of effective intervention	Less than 10%	10–20%	Above 20%
Unfavorable scenario	Austria, France, Spain, Germany, Great Britain, Italy	Belgium, Czech Republic, Denmark, Finland, Greece, Netherlands, Sweden	Bulgaria, Croatia, Cyprus, Estonia, Ireland, Lithuania, Luxembourg, Latvia, Malta, Poland, Portugal, Romania, Slovakia, Slovenia, Hungary
Number of countries	6	7	15
Favorable scenario	Austria, Denmark, France, Greece, Spain, Germany, Poland, Slovenia, Sweden, Hungary, Great Britain, Italy	Belgium, Bulgaria, Croatia, Czech Republic, Finland, Netherlands, Luxembourg, Portugal, Romania	Cyprus, Estonia, Ireland, Lithuania, Latvia, Malta, Slovakia
Number of countries	12	9	7

Source: Author's own formulation based on results of the study presented in Tables A.9 and A.10 of Annex VII

financial sectors, such as Germany, Great Britain, Spain, or France. The results may be accredited to the high number of financial entities existent in these countries. As for states will a small sector, such as Malta, Estonia, Lithuania, or Slovenia, the absence (being outside resolution scope) of even a couple entities creates a high percentage of entities outside intervention capabilities. An important conclusion for countries, where there is a large number of banks—such as Germany (1,790), Italy (592), or Great Britain (383)—is that many deposits have been dispersed among hundreds of financial entities. Thus, it may be expected that the concentration of deposits is more favorable for resolution than, for instance, in Estonia or Slovakia, where there are, respectively, nine and 16 financial institutions covered by resolution authority. Nevertheless, such is the specificity of particular countries—numerosity of financial institutions does not guarantee a diversified covered deposits' structure. Examples of such a situation are Deutsche Bank AG of Germany with €577 billion in covered deposits, HSBC Bank of Great Britain with €389 billion in covered deposits, and Unicredit of Italy with €368 billion from clients. This, despite a big number of financial entities in the previously mentioned countries, results in high guarantee figures for the insurance agencies and causes restructuring difficulties.

The second of the previously mentioned supplementary components is the content of the last (seventh) column of Tables A.9 and A.10 of Annex VII, which present the analysis of the influence of deposit guarantee scheme funds on resolution in reference to the levels of covered deposits of a given financial institution in need of assistance. Unfortunately, after the analysis had been carried out, it was revealed that—despite initial assumptions—formulation of general conclusions is difficult. The only remark that may be made is that in EU countries, the situation differs greatly and depends strictly on the structure of a given entity's balance. Deposit guarantee scheme resources do not necessarily need to be utilized (Finland), or may cover 100 per cent (Cyprus, the Netherlands) or even much more (Hungary) of covered deposits' value of a given institution. The median of the unfavorable scenario is 9.3 per cent, while the favorable—5.1 per cent. Nevertheless, a general rule applies that the higher the position of the institution in line for resolution, the more covered deposits collected by the bank, and the bigger the expected deposit insurance agency participation in resolution. Simultaneously, a lower percentage of covered deposits amortization from deposit guarantee scheme funds may be expected.

6.6   Analysis of Implementing Simultaneous Resolution of Two Institutions

Section 6.5 analyzes two basic variants in two scenarios, in which the necessity of commencing resolution occurred toward a single entity. Nevertheless, the ambition of the BRR and DGS Directive authors was to equip EU member states not only in tools that would enable them to deal with intervention in a single event, but also for multiple crises of systemic character. This is apparent in the declaration that countries must be capable of taking control over a failing institution and carry out its resolution. In order to deal with situations of insolvency of specific institutions and systemic crises, member states ought to be ready and equipped in necessary reparatory and resolution instruments (Preamble of the BRR Directive, Recitals 3 and 6).

Providing countries the possibility to act in times of turmoil would undoubtedly be favorable. Namely, it may be expected that the insolvency of a single financial institution is a less complicated situation from the point of view of financial safety net functioning than complex, simultaneous actions toward multiple financial institutions. Still, intervention toward several entities during systemic crisis cannot be ruled out. Situations, in which intervention toward a greater number of entities too place in the same period with the use of tools similar to those specified in the BRR Directive, are presented in Table 6.7.

The analysis of Table 6.7 reveals that the need of carrying out intervention toward several entities within the financial safety net takes place often and within a short time frame. A particularly interesting example of such a situation is Spain, which restructured its savings banks extensively (13), as well as, for instance, Denmark (11), where "bank packages" were subsequently introduced in reference to financial institutions. Tools for resolution of savings and credit unions were also applied in Poland in the year 2014 in the form of complete takeover of the above-mentioned institutions, with the donation on behalf of the BGF.

Taking into consideration the necessity of simultaneous (or subsequent) resolution organ intervention toward a greater number of financial entities, it has been decided to evaluate an additional situation—the

Table 6.7 EU countries with the number of entities under resolution between the years 2007 and 2014

Country	Number of events	Country	Number of events
Spain	13	France	4
Denmark	11	Italy	4
Germany	10	Belgium	3
Austria	7	Cyprus	3
Greece	7	Netherlands	3
Portugal	6	Latvia	2
Ireland	6	Poland	2
Great Britain	5	Lithuania	1
Slovenia	5	Sweden	1

Source: Iwanicz-Drozdowska et al. (2016), IMF (2014, p. 41)

insolvency of multiple financial institutions. Specifically, it concerned the substitution of a single insolvency (tested in Section 6.4) with the possibility of assessing intervention scope toward two banks—subsequent financial institutions in terms of the size of their own capital. The concept is illustrated in Fig. 6.3 and presented in Section 6.2.

The remaining concepts are unchanged, namely, in case two financial institutions become bankrupt, two financing variants are evaluated (RF and RF+DGS), as well as the unfavorable (need of engaging resources equivalent to 100 per cent of own capital) and favorable (applying the value of 50 per cent of own capital) scenarios.

6.6.1   RF Variant Only

Table 6.8 demonstrates the division of EU countries based on the maximum intervention scope in relation to two subsequent financial entities covered by the procedure (two consecutive financial institutions similar in terms of the size of own capital). A result which, for instance, assesses the scope at eight or nine points, means that two banks that took the eight and ninth spots in the country financial sector (in terms of own capital) may be restructured simultaneously with the use of resolution funds. Naturally, costs of resolution of both financial institutions are bigger than for a single entity, and the resolution fund budget was set permanently at one per cent of covered

Table 6.8 Division of EU countries based on their resolution scopes when two failing financial institutions are being restructured in the RF variant only

Evaluation of resolution capabilities	High	Moderate	Low
Range in which the two subsequent institutions are present	1–5	6–10	Above 10
Unfavorable scenario	Greece	Croatia, Czech Republic, Estonia, Finland, Lithuania	Austria, Belgium, Bulgaria, Cyprus, Denmark, France, Spain, Netherlands, Ireland, Luxembourg, Latvia, Malta, Germany, Poland, Portugal, Romania, Slovakia, Slovenia, Sweden, Hungary, Great Britain, Italy
Number of countries	1	5	22
Favorable scenario	Greece	Croatia, Cyprus, Czech Republic, Estonia, Finland, Spain, Netherlands, Lithuania, Latvia, Malta, Portugal, Romania, Slovakia	Austria, Belgium, Bulgaria, Denmark, France, Ireland, Luxembourg, Germany, Poland, Slovenia, Sweden, Hungary, Great Britain, Italy
Number of countries	1	13	14

Source: Author's own formulation based on results of the study presented in Table A.11 of Annex VII

deposits. The BRR Directive assumes that countries with such a resolution fund will be capable of eliminating financial institutions on the brink of bankruptcy, as long as normal market conditions apply. Nevertheless, verification of data on particular countries brings less optimistic results.

Unfavorable Scenario

As revealed by data presented in Table 6.8, it is only a theoretical assumption, as—in the case of two insolvencies in a banking sector—most EU countries (22) have a low scope of intervention. There is only one country in the group with high resolution capabilities—Greece. As mentioned earlier, the state is already engaged in the process of restructuring its financial sector, thus positively influencing the results of the study (low own capital of many institutions). The group with an average evaluation is comprised of five states, which are additionally characterized by small banking sectors. In the group, Estonia and Lithuania marked best as capable of restructuring banks with the sixth and seventh positions in the country financing sector. The last group is constituted by the majority of EU countries. What is especially disturbing is the fact that Great Britain is not capable of carrying out resolution of two financial institutions higher than positions 24 and 25. Respectively, Italy could restructure institutions with positions 17 and 18, and France—16 and 17.

Favorable Scenario

In the more favorable scenario, due to forecasted lower resolution costs, the scope of potential intervention increases. The resolution capability does not, in fact, improve for the top states, and Greece once again is the only country in the first group. This reflects negatively on the planned reform, because even with a mild outbreak of problems at financial institutions, virtually no country will be capable of supporting two banks that are among the top five players of the sector. However, the size of the middle group, capable of restructuring two entities that scored between six and ten on the financial sector scale, has increased. The fact that Spain and the Netherlands have advanced into the group of countries with a mid-sized financial sector, and are capable of carrying out resolution of the eight and ninth, and, respectively, ninth and tenth banks or investment companies, is especially worth noting.

Summary

The analysis of the results of the RF variant in both scenarios presented in Table 6.8 (in case two subsequent entities become insolvent in a short time) leads to the conclusion that EU member states, while agreeing on the resolution fund level of one per cent of covered deposits, will find themselves in deficit should a crisis event occur. While the favorable scenario assumes that Greece will be capable of carrying out resolution of two biggest entities (Marfin Investment Group Holdings SA and Alpha Bank AE), it is the only country to achieve such a high result. The last state on the list, Luxembourg, is, in the given conditions, capable of carrying out resolution only in regard to the 32nd and 33rd entities (Banco Bradesco Europa SA and Banque Raiffeisen). Countries with big financial sectors, such as France, Germany, Great Britain, or Spain, witness unsatisfactory results if only the RF variant is applied. It must also be kept in mind that simultaneous insolvency of more than two entitles is possible, as it occurred in certain EU countries in the years 2007–14. At this level of the study, if more than one entity becomes insolvent, it is apparent that many institutions will clearly remain outside the scope of resolution in both scenarios. Therefore, while it may be assumed that resolution has a high change of success in case a single institution is salvaged, it becomes highly unlikely if two or more institutions require simultaneous assistance.

6.6.2 RF+DGS Variant

Further on, it was required that the scope of successful intervention during insolvency of two consecutive institutions in the RF+DGS variant be evaluated. It must be noticed that in such a situation it is much more difficult to assess whether the deposit guarantee scheme will be obliged to take action (hence, if legal premises will be fulfilled), because the condition of deposit ownership in two entities requires a simultaneous analysis.

In case two financial institutions become insolvent, it is possible that one of them will possess many, and the other few covered deposits. An example of such a situation is Cyprus and the SIB Cyprus Ltd. entity (with €3 billion in covered deposits), as well as the "neighboring" Eurobank Cyprus Ltd. (with €2.1 billion in covered deposits). The banks' own capital are, respectively, €558 million and €529 million. One per cent of resolution fund in Cyprus corresponds to €519 million only, while the resources of the deposit guarantee scheme account for another €208 million. It may be acknowledged that in such a situation in the favorable scenario, a sum of €544 million will be required for resolution purposes of both entities. Due to the fact that the Eurobank Cyprus Ltd. entity possesses covered deposits, the participation of the deposit guarantee scheme in its resolution may be increased, and a greater amount of the resolution budget may be used—with scarce deposit use. In the above situation, SIB Cyprus Ltd. will receive more resources from the resolution fund, and Eurobank Cyprus Ltd. will be supported more prominently by the deposit guarantee scheme. Hence, flow between resolution and deposit guarantee scheme funds is possible during the simultaneous resolution of more than one entity. It means that including the deposit guarantee scheme in the resolution process, with the expected insolvency of more than one financial institution, grants the financial safety net a bigger flexibility and more capacity for action in case a crisis event occurs. A similar situation would take place, for instance, in Finland and its "neighboring" entities Finnvera Plc (investment company without covered deposits) and Aktia Bank Plc (bank with covered deposits), or in France (Amundi Group SA and HSBC France SA). Engaging funds of the deposit guarantee scheme in restructuring several financial entities makes its relation with the resolution organ a crucial determinant of the effectiveness of the entire process. Also, the cooperation between the two financial safety net bodies becomes extremely important. A detailed division of the scope of successful intervention in case the RF +DGS variant is applied is presented in Table 6.9.

Unfavorable Scenario

`The scope of intervention with an increased budget of resolution and deposit guarantee scheme funds provides much better results than the RF variant alone. Despite Greece still being the only country of the first group,

Table 6.9 Division of EU countries based on their resolution scopes in the RF+DGS variant, when two failing financial institutions require restructuring

Evaluation of resolution capabilities	High	Moderate	Low
Range in which the two subsequent institutions are present	1–5	6–10	Above 10
Unfavorable scenario	Greece	Croatia, Cyprus, Czech Republic, Estonia, Finland, Spain, Lithuania, Malta	Austria, Belgium, Bulgaria, Denmark, France, Netherlands, Ireland, Luxembourg, Latvia, Germany, Poland, Portugal, Romania, Slovakia, Slovenia, Sweden, Hungary, Great Britain, Italy
Number of countries	1	8	19
Favorable scenario	Cyprus, Estonia, Greece,	Lithuania	Belgium, Bulgaria, Croatia, Czech Republic, Finland, Spain, Netherlands, Latvia, Malta, Germany, Poland, Portugal, Romania, Slovakia, Slovenia, Sweden, Hungary, Italy
Austria, Denmark, France, Ireland, Luxembourg, Great Britain			
Number of countries	4	18	6

Source: Author's own formulation based on results of the study presented in Table A.11 of Annex VII

the numerosity of the second has grown significantly in comparison to the application of the RF variant (from five to eight institutions), with Cyprus, Spain, and Malta joining the category. The last group remains numerous and is constituted by as many as 19 countries—all with big financial sectors.

Favorable Scenario

Due to the predicted lower costs of resolution, the arrangement of countries in particular groups changes in the favorable scenario. In the first party, apart from Greece, there are three countries—Cyprus, Estonia, and Lithuania. The big rise of the second group—countries that may restructure two consecutive institutions of the range 6–10—ought to be evaluated most positively. Altogether, the group is comprised of 18 countries, including Belgium, Spain, the Netherlands, Germany, Poland, Sweden, and Italy, which all have big influence on the stability of the unified EU market. The last group, hence, countries with a low score, is made of six states, including Denmark, France, and Great Britain. What is most disturbing in case of the latter mentioned is that with such lowered conditions, it is only capable of carrying out resolution of the 15th and 16th entities. Taking into consideration that in the years 2008–14 Great Britain recapitalized banks with a sum of €100 to €113 billion (depending on the source), it seems that even after the introduction of the BRR Directive, the country will be condemned once again to public aid (Iwanicz-Drozdowska et al. 2016).

Summary

The analysis of the results of the RF+DGS variant evaluation inclines that thanks to resources of the deposit guarantee scheme, the scope of successful intervention toward two banks, which require simultaneous aid, is constantly increasing. The rise of effective interventions' scope needs to be evaluated positively. The extension of the middle group (6–10 range) deserves special recognition. It may also be assumed, with strong probability, that in case more than one institution becomes insolvent, chances for the lowering of assembly costs will rise. This is due to the fact that the entire administrative apparatus is initiated once for several institutions, for instance, through the creation of a single bridge institution or asset management tool. This, in turn, shall positively augur for the resolution of multiple entities. In summary, the analysis of changes in the scope of successful intervention (hence, the comparison of results of the RF and RF+DGS variants in case two financial institutions fail) may be referred to. Details are provided in Table 6.10.

Table 6.10 Division of EU countries based on the changes of the resolution scope after the deposit guarantee scheme becomes a co-financing side

Change of scope of successful intervention	Significant	Moderate	No influence
Scale of rise of successful intervention scope	Above 2	1–2	0
Unfavorable scenario	Austria, Belgium, Netherlands, Ireland, Luxembourg, Latvia, Poland, Romania, Great Britain, Italy	Bulgaria, Croatia, Cyprus, Czech Republic, Denmark, Finland, France, Spain, Lithuania, Malta, Germany, Portugal, Slovakia, Slovenia, Hungary	Estonia, Greece
Number of countries	10	16	2
Favorable scenario	Bulgaria, Denmark, Ireland, Luxembourg, Malta, Germany, Poland, Romania, Slovenia, Sweden, Great Britain, Italy	Austria, Belgium, Cyprus, Estonia, France, Spain, Netherlands, Lithuania, Latvia, Portugal, Slovakia, Hungary	Croatia, Czech Republic, Finland, Greece
Number of countries	12	12	4

Source: Author's own formulation based on results of the study presented in Table A.11 of Annex VII

The analysis of data presented in Table 6.10 reveals that EU countries gain notably on the inclusion of deposit guarantee scheme funds in resolution. The biggest beneficiaries in the unfavorable scenario are Luxembourg and Belgium, which note changes of seven and five positions, respectively. As for the favorable scenario, Germany, Denmark, and Ireland note the increase in successful interventions by four institutions each. Lack of influence in the case of certain countries also deserves explanation. Such an occurrence is caused most often either by the achievement of maximum restructuring capabilities prior to the inclusion of the deposit guarantee scheme in the process (Greece), or the specificity of the financial market structure. For instance, in the Czech Republic, the latter case is caused by the big value of own capital of the subsequent entity (Hypotecni banka a.s.), which, given the budgets, does not fulfill the requirements of effective resolution.

Finally, in reference to the thread on supplementary analyses mentioned in Section 6.5.3, it would be fruitless to carry out similar studies for bank groups. Such a situation would create a need for an excessive number of theoretical assumptions and, as an effect, cause low applicability and a scarce informative value of the analysis.

6.7 Calibration of National Target Levels

Analyses concerning the effective interventions of country resolution organs lead to a general conclusion that the majority of over 4,000 studied financial institutions are covered by resolution scope and—as a result of resolution organ financial capabilities—the deposit guarantee scheme financial aid as well. Nevertheless, due to their size, a certain part of institutions remains outside the scope of successful intervention in such an event, and their successful restructuring is still impossible. The EU, by setting the resolution fund budget at one per cent, and the deposit guarantee scheme budget at 0.8 per cent of covered funds, indicated target levels of both funds and determined their relationship (target level of the resolution fund higher than that of the deposit guarantee scheme). Although according to global provisions (of the financial safety net in the EU) the above levels are set accurately, after their evaluation on country ground and testing in specific financial market structures, it becomes apparent that the reform does not provide assumed goals, and a big part of institutions still requires alternative support measures—most probably, the recapitalization from public resources.

A solution to the above problem may be the country calibration of target levels of both funds and their respective adjustment to the financial market, so that intervention capabilities in the financial safety net are expanded. Poland may serve as an example of calibration attempt. In the legislation project of the BRR Directive, the Polish legal order was to be calibrated as follows (Ministerstwo Finansów 2016):

– the target level of deposit guarantee scheme resources is equivalent to 2.8 per cent of covered resources provided by the obligatory deposit guarantee scheme,
– the target level of resolution financing resources is equivalent to 1.4 per cent of the value of covered funds.

In the above example, the level of deposit guarantee scheme funds in Poland amounts to €2.9 billion, and the resolution fund—€1.4 billion. Detailed intervention scope of the BRR Directive and national calibration levels are presented in Fig. 6.4.

While analyzing Fig. 6.4, it must be noted that minimal DGS and BRR Directive levels are far from what is required in order to pay out lost deposits or carry out resolution at the top of the financial sector in Poland. As mentioned earlier, the literal implementation of financing as specified in the DGS Directive (with the proposed target level) would allow for the pay out of the 21st biggest financial institution in Poland. Whereas, after country calibration to the level of 2.8 per cent of the value of country covered deposits, the result improve and payouts are already possible for the 12th biggest institution in the country, as measured by its covered deposits' size. In the case of resolution fund levels, the implementation of the directive with the one per cent level of covered deposits' value would allow for the restructuring of the 13th biggest institution. After national calibration to 1.4 per cent of covered deposits' value, salvaging the ninth institution, at most, would thus be possible, and eight remaining entities would be outside successful intervention scope. What is more, combining

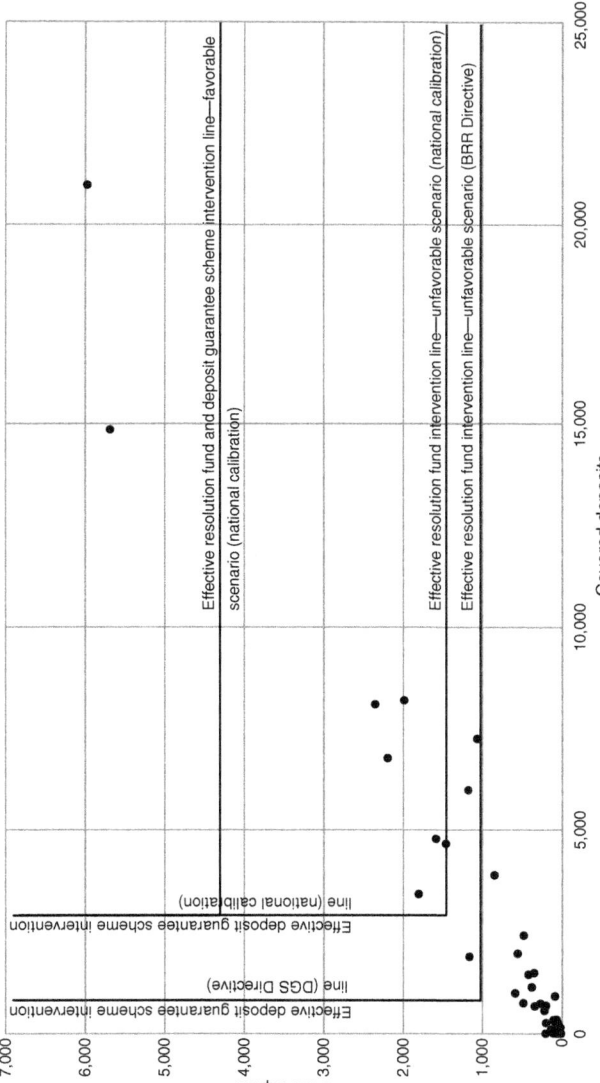

Fig. 6.4   Concentration of financial institutions in Poland and the possibilities of carrying out intervention of the deposit guarantee scheme and the resolution organ (data in millions of euros)

Source: Ministerstwo Finansów (2016)

deposit guarantee and resolution funds would create a budget of €4.3 billion for the sake of potential interventions. Thus (as shown by the highest line, marked in parallel to abscissae), practically all institutions are within intervention scope in the unfavorable scenario (costs of 100 per cent of own capital of institutions), with the exception of two biggest banks in Poland. In the favorable scenarios (costs of 50 per cent of own capital of institutions), intervention possibilities are even more significant, and all financial institutions find themselves within the scope of successful intervention of the resolution authority, supported by resources of the deposit guarantee scheme. It may thus be assumed that the calibration projected in the legislation is accurate and effectively guarantees the proper functioning of the financial safety net in Poland.

Also, another separate issue is the determination of the paths of achieving target levels of resolution and deposit guarantee scheme funds. Rebuilding financial potential after payouts, ensuring the counter-cyclical character of the process, and the orderly definition of the basis of contribution, dependent on the risks a given institution brings into the system, ought to be all predicted. Nevertheless, the above topics exceed the thematic scope of the book (Marcinkowska 2010a, pp. 93–104).

6.8   Conclusion

This chapter verifies the role of the deposit guarantee scheme and its effectiveness in interventions performed toward banks. Two scenarios, favorable and unfavorable, were assumed in resolution effectiveness study, which concern the costs of carrying out the procedure. Both scenarios also included several financing variants: limited, which does not include the role of the deposit guarantee scheme, and extended, which, in accordance with the new approach, assumes the participation of the deposit insurer in financial institutions' restructuring. Furthermore, a simulation of two situations was made—insolvency of a single bank, as well as two similar in terms of own capital size. The analysis revealed that EU countries, due to their varying financial sector structures, differ significantly from one another in terms of financial sector restructuring capabilities. In both scenarios, many entities were proved incapable of effective restructuring. In over 4,000 studied banks and investment companies in the EU, depending on the cost scenario, 160 or 268 of the biggest entities remained outside the scope. Still, as a rule, countries with big financial sectors have unsatisfactory results in terms of financial sector restructuring. The study showed that resolution, in which only own funds are applied, is insufficient, because lack of adequate funds disqualifies a large, remaining group of institutions from successful intervention. Inclusion of the deposit insurance agency in resolution procedures shows that successful restructuring interventions in the EU shall rise, respectively, by 34 and 42 institutions in favorable and unfavorable scenarios. These results are of great importance, because such an extended intervention scope covers the biggest institutions. Nevertheless, it is the great diversity of potential intervention scopes among EU member states, and the fact that— despite the implementation of resolution—226 and 126 entities (in the unfavorable and favorable scenarios) still remain outside the scope of intervention that deserve recognition. Even if costs of potential restructuring will be lower than assumed in the study and part of responsibilities will be taken over by the SRB, it still leads to the conclusion that some of the biggest EU banks and investment companies will remain outside successful intervention scope. Hence, it may be acknowledged that resolution intervention planned on a union level reveals shortcomings toward the biggest entities, thus casting the bank union in negative light.

In light of the studies above, offering a new functioning model of deposit insurance agencies through their inclusion in resolution procedures is of great practical importance. Acknowledging the validity of the above institutions' participation in restructuring and resolution of financial institutions allows for a partial solution to the problem of insufficient financial potential of deposit guarantee schemes.

References

Bennett, R.L.; Unal, H. (2014). *Understanding the Components of Bank Failure Resolution Costs*, Working Paper Series, FDIC.

Bhattacharya, K. (2003). *How Good Is the BankScope Database? A Cross-Validation Exercise with Correction Factors for Market Concentration*

Measures, Monetary and Economic Department, BIS Working Papers, no. 133, September.

BoE. (2014). *Making Resolution Work in Europe and beyond – The Case for Gone Concern Loss Absorbing Capacity*, 17 July.

Bolzico, J.; Mascaró, Y.; Granata, P. (2007). *Practical Guidelines for Effective Bank Resolution*, Policy Research Working Paper, WPS 4389, World Bank, November.

Bureau van Dijk. (2015). *Bankscope Database, World Banking Information Source*, www.bvdinfo.com.

Cannas, G.; Cariboni, J.; Veisari, L.K.; Pagano, A. (2014). *Updated Estimates of EU Eligible and Covered Deposits*, JRC Technical Reports, Report EUR 26469 EN.

DAB. (2015). *Deposit Insurance, Numbers at a Glance*, State Agency for Deposit Insurance and Bank Resolution www.dab.hr (access 24.08.2015).

EC. (2011a). *JRC Report under Article 12 of Directive 94/19/EC as amended by Directive 2009/14/EC*, JRC, Unit G09, Ispra (Italy).

European Council. (2012). *Towards a Genuine Economic and Monetary Union, Report by President of the* European Council *Herman van Rompuy*, Brussels, 26 June, EUCO 120/12.

FDIC. (1997). *Managing the Crisis: The FDIC and RTC Experience*, Washington.

Fonteyne, W.; Bossu, W.; Cortavarria, L.; Giustiniani, A.; Gullo, A.; Hardy, D.; Kerr S. (2010). *Management and Resolution for a European Banking System*, IMF Working Papers, March.

FSB. (2012). *Thematic Review on Deposit Insurance Systems. Peer Review Report*, Basel.

IADI. (2008a). *Annual Survey*, BIS, Basel.

IADI. (2013). *Annual Survey*, BIS, Basel.

IMF. (2014). *Denmark. Financial Sector Assessment Program. Crisis Management, Bank Resolution, and Financial Sector Safety Nets*, Technical Note, Country Report no. 14/351.

Iwanicz-Drozdowska, M.; Kerlin, J.; Smaga, P.; Tomasik, M. (2015). *EU Guarantee Schemes: Status Quo and Policy Implications*, "Journal of Banking Regulation", vol. 16, no. 3.

Iwanicz-Drozdowska, M. (ed.); Kerlin, J.; Kozłowska, A.; Malinowska-Misiąg, E.; Nowak, A.; Smaga, P.; Wisniewski, P.; Witkowski, B. (2016). *European Bank Restructuring During the Global Financial Crisis*, Palgrave Macmillan.

Klingebiel, D.; Laeven, L. (2002). *Managing the Real and Fiscal Effects of Banking Crises*, Discussion Paper no. 428, Washington.

Laeven, L.; Valencia, F. (2013). *Systemic Banking Crises Database: An Update*, IMF Working Paper, WP/12/163, IMF.

Marcinkowska, M. (2010a). *Analizy ryzyka banków dokonywane przez polskie instytucje sieci bezpieczeństwa*, "Zeszyty Naukowe Wyższej Szkoły Bankowej w Poznaniu", nr 29.

Ministerstwo Finansów. (2016). Ocena skutków regulacji projektu z dnia 23 października 2015 r. ustawy o Bankowym Funduszu Gwarancyjnym, systemie gwarantowania depozytów oraz przymusowej restrukturyzacji, Komisja Prawnicza, RCL, 19.01.

Schich, S.; Kim B. (2010). *Systemic Financial Crisis: How to Fund Resolution*, "OECD Journal: Financial Market Trends", vol. 2010, issue 2, December.

Zoli E. (2001). *Cost and Effectivness of Banking Sector Restructuring in Transinion Economies*, IMF Working Paper, WP/01/157, IMF.

7

Readiness of Deposit Guarantee Schemes to Participate in Resolution

7.1 Introduction

This chapter analyzes the readiness of EU deposit guarantee schemes for the participation in resolution. An original method of determining whether deposit insurers are ready for taking on new roles in EU financial safety net is also presented. The procedure, based on the creation of a proprietary readiness index for deposit insurance agencies, allowed for the classification of countries depending on their results. The index was built through the selection of specific deposit guarantee scheme characteristics which determine their readiness for resolution proceedings—among them fund accumulation levels, political position, and legislative authority. The chapter concludes this book with practical recommendations for specific EU member states' groups.

© The Author(s) 2017   251
J. Kerlin, *The Role of Deposit Guarantee Schemes as a Financial Safety Net in the European Union*, Palgrave Macmillan Studies in Banking and Financial Institutions, DOI 10.1007/978-3-319-54163-1_7

7.2   Background and Purpose of the Study

The EU financial safety net has greatly expanded in the post-crisis period. An important institutional change was the creation and inclusion of a new resolution authority in the financial safety net. The above institution, as well as authority related to resolution, might in fact be located in any given place of the financial safety net. Nevertheless, as described in Sections 6.5.2 and 6.6.2, it goes without saying that participants of the safety net ought to cooperate with one another in order to bring positive effects. It seems that the supervisor and deposit insurer will be the most important partners of the resolution organ in the financial safety net. It may be expected that the role of the central bank as the lender of last resort will weaken to some extent, because the BRR Directive oversees in its place the priority of resolution procedures and forbids granting help by the central bank under certain conditions (provisions may be found in Articles 10(3), 15(1), and 36(5) of the BRR Directive). The relationship of the resolution authority with the supervisor will be based mostly on the takeover of problematic entity management duties (after futile early intervention, which lies in the authority of the supervisor), as well the determination of fulfillment of certain conditions required for resolution initiation.

Nevertheless, it seems that the deposit guarantee scheme is a more important financial safety net partner, from which increased engagement in financial market stability maintenance will be henceforth expected. First and foremost, greater commitment of the deposit guarantee scheme in resolution will be compulsory, because, as long as moving from the first (unsuccessful), early intervention phase into resolution is nearly always possible, reaching the deposit payout stage by a failing resolution procedure will not always be probable due to an excessive number of covered deposits in the restructured institution and lack of deposit insurer funds. Such circumstances determine the situation of the deposit guarantee scheme from the actions of the resolution authority and encourage the coordination of actions of both institutions. Secondly, the deposit insurer may significantly support actions of the resolution authority through the application of its capital in resolution tools, thus simultaneously providing depositor protection. It is a completely new, thus far unknown role of the deposit guarantee scheme, triggered by the endurance of the global financial crisis and certain actions of deposits insurers prior to payouts. Thirdly, supporting the transfer of covered funds during resolution strongly enhances intervention capabilities of the resolution organ and lowers costs of deposit guarantee scheme actions (in comparison to those it would have been burdened with in the case of standard payouts). Hence, it is crucial that the role of the deposit guarantee scheme in country financial safety nets in the EU be strengthened through its inclusion in resolution proceedings.

In light of the above, it seems reasonable to determine resolution readiness of EU deposit insurance agencies, as well their potential roles in the procedure. Through the analysis of discrepancies among deposit insurance agencies in the EU, it may be expected that they will represent varying states of preparedness. This, in turn, will influence—positively or negatively—the foreseen effectiveness of the entire procedure.

The study presented in Chapter 7 aims at the verification of the level of EU deposit insurance agencies' preparedness to participate in resolution (resolution readiness) and the evaluation of the different stages in various countries.

Verification of the deposit guarantee scheme's readiness to participate in resolution is justified in light of the new BRR and DGS regulations. Although they foresee the participation of the deposit guarantee fund in the restructuring of financial institutions, the form of participation has not been clearly defined. It is too early to determine the preparation of resolution organs for fulfillment of its designated tasks, because such institutions are in the creation phase, and new provisions and regulations have not been tested in real life. Nevertheless, due to the fact that cooperation between the resolution authority and deposit guarantee scheme in the financial safety net is crucial, it is justified that readiness of the already well-established, existent deposit guarantee schemes in the European financial safety net be verified.

A broad diversification of deposit insurance agencies' resolution readiness levels was expected among various member states. The results of the study have critical implications for the financial safety net in EU countries, because they indicate its weakest elements, as well as the direction reformed country financial safety nets should take in order to make place for more effective financial institution restructuring efforts.

7.3 Method Description

Post-crisis reforms paved the way for new roles of deposit insurance agencies in ensuring the stability of the financial market through its participation in resolution. Thus, an attempt was made of creating an index that would help in the evaluation of the readiness levels of EU deposit insurance agencies for the participation in resolution in accordance with the BRR and DGS Directives. Hence the proposition of the assessment of basic components that shape the institutional construction of the deposit guarantee scheme and, in effect, its successful resolution potential.

During analysis preparations, it was noticed that several distinctive characteristics of deposit guarantee schemes may be indicated. These features are extensively described in Sections 2.3–2.4 and Chapter 3. It may be assumed that some universal characteristics of the deposit insurer, as well as the intensification of certain characteristics, may trigger the increase of deposit insurance agency preparedness for the role of an active resolution participant. Numerous criteria, in which readiness for resolution actions is visible, may be distinguished and include:

- political position of the deposit fund;
- mandate scope (extensiveness of granted authority);
- right to control financial institutions, demand information, and their verification;
- scope of aid and restructuring competences;
- experience in restructuring financial institutions;
- type of management and the independence from pressure on behalf of politicians and other members of the financial safety net;
- organizational and financial resources;
- internal organization method;
- institutional consistency of the deposit guarantee scheme in a given country;

- financial potential of the fund (*ex post* or *ex ante* financing method and the size of accumulated funds);
- freedom of determination of target and bank encumbrance levels;
- institutional engagement in crisis management;
- integration of various guarantee schemes into a single institution (aggregation of depositor, insured, and investors' protection).

Only several of the above-listed characteristics of national deposit guarantee schemes were selected for components of the index in order to determine the readiness of insurance agencies for the participation in resolution, as well a cross-country results comparison. The method of indexing deposit insurers may also be found in the study authored by Demirgüç-Kunt et al. (2014). The so-called Safety Net Index indicates, on the basis of data of country guarantee schemes, the level of generosity of the deposit insurance scheme guarantee granted to depositors.

Eight deposit guarantee scheme characteristics were selected after the analysis in accordance with the availability of data and country comparison possibilities. Altogether, they constitute the Deposit Insurance Agency Readiness for Resolution Index (DIA RRI, as mentioned in the book's introduction). Presented below is a list of arguments justifying the selection of chosen characteristics of the deposit guarantee scheme from the perspective of their added value in resolution procedures. Most index components have been analyzed on a national level in earlier parts of the book, and detailed references to the studies were singled out in Section 7.3. Only two components, the system management method and concentration of guarantee schemes, were not analyzed—hence their detailed study in the following chapter. Chosen components and scoring conditions are presented in Table 7.1.

Scope of mandate of the deposit insurance agency is described more extensively in Section 3.5.1. In order to avoid repetition, it is hereby only stated that the scope of deposit guarantee scheme authority determines its significance for the financial safety net. Hence, it may be assumed that its mandate is an important component of the index. The deposit insurer may be a passive observer of events on the financial market, who anticipates the fulfillment of guarantee requirements prior to taking action after the insolvency of a given financial institution

Table 7.1 Choice of components used for the index establishment along with respective scores

Number	Component name	Classification		Score
1.	Mandate scope	Paybox		0 pts
		Paybox plus		1 pts
		Loss minimizer		2 pts
		Risk minimizer		3 pts
2.	Position in financial safety net	Separate entity of private law		0 pts
		Part of the Ministry of Finance		1 pts
		Part of the financial market		1 pts
		Part of the central bank		2 pts
		Separate public authority entity		3 pts
3.	Coverage ratio	Up to 0 (inclusive)	insufficient	0 pts
		From 0 to 0.5% (inclusive)	scarce	1 pts
		From 0.5% to 0.8% (inclusive)	moderate	2 pts
		From 0.8% to 1.5% (inclusive)	good	3 pts
		Above 1.5%	very good	4 pts
4.	Restructuring experience	None		0 pts
		Moderate		2 pts
		Significant		4 pts
5.	Governance	Private		0 pts
		Mixed		1 pts
		Public		3 pts
6.	Organizational background	0 persons	none	0 pts
		From 0 to 5 persons	scarce	1 pts
		From 6 to 15 persons	moderate	2 pts
		More than 15 persons	good	3 pts
7.	Systemic structure	Multi-entity system		0 pts
		Unified system		1 pts
8.	Concentration	Solo system		0 pts
		Integrated system		1 pts

Source: Author's own formulation

(paybox). Still, it may also actively take steps toward the improvement of the struggling bank's situation (risk minimizer). The scope of deposit fund competences, evaluated in the study, was determined by local member state law. It may not be ruled out that a situation will take place, in which the deposit insurer mandate—despite its broad scope and formal authority (for example France)—will not take action during crisis events. Adequate legal conditions regulating fund activities are crucial for the perception of its role, as well as ensuring an uninterrupted, reliable intervention. A detailed explanation of the mandate determination process in particular countries may be found in Section 3.5.1 and Table A.3 of Annex III. The fact that the closer the risk minimizer mandate to the deposit guarantee scheme in the financial safety net, the better its readiness for resolution, requires recognition. Deposit insurers with a broad scope of capabilities (such as aid, monitoring, and control) and the authority to act as forced administrator or intermediary in the sale or transfer of assets of a bankrupt financial institution are closer to the entire restructuring process (as presented in the BRR Directive) and will, most probably, be better support for the resolution organ throughout the entire process.

Hence, the broader the authority scope of the deposit insurance agency, the higher the evaluation of components. Three points were granted to the broadest of mandates (risk minimizer), while each of the remaining chosen authority scopes was given one point less. In order to increase its role for the index, it has not been decided to raise score of this—apparently—most important component. Firstly, the mandate is only a legal, not factual, exercise. Hence, it may be relatively quickly extended by the enactment of proper law. Secondly, although it is formally broad, it may remain unused—hence, its excessive formal state appreciation would not be valid in reference to the index.

The institutional position of the deposit guarantee scheme in the financial safety net is described in more detail in Section 3.5.3. Here, the only topic indicated is the relation between the insurer and readiness for the participation in resolution. As long as a general analysis is conducted, it is difficult to find direct relations between the two topics. Nevertheless, the deposit guarantee scheme functioning as a separate legal entity has greater chances for participating in resolution proceedings. As a separate entity, its interests (goals) are taken into account with the same consideration as those of remaining participants of the financial safety net. Whereas, if the deposit insurer is an institution existent within the central bank, ministry of finance, or supervisory body, it is treated as a subsidiary, subordinated to the supervisor's or central bank's interest, which regulates its functioning (for instance, as in the case of Slovenia). A lesser conflict of interests takes place when the entity is in the central bank, because goals of both institutions are separate and mostly non-conflicting. Still, the location of deposit insurance functions in the ministry of finance or the supervisor causes a situation, where the insurance agency's concerns are not always taken into account. Thus, the direction of actions in the safety net may be disturbed by the weak position of the deposit guarantee scheme. In case the deposit insurance agency is a subject of commercial law (a separate private company), the situation of the deposit guarantee scheme is evened with other commercial entities, including banks. This means that in practice it may not act from the position of public authority. This, in turn, distances the deposit insurer from the possibility of participating in an authoritative, administrative resolution procedure, in which the state plays the dominant role. The economical practice outside the European continent, where deposit guarantee schemes engaged in resolution procedures are present only in the form of independent public law entities (for example, the United States, Japan, Canada, South Korea, and Malaysia) are also a confirmation of the theses above.

With the above in mind, three points of the index were granted if the deposit insurer was a separate public law entity, two points—if it functioned within the central bank (due to the fact that conflict of interest of these participants were lowest in this case), and one point—if the deposit insurer was located within other public law organs (such as the ministry of finance or the supervisor). No points were appointed to countries, where the deposit insurance agency was entirely private, and were treated simply as "officially recognized". Though burdening for the result of a given country, such a score system is justified, because the institutional position of the deposit guarantee scheme is crucial in this regard. Also, its fast alteration is not possible, because potential reform of the current state-of-being requires the consent of multiple stakeholders.

In this chapter, **coverage ratio** is described only in reference to its choice as an index component. As inclined in Chapter 6, it is most expected of the deposit insurance agency that it aids the resolution procedure should a crisis situation occur. Thus, it increases the scope of successful resolution intervention. The better the financial potential of the deposit guarantee scheme fund, the higher the capabilities of supporting resolution efforts. In the evaluation of the component above, hypothetical indicators of the BRR Directive (hence, equal results for all countries) were not taken into account. Instead, the EU *status quo* as of 2012 was applied, because the inclusion of previous state of affairs clearly accentuates the differences in readiness for resolution of particular insurance agencies. It must hereby be noted that nil coverage ratios lower the results of the component, especially for deposit guarantee schemes operating in the *ex post* system. Nevertheless, its evaluation shall be approached with certain cautiousness, because resolution processes will not always require financial aid on behalf of the deposit insurer or resolution authority, and the procedure may be financed from the restructured fund's resources (for instance, through high values of the MREL index).

Although details on particular score ranges are expressed in Table 7.1, it is the choice of their limiting values that deserves special attention. The levels of 0.5 and 0.8 per cent of covered funds are directly derived for the DGS Directive. The first is the minimum required for achieving action capabilities by a given system (with lowered requirements), while the second value expresses the minimum target level of the deposit guarantee scheme under standard conditions. Meanwhile, the level of 1.5 per cent is a result of the initial proposition of the directive in 2010 (described thoroughly in Section 3.6.4) and is believed to guarantee a proper scope of intervention and freedom of action for the deposit insurer. Nevertheless, the threshold was eventually rejected in legal acts, as it was decided that it would burden banks excessively.

The **resolution experience** is briefly mentioned in Sections 5.6 and 6.2, despite being an important component of the index due to its disclosure of whether deposit insurers have participated in resolution previously. The years 2007–14 were chosen for the analysis, because it was a period of resolution tool use in their new forms. For example, restructuring experiences during bank crises in the 1990s were of different specificity and would have been an erroneous indicator of current readiness of deposit insurance agencies for the participation in a refreshed, post-crisis procedure (including the use of tools such as bail in). Firstly, countries where resolution of financial entities took place were identified. Secondly, the number of events was assessed, scrutinized, and counted with regard to the engagement of covered funds in restructuring procedures.

The score was assigned as follows: zero points—if the deposit guarantee scheme has not thus far participated in restructuring procedures; two points—if it took part in a limited form (for instance, was confined to the transfer of funds and did not take true action in the process), and four points—if the engagement of the deposit guarantee scheme was prominent (for example, the insurer took on various roles, engaged in the creation of the bridge institution, arranged bail in management, bond emission guarantee, and so on). It must be underlined that the allocation of points in the category was most discretionary, because it is difficult to evaluate clearly the actions of deposit guarantee schemes (including the restructuration of cooperative savings and credit unions by the BGF in Poland).

The mode of deposit guarantee scheme management (governance) was not known or analyzed broadly thus far, apart from literature overview and a presentation of views on the subject. Public or mixed governance management in EU countries has taken place in the past evenly among countries and referred to 11 cases in total. Mixed type of governance was dominant among the so-called new EU countries (eight of 11 mixed system cases). Most probably, it was caused by a trend in the 1990s, which relied on the inclusion of the banking sector into deposit guarantee scheme management in economies in their early transition stages. Private management method was present in the majority of small EU economies and concerned six cases. Interestingly, such a system was dominant in German-speaking countries (Austria and Germany).

Methods of management in a deposit insurance agency are a key factor of the preparedness of the deposit guarantee scheme for resolution. Varying management and targeted supervision methods may be hereby distinguished. Depending on the composition of the fund executing body, it may be, respectively, public, mixed, or private governance. Similarly to the legal functioning form, the relation of the composition of the board and resolution is unclear. The participation of banking sector representatives (hence, private board) creates problems in regard to deciding on the mobilization of funds and resolution method choice. As far as supervisors and central banks are concerned, due to obvious conflict of interest, they are not authorized to govern the institutions. Meanwhile, in the case of deposit insurance agencies, an often encountered solution is the inclusion of representatives of the banking sector in the decision process, or even granting a commercial entity total management authority over the fund, as, for instance, in the case of Germany.

For this reason, the scope of the given criterion is adjusted in a way that the private sector, whose board is not public authority, receives the lowest score (0 points). This contests the character of the entire resolution procedure, which is subordinated entirely to public jurisdiction, and enacts administrative decisions. Obstacles of legal nature were also caused by mutual relations of financial safety net participants, in which one institution was under banking sector legislature, while the rest—in terms of organizational hierarchy—represented a superior position (public administration). Mixed governance (present, for instance, in Poland) also creates certain obstacles for guarantee scheme participation in resolution, because members of the sector are directly engaged in the making of strategic decisions (for example, their acceptance) and receive data the deposit insurance agency is authorized for, thus weakening its negotiation position (for example, in asset separation transactions aimed at market sale in the form of auction). The most desired position is such, where the deposit insurance agency has a board resembling the central bank, hence, is formally independent from pressure from the banking sector. On the other hand, deposit guarantees are different than supervisory relations and are not subject to such restrictive legal frameworks. The system management concerns mentioned above are not an isolated case and were also expressed, for instance, by G. Garcia (1999) and the IMF, which recommended Poland the change of BGF council members

(World Bank 2013, p. 9). A certain compromise solution is the maintenance of engagement of the banking sector in the relations with the deposit guarantee scheme, but through an external monitoring and advisory committee.

For this reason, private governance received 0 points as the least applicable solution from the resolution perspective. Mixed governance, comprised of representatives of public authorities and the banking sector, received 1 point, and an entirely public board was given 3 points as most effective in resolution decision making processes.

Organizational capacity of the deposit insurance agency is a component of the index described broadly in Section 3.5.2. In order to clarify its significance for the index, its application methods ought to be clarified. In the following book, organizational capacity is perceived solely through the prism of its human capacity—hence, employees dedicated to deposit guarantee issues. Moreover, it may not be said that a given deposit insurance agency is ready for resolution, if it has scarce organizational potential at its service. Additional troubles for the given category are caused by the fact that deposit insurance agencies in certain countries are strongly supported by other participants of the financial safety net (for example, in France). Analyzing operative potential of the entire country deposit guarantee scheme would be a certain solution to the problem. Nevertheless, first and foremost, it would not create an entirely accurate component of the index, because it is focused primarily on the analysis of the given deposit insurance agency's condition as a separate legal entity. Secondly, a supportive participation of other members of the financial safety net would be difficult for the proper quantification in all EU countries, making space for the allegation of broad discretion of category treatment.

Setting score boundaries for this category was the biggest challenge, because it is difficult to valuate objectively when operational capabilities of the deposit insurer, expressed in human potential, become moderate, and at what employment point they transform permanently. In addition, a modification possibility of the system exists, based on the comparison of human resources in relation to the banking sector of a given country. This is true, because personnel are perceived differently in the case of the four employees in France (where guarantee procedures are additionally supported by the supervisor) and distinctively in the Czech Republic. Regardless, it is difficult to assess the advantages of the scale in such a situation. EBA assessments indicate that operation of resolution functions in their minimal state will be, depending on the state, from five to 18 people in countries, where institutions of systemic gravity (from the perspective of EU stability) do not exist. As for countries, where such entities are present, the EBA did not even indicate the expected or recommended levels of employment (EBA 2015e). During the evaluation of the implementation process of the BRR Directive in Poland, an assessment of regulation effects has been prepared (Ministerstwo Finansów 2016), which revealed that employment resulting from the assignment of resolution functions to the BGF shall increase by 50 per cent (hence, from 100 to 150 people). Eventually, three thresholds were assigned: zero, five, and 15 persons. Thus, EU countries were divided into nearly even groups (five, ten, five, and eight countries, respectively). Points were allocated depending on the range, and funds with a greater number of employees were promoted.

For this reason, zero points were assigned in case a given deposit insurance agency had no employees holding permanent positions (such a situation took place mainly when the deposit insurer functioned within a different institution of the financial safety net). One point was assigned when the organizational base was scarce, and employment did not exceed five persons. Two points were granted, when the potential of human resources in deposit insurance agencies ranged from 6 to 15 individuals, and 3 points, when it exceeded 15 people.

The systemic structure of the deposit guarantee scheme is described thoroughly in Section 3.3.2., still, its relation to the preparedness of the guarantee scheme for participation in resolution is important. In the case of multi-stakeholder systems, a complication arises in crisis management during resolution procedures. More than one representative of the deposit guarantee scheme, which is comprised of multiple institutions, ought to be engaged (for instance, in Germany). It means that it is potentially more difficult to work out a common position, because more participants who—paradoxically—may have conflicting goals become engaged in the process. A situation may occur, where one deposit guarantee fund (responsible for the institution on the brink of bankruptcy), appropriate, for instance, for savings unions, wants its complete takeover be another financial institution such as a bank (healthy entity), which is under jurisdiction of a different, separate deposit insurance agency. From the second institution's point of view the situation may be unfavorable, because it increases its responsibility in case the takeover does not salvage the failing institution. When the guarantee scheme is unified (namely, run by a single insurance agency), and its responsibility is concentrated in one institution, its readiness for successful resolution participation rises.

Scoring of the above criterion was limited to granting either zero or one point. Zero points were granted in the case of the multiple systems, while unified systems—as a solution better fitting for resolution purposes—were given one point.

Concentration of guarantee schemes is the last component of the index, whose importance was accredited in Chapter 2, but requires further explanation. In case a single entity is authorized not only to provide protection of depositors, but also investors and insurance holders, the deposit guarantee scheme gains new perspectives and a broader authority scope. Thus, the agency is better prepared for the participation in resolution of not only banks, but also, for instance, investment companies. Knowing the specificity of investment firms through providing protection services for its participants, the entire system is more efficient. Also, the occurrence of synergy, created by the aggregation of experiences of various financial institutions, the effective information flow, and administrative savings may all be indicated (IADI 2015c). In the case of authority concentration (present, for instance, in Great Britain) in one entity, it is easier to coordinate resolution actions—especially when a problematic institution holds not only covered deposits, but also protected investments. Through the concentration of multiple functions in the British deposit insurance agency (FSCS), Great Britain also introduced the participation of resources from the investor protection scheme, which will be used for the resolution of investment companies. While the solution is not required by the BRR Directive, it resembles participation of deposit guarantee scheme funds presented in Article 109 of the document.

18 EU countries chose the solo system, while the integrated scheme was present in ten member states. An example of the largest aggregate combining all the guarantee institutions (policy holders, investors, and depositors) is the above-mentioned FSCS. Integrated systems exist only in countries of the old EU, apart from Malta, where all guarantors are aggregated under the supervisory agency.

It seems that the component of concentration of the scheme is of lesser importance for the index and resembles the element describing the systemic structure of the system. Hence, either zero or one point was assigned.

As a summary of the description of index components and scores, it must be underlined that rating was adjusted to components of various ranges, so that their gravity and importance are differentiated. The highest rating in a given category means the best fulfillment of given criteria by the deposit insurance agency—hence, its readiness for participation in resolution. While the assessments are largely qualitative and discretionary, the assignment of points was an attempt at justifying the choice of components and indicating index construction weaknesses. Translating specific results of the description of deposit insurance agency characteristics into scores allows for the more synthetic, transparent presentation method of the analysis, as well as the indication of deposit insurers best fit for the important EU financial safety net resolution role.

Lastly, the omission of certain deposit insurance agency characteristics and lack of their inclusion in the index also deserve clarification. These include, among others, auditing power and supervision over the fund, which may, theoretically, be incorporated in every—even the narrowest—mandate. Nevertheless, it has been decided that they are moderate traits, despite being extensively included in the scheme's mandate scope. As for the organizational capability, only human potential has been taken into account, despite the fact that studies (featured in Section 3.5.2) enabled the classification of annual administrative budget to their category. Nevertheless, inclusion of the second component would lead to the monetary value problem in various EU states and would complicate comparisons due to the fact that budget is not determined often through the prism of capabilities and competences of the fund, but country systemic objectives and the institutional form of deposit insurance agencies. Similarly, method of internal organization of the fund would not be a good component of the index, although, in certain studies, such factors as the presence of an analyses or crises management department at the deposit insurance agency are perceived as important. As far as limited analysis is concerned, it may be assumed that it is partially included in the human resources factor.

7.4   Data Sources

Before the analysis, it is necessary to clarify sources of data used for the evaluation and scoring of each component of the index. The primary source of data was the author's own research, based on an analysis of national laws that stipulate the existence of certain insurance agencies. The data were also supported with results of other analyses, whose author's published data corresponding to the research. Detailed data sources may be found in Table 7.2.

The findings of the author were cross-verified with multiple databases corresponding with the study area. Checking and verifying information was necessary because of numerous doubts about the eligibility of

Table 7.2 Sources of data used in the research, divided by components

Number	Component	Data sources subsidiary to the author's own research	State as of the end
1.	Mandate scope	– Iwanicz-Drozdowska et al. (2015)	2012
2.	Position in the finan-cial safety net	– FSB (2014).	
3.	Coverage ratio value	– IADI (2013)	
4.	Restructuring experience	– Iwanicz-Drozdowska et al. (2016)	Period of 2007–15
5.	Governance method	– Iadi (2013) – Demirgüç-Kunt Et Al. (2014)	2012
6.	Organizational capacity	– EC (2011a)	2007
7.	Deposit guarantee scheme structure	– IADI (2015b)	2013
8.	Concentration of the guarantee scheme	– IADI (2015c)	2012

Source: Author's own research

individual deposit insurance agencies for their respective categories and assigning them appropriate characteristics.

An example of dilemmas and inconsistencies is the case of Germany, where the deposit insurance agency mandate was classified by IADI and FSB as paybox, whereas the IMF categorized it as paybox plus and loss or risk minimizer. The situation is similar in the case of Poland and the evaluation of the governance component. The management body of the Polish BGF is constituted by representatives of the Minister of Finance, members of the financials safety net (supervisor—*Komisja Nadzoru Finansowego* (KNF) and the central bank—*Narodowy Bank Polski* (NBP)), as well as two representatives of banks. As a result, a mixed type of board was established, because some of its members are representatives of public authorities, while others come from banks—hence, the private sector. Still, the IMF classified the Polish deposit insurance agency as one existing under public governance. An example of a different approach to the vision of the position of deposit insurance agencies in the safety net may be Cyprus. Although the country's deposit insurance agency is part of the central bank (there is a separate department dedicated to this purpose), the IMF recognized it as an independent, separate entity. The author's experience, including data gathered in previous studies focused on the analysis of insurance agencies in the years 2013–15, was helpful in coding the specific features of deposit insurance agencies.

In order to maintain a consistent approach, all components and their multiple variants were, after a thorough analysis, scored and evaluated in reference to particular countries. The values of the above constituents for given countries may be found in Tables A.13 and A.14 of Annex VIII. Hence detailed justification may be found as follows:

- mandate scope is presented in Table A.3 of Annex III,
- position in the financial safety net is presented in Section 3.5.3,
- coverage ratio is presented in Table 4.2,
- restructuring experience is presented in Sections 5.6 and 6.2, as well as Table 6.7,
- governance method is presented in Chapter 2,
- organizational capacity is presented in Table A.4 of Annex III,

- deposit guarantee scheme structure is presented in Section 3.3,
- concentration of the guarantee scheme is presented in Section 7.2.

The choice of reference year, as well as the application of data, deserves special recognition. With two exceptions regarding the number of employees and the structure of the deposit guarantee scheme, information concerns the year 2012. The reason behind this is the fact that by the end of 2012, most deposit insurance agencies in the EU were already publicly reporting data derived from the extensive works of the European Commission on the new directives, as well as the efforts of the FSB on new regulatory key attributes. Selecting the end of 2012 for most of the components of the index allowed to keep the completeness of data for all countries and to maintain comparability among insurance agencies. Unfortunately, current data on the number of employees of individual insurance agencies are not available. Nevertheless, it must be noted that since the year 2007, there were no significant changes in deposit guarantee scheme organizational structures in the EU.

7.5   Analysis of Results and Concluding Remarks

Both complete and partial results are presented in Annex VIII. Moreover, two tables have been complied: Table A.13—for components one to four, and Table A.14—for components five to eight of the index, as well as the final result. The higher the score (higher value of the index), the better, as a rule, the preparedness of the deposit insurance agency for resolution. The maximum possible value was 22, and the minimum—zero points. The value of the index for each EU country is presented in Fig. 7.1. EU countries scored between four and 18 points, with the arithmetic mean of 9.4 points (marked black on the chart). Looking at the results obtained in DIA RRI, EU countries can be divided into three basic groups:

- group 1—countries with deposit insurance agencies well prepared for the participation in resolution; includes Denmark, Poland, and Spain (results ranging from 15 to 18 points),

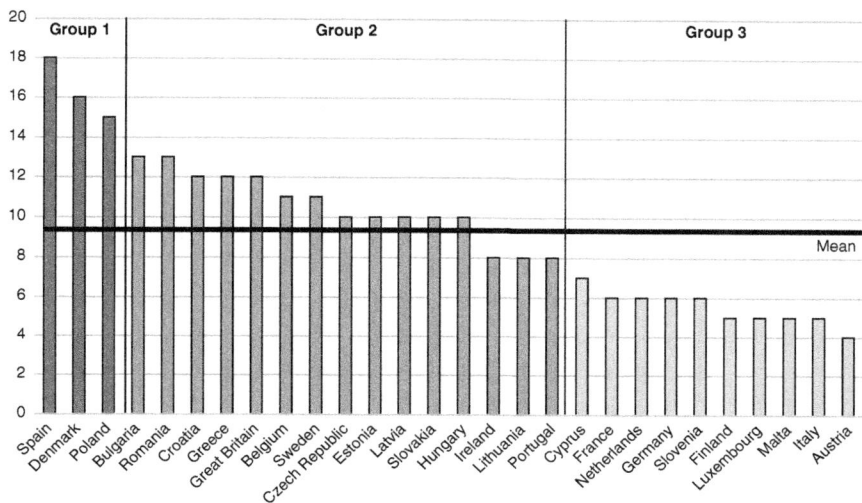

Fig. 7.1 Results of DIA RRI analysis
Source: Author's own formulation based on data from Annex VIII

- group 2—countries with deposit insurance agencies moderately prepared for participation in resolution, which can further be divided in
  three subgroups:

  • above average, which includes: Bulgaria, Romania, Croatia,
    Greece, Great Britain, Belgium, and Sweden (results of 11–13
    points),
  • average, which includes: Czech Republic, Estonia, Latvia, Slovakia,
    and Hungary (10 points each),
  • below average, which includes: Ireland, Lithuania, and Portugal
    (results equal to 7 points),

- group 3—countries with deposit insurance agencies insufficiently prepared for participation in resolution, among them: Cyprus, France, the
  Netherlands, Germany, Slovenia, Finland, Luxembourg, Malta, Italy,
  and Austria (results within the 4–7 point range).

The results of DIA RRI indicate high diversity among EU countries. It reveals that Spain and Denmark are best prepared, while Austria is at the opposite edge. It is difficult to identify clear regularities in index results. Nevertheless, there is a visible pattern in the poor final results of countries with an *ex post* guarantee scheme, such as Italy, Austria, Germany, Luxembourg, and Slovenia. The above countries bring up the rear with worst results. Financing in the *ex post* variant directly influences the coverage ratio component. Still, the decision on *ex post* financing also indirectly influenced other characteristics of the deposit insurance agency, such as the way of governing the scheme (mostly private) or the scarce organizational capacity (modest number of employees). The second indicator is the separation of the old EU into two groups. Countries such as Spain, Denmark, Greece, or Sweden are characterized by a relatively big value of the readiness factor and are at the top of the ranking. As for the second group (countries on the opposite edge), these are the earlier mentioned countries with *ex post* financing variants, as well as Finland, France, and Cyprus. The majority of new EU countries are situated in the middle of the result list. The mean for old EU countries is 8.9 points, whereas new EU scored, on average, 9.9 points. When drawing conclusions, it is also important to refer to EU country plans in regard to the engagement of their deposit insurance agencies in resolution. As indicated earlier (in Table 5.8), four countries have foreseen the role of the resolution organ, related to the deposit insurance agency. These countries are Poland, Croatia, Sweden, and Finland, which received, respectively, 15, 12, 11, and as little as five points. In the case of Poland and Croatia, the planned participation of the deposit insurer in resolution is significant and is accredited with a dominant role, because it will perform part of resolution functions. As for Finland and Sweden, the role of the deposit insurance agency is scarce, nevertheless, along with the resolution organ, they will be located in the same entity.

As the evaluation of readiness of deposit insurance agencies for the participation in resolution brought results that indicate a wide diversification in the field, the presentation of two deposit insurer engagement concepts, corresponding with each recognized country group, was required. The analysis of each of the three groups leads to the conclusion that EU countries can choose from two target scenarios of their respective financial safety nets' development, as seen through the prism of the deposit guarantee scheme role.

Each country—as indicted in Chapter 6—ought to mandatorily include the deposit insurer in resolution financing procedures. The BRR Directive requires such an act, nevertheless, the anticipation of financial participation only is insufficient. Thus, the inclusion of the deposit insurer to the orderly liquidation procedure ought to be taken into consideration in two basic scenarios:

- deposit insurance agency in the risk minimizer or resolution authority role, as well as the leading resolution institution,
- deposit insurance agency in the paybox model, with a subsidiary resolution role.

Two deposit insurer placement capabilities are presented in Fig. 7.2. The above-proposed inclusion of deposit insurance agencies in crisis management may redefine their role and mark a new chapter in their development history. The guarantee fund may:

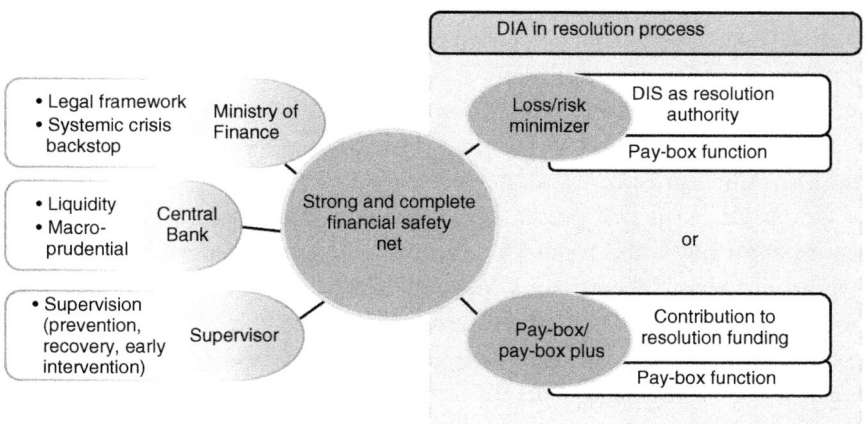

Fig. 7.2 Institutional system of the financial safety net and the role of the deposit insurance agency in resolution

Source: Pruski (2014b)

- become a prominent entity in resolution procedures, as well as perform the role of resolution organ, or—alternatively—share these functions with another financial safety net entity, for example, the supervisor,
- be marginalized; its role may be narrowed down to a procedure financing body, without a decisive authority scope.

It seems that other scopes of authority of the deposit guarantee scheme may be impossible to maintain in light of upcoming reform. Restructuring competences would duplicate during resolution procedures and for an independent deposit insurance agency with a wide authority scope. It would not be known when the fund would be capable of starting its intervention, and in what relation to resolution organ intervention it would be (Schich 2011). Furthermore, it would be an uneven form of depositor situation creation in EU countries.

Certain practical solutions applied by particular countries indicate the interest of leaders in the inclusion of deposit insurance agencies in resolution in the financial safety net (Singh and Walker 2009). An example is Croatia (where part of resolution procedure authority was granted to the national guarantee scheme), Slovakia (where an independent entity was established during resolution organ establishing efforts, with active participation of the guarantee scheme), and Poland (where, according to the macroprudential supervision act, resolution authority was granted to the deposit insurer—BGF).

With the above in mind, Table 7.3 includes recommendations aimed at all specified groups.

Countries of the first group (hence, with good deposit insurance agency readiness for resolution results) are recommended the strengthening of their deposit insurers to the extent, which will allow to perform a significant—if not leading—role in the whole resolution process. It seems possible to combine tasks and responsibilities of the deposit insurer and resolution organ in one institution. This, in turn, may bring benefits in the form of facilitating crisis management in the financial safety net, as well as have a positive influence on the efficiency and reduction of administrative costs of deposit insurance agencies (FSB 2011). Housing of two members in a single entity has occurred in the past in the financial safety net of the EU.

Table 7.3 Division of deposit insurance agencies on the basis of their readiness for resolution evaluation

Group number	Evaluation of readiness of the deposit insurance agency to participate in resolution	Average group score	Countries	Recommendation
First	Good	16.33	Spain, Denmark, Poland	Strengthening of deposit insurance agencies and the merger of functions with the resolution authority
Second	moderate (above average)	12.40	Bulgaria, Romania, Croatia, Greece, Great Britain	Strengthening of the deposit insurance agency and the unification of its functions with the resolution organ or limiting the deposit insurer authority (winding up of aid activities) and caring for its financial condition only
	Moderate (average)	10.29	Sweden, Belgium, Latvia, Estonia, Czech Republic, Slovakia, Hungary	
	Moderate (below average)	8.00	Ireland, Lithuania, Portugal	
Third	Insufficient	5.50	Cyprus, Netherlands, Slovenia, France, Germany, Malta, Finland, Luxembourg, Italy, Austria	Reform of the deposit insurance agency and its adjustment to global standards, as well as making it a reliable resolution organ partner in the financial safety net

Source: Author's own formulation

An example of such a solution may be, for instance, granting supervisory rights and their location in the central bank (the lender of last resort) in Great Britain and Spain. Although the concept of the dominant role of the deposit insurance agency in the financial safety net is not, as it seems, popular in the EU, it is successfully applied in other world countries (the United States, Canada, Japan), and could be transposed to European ground. The inclusion of the above institutions has solid grounds, supported by positive experiences of other countries. On this occasion, it is worth noticing Poland, where the resolution organ role was granted to the deposit insurance agency. The high evaluation of the BGF in the index indicates that merging two institutions into one organization is justifiable and provides good future prospects.

Countries of the second group (with an average evaluation of deposit insurance agency readiness for the participation in resolution) are recommended one of two scenarios. The first could be advantageous for countries of the above average group (Bulgaria and Romania), where strengthening of the deposit insurer to the extent, in which it would be capable of playing a dominant role in resolution, is possible. Still, it is realistic only if the deposit insurer has a separate institutional structure. It would be particularly justified in Sweden, where the planned location of resolution authority is one of the Ministry of Finance agencies—*Riksgälden* (the Swedish National Debt Office). Hence, in the country, the resolution and deposit insurance authorities will belong to one institution, despite it being highly dependent on the government. In the second scenario, it may be recommended to preserve limited authority of deposit insurance agencies and marginalize their role, so that their financial stability is only cared for. Such an approach is particularly recommended to countries that reached a below average score (for instance, Ireland and Portugal), where the resolution organ role will be taken over by stronger and more experienced participants of the financial safety net. In these two countries, deposit insurance and resolution authorities will be granted to country central banks and will be unified in a single institution.

The third group of countries (with an insufficient assessment of deposit insurance agency readiness for resolution participation) ought to remodel their financial safety net in the fastest possible mode, as well as care for the proper construction of the deposit insurance agency structure. Deposit insurance institutions in these countries are usually very limited in operational form and are not, as a rule, ready either for resolution, or payouts of covered deposits. It fulfills the psychological component only, which—as revealed by the recent financial crisis—cannot succeed alone. In countries such as France, Germany, or Italy, it is necessary to remodel the financial safety net and adapt the role of the deposit insurance agency at least in its minimal form to post-crisis reform trends. It is worth noting that countries with the lowest results in the index start from a difficult position, but—if sufficient reformatory efforts are made, and one of the deposit insurance agency development paths is chosen—they may quickly remedy their financial safety net shortcomings. The only exception is the accumulation of funds from banks, which is usually a long-term commitment. It may be anticipated that deposit insurance agencies in the EU will not have leading roles in their countries, nevertheless, they need to be remodeled into reliable partners of the resolution organ to the biggest possible extent.

The comparison of results of countries in Chapter 6 (RF and RF+DGS variant scope) with the analysis outcome in Chapter 7 (Deposit Insurance Agency Readiness for Resolution Index) does not allow for the formulation of clear conclusions and disclosure of dominant relations. Countries with high rise of intervention effectiveness (in the RF+DGS variant) achieved both high and low scores in the readiness index.

7.6   Conclusion

This chapter tackles the problem of EU deposit insurance agencies' readiness for the participation in resolution. The proposed index includes basic characteristics of deposit insurers, which reflect their readiness for the procedure. These include, among others, financial potential, management method, and legislative authority. The analysis of index results allowed for the distinction of three basic groups of countries, divided on the basis of the readiness of their deposit insurance agencies for resolution. These groups represent deposit guarantee schemes with good, moderate, and insufficient preparedness for resolution. Analysis of all three groups leads to the conclusion that in terms of deposit guarantee scheme roles, EU countries may choose between two scenarios of financial safety net development. These may be either creating a deposit insurance agency with the role of a risk minimizer entity or resolution organ with a leading resolution role, or a deposit insurance agency acting solely, in terms of financing resolution, as a paybox participant. An important conclusion is the fact that other scopes (scenarios of role development) of deposit guarantee schemes are impossible to maintain in light of upcoming reform. If resolution and an independent deposit insurance agency were to act simultaneously, their restructuring competences would have overlapped. Thus, the appropriate time for fund intervention would not be known, and its relation to the resolution organ would remain undetermined.

References

Demirgüç-Kunt, A.; Kane, E.; Laeven, L. (2014). *Deposit Insurance Database*, IMF Working Paper, no. 14/118.

EBA. (2015e). *Resourcing and Skillset, Survey Results*, February.

EC. (2011a). *JRC Report under Article 12 of Directive 94/19/EC as amended by Directive 2009/14/EC*, JRC, Unit G09, Ispra (Italy).

FSB. (2011). *Key Attributes of Effective Resolution Regimes for Financial Institutions*, Basel, October.

FSB. (2014). *Towards Full Implementation of the FSB Key Attributes of Effective Resolution Regimes for Financial Institutions*. Report to the G20 on Progress in Reform of Resolution Regimes and Resolution Planning for Global Systemically Important Financial Institutions *(G-SIFIs)*, 12 November.

Garcia, G. (1999). *Deposit Insurance: A Survey of Actual and Best Practices*, IMF, WP/99/54, April.

IADI. (2013). *Annual Survey*, BIS, Basel.

IADI. (2015b). *(nce Systems: Multiple Deposit Insurance Organizations)*, Guidance Paper, June.

IADI. (2015c). *Integrated Protection Schemes*, Research Paper, March.

Iwanicz-Drozdowska, M.; Kerlin, J.; Smaga, P.; Tomasik, M. (2015). *EU Guarantee Schemes: Status Quo and Policy Implications*, "Journal of Banking Regulation", vol. 16, no. 3.

Iwanicz-Drozdowska, M. (ed.); Kerlin, J.; Kozłowska, A.; Malinowska-Misiąg, E.; Nowak, A.; Smaga, P.; Wisniewski, P.; Witkowski, B. (2016). *European Bank Restructuring During the Global Financial Crisis*, Palgrave Macmillan.

Ministerstwo Finansów. (2016). Ocena skutków regulacji projektu z dnia 23 października 2015 r. ustawy o Bankowym Funduszu Gwarancyjnym, systemie gwarantowania depozytów oraz przymusowej restrukturyzacji, Komisja Prawnicza, RCL, 19.01.

Pruski, J. (2014b). *Ewolucja światowego systemu ochrony depozytów oraz systemu recovery i resolution*, BFG, Warszawa.

Schich, S. (2011). *Financial Crisis: Deposit Insurance and Related Financial Safety Net Aspects*, OECD.

Singh, D.; Walker, D. (2009). *The European Deposit Guarantee Directive: An Appraisal of the Reforms, Financial Crisis Management and Bank Resolution*, Chapter 10, September 2009.

World Bank. (2013). *Financial Sector Assessment Program. Poland. BCBS–IADI Core Principles for Effective Deposit Insurance Systems, Detailed Assessment of Observance*, May.

8

Conclusion

The following publication presented the analysis of the changing deposit insurance agency role in the safety net of EU member states in light of postcrisis reform.

Research areas, which have become consolidated throughout the years, have undergone fundamental changes due to global financial crisis experiences. The inadequate financial safety net structure in many countries, including the EU, forced the change of institutional construction of participants of the financial safety net. Since the year 2007, deposit insurance agencies have been dynamically transforming toward more complex action forms. Taking into consideration the history of deposit guarantee, it must be underlined that evolution of deposit insurance agencies is constantly accelerating.

The financial crisis revised numerous functioning concepts of the above institutions, thus approximating them to the issue of bank resolution, which directly antecedes the payout of deposits. Through the analysis of the scope of resolution (created in response to crisis) and the extended tasks of deposit insurers, it may be acknowledged that merger of the two functions took place, and they cooperate in financial safety net bank interventions.

© The Author(s) 2017   **279**
J. Kerlin, *The Role of Deposit Guarantee Schemes as a Financial Safety
Net in the European Union*, Palgrave Macmillan Studies in Banking
and Financial Institutions, DOI 10.1007/978-3-319-54163-1_8

The issue of deposit insurance agency participation in resolution still seems to be insufficiently analyzed. The global financial crisis and changes in EU regulations started an entirely new chapter in deposit insurance agency involvement in the financial safety net.

Until this point, data on deposit insurance agency characteristics were irregularly aggregated. Reasons behind the establishment of guarantee schemes were analyzed with scrutiny, while studies on deposit insurer characteristics, which influence their effectiveness, were only their derivatives. Research achievements have been analyzed, and, on the basis of historical data, stages of deposit guarantee scheme establishment were indicated both for the EU and world countries. Namely, examining the evolution of deposit insurance agencies in the financial safety net of the EU would have been a difficult task without international context. The global financial crisis allowed for the systematization of deposit insurance agency functioning models from a previously unknown perspective—showcasing their increased responsibility, new roles, and tasks.

The scope of scheme authority, their organizational potential, and the allocation of deposit insurers in the financial safety net are examples of key institutional solutions of deposit insurance agencies. Even the analysis of only these results leads to the conclusion that deposit insurers in EU countries differ greatly, despite partial harmonization of solutions created by the DGS Directive of 1994.

Due to ongoing legislative works on the EU forum, the evolution of deposit insurance agencies took place at alternating paces, which were conditioned upon the situation of the financial market. Various approaches toward the above context of deposit insurance agency design have been underlined along with views, which eventually gained approval. These included the necessity of establishing schemes in 1994, the harmonization of guarantee levels in 2009, and, in 2014, the indication of target levels, which ought be achieved by deposit funds, as well as the necessity of collecting bank contributions in an *ex ante* model. As an effect, various deposit insurance agency functioning models have evolved, with significantly diversified competences and varying positions in the financial safety net.

As part of the study, the *status quo* of deposit guarantee schemes' effectiveness has been compared, along with the evaluation of the situation, which will take place after reforms had been introduced (hence, the establishment of DGS and BRR Directives). For this reason, the financial potential of deposit insurance agencies has been analyzed, and the effectiveness of their interventions in a given country evaluated (with the inclusion of the market structure). The evaluation of successful interventions of the deposit insurer indicates that—by the end of 2012—the situation was not favorable. In the majority of EU countries, deposit insurance agencies are incapable of fulfilling designated tasks. The analysis of the existing state of the financial potential of deposit insurers as of the end of 2012 allowed for the conclusion that EU countries may be divided into four basic groups.

The first is comprised of countries with good intervention scope results—hence, their deposit insurance agencies are capable of successfully intervening (paying out deposits) toward banks from the top ten, according to the size of covered deposits. These countries include, among others, Bulgaria, Finland, Sweden, and Romania. The second group with intervention capabilities toward banks that ranked 11–20 includes nine countries, such as Belgium, Poland, and Slovakia. The third group is comprised of countries, whose insurance agencies had insufficient funds and were capable of carrying out payouts for banks which ranked below the 20th place, measured by their covered deposits' value. The last group is constituted by countries, in which deposit insurance agencies operating in the *ex post* model were present. In accordance with the provisions of the study, they were characterized by lack of intervention capabilities, due to the fact that they did not previously accumulate funds. These countries were, among others, the Netherlands, Austria, and Italy.

After the introduction of reforms related to the DGS Directive of 2014, the situation described above shall enhance. Due to the fact that the directive requires accumulation of funds equivalent to 0.8 per cent of covered deposits' value, the scope of successful intervention capabilities of the deposit insurer will rise significantly in some EU countries. The planned reform will have the biggest impact in countries, where the insurance agency has been, thus far, financed in an *ex post* mode (for instance, Italy and the Netherlands). Improved results of big EU economies, such as Germany, France, and Great Britain, also deserve recognition due to the fact that they are to witness a payout improvement by 62, 107, and 149 banks, respectively. Nevertheless, the first two groups (countries capable of successful interventions towards the top 20 banks) are comprised of only 18 countries in total. Nevertheless, a big group of countries still remains capable of dealing with bankruptcy of mid-sized banks only. Despite the improvement of intervention capabilities, countries with low deposit payout capabilities include big EU economies such as Italy, Spain, Great Britain, and Germany. Hence, the reform of EU deposit insurance agencies will not have much impact due to its insufficiently ambitious character. Analyses reveal that changes introduced by the DGS Directive of 2014 will allow for intervention and payout of deposits mainly toward small and mid-sized EU banks, whereas big banks will still remain outside deposit insurance agency capabilities.

It must also be underlined that the long-established concept of deposit guarantee, whose beginnings may be traced to the 1930s, was not reformed for multiple years and does not apply to the scale of problems present on the financial market nowadays, with the existence of modern big banks. The effectiveness of deposit insurance agencies had been declining for years for several reasons. These include, among others, the dynamic development of the banking sector and its current size, big values of covered deposits, the rising concentration in the banking sector, and the low effectiveness of bank insolvency proceedings. Potential obligations of guarantee funds toward the biggest banks in EU countries are too big for the payout of deposits by the guarantee scheme functioning in the pay-box model. As shown in the study, even after the DGS reform as many as 516 of the approximately 8,500 banks in the EU will remain outside deposit insurance agency intervention scope. Thus, new solutions must be sought for in order to enhance the effectiveness of deposit insurance agency operations or to improve their functioning with a new, bank targeted toolkit. In light of analyses' results, it is clear that deposit guarantee schemes in the EU may be unable to properly perform their basic roles, because they do not have sufficient financial potential for the sake of payouts at their disposal—especially in the case of big financial institutions' insolvency.

The analysis of new BRR Directive regulations and their basic goals, provisions, and resolution tools brings several conclusions. One of the most important remarks is the fact that the deposit guarantee scheme role has been recognized as an institutional form of the financial safety net, and insurers became its fully fledged members. It may be concluded from new legal, resolution-related solutions that the situation and scale of public fund use, as seen during the previous global financial crisis, nowadays shall not be as prominent. This is caused by the fact that new regulations limit significantly such intervention capabilities toward financial institutions. Nevertheless, detailed analysis of BRR Directive provisions reveals that certain regulations were worked out on the union level solely to a minimal degree. These include, among others, the creation of a financing mechanism for the new procedure. It may be expected that setting a unified target level of 1 per cent of covered deposit value will be too low for carrying out of successful resolution interventions. In light of the resolution procedure, a greater role of the deposit insurer ought to be noticed throughout the whole process, because goals of both participants of the financial safety net (deposit insurer and the resolution organ) are concurrent and aimed at the same goal—continuity of bank actions and customer service, with special attention to depositors. The latter function is also related to the introduced depositor preference rule, whose effects are not entirely predictable. Analysis of BRR Directive regulations leads to the conclusion that new tasks were foreseen in the financial safety net, which may be fulfilled successfully by the deposit insurance agency. This, in turn, may mean a new functioning model, and a further stage of evolution, mentioned in the title of the following book.

Significance of the deposit insurance agency role and its effectiveness were verified by quantitative measure methods. In the resolution effectiveness study, two scenarios—favorable and unfavorable—were assumed in reference to resolution costs. Both scenarios included different financing variants: limited (exclusive of deposit insurer role) and extended (assuming the participation of the insurer in financial institution restructuring, in accordance with the new approach). Additionally, a simulation of two situations was performed: respectively, the insolvency of one and two banks, similar in size in terms of own capital.

The analysis revealed that EU countries—due to variations of financial sector structure—differ greatly from one another in terms of restructuring capabilities. In case a single entity becomes insolvent in the RF variant (without deposit insurer participation), countries with big financial sectors, such as France, Germany, Great Britain, and Spain, achieve unsatisfactory results in terms of possible financial sector restructuration. In both cost scenarios multiple entities remain outside successful restructuring possibilities. Out of a total of 4,000 analyzed banks and investment companies in EU countries, 160 or 268 biggest entities (depending on the cost scenario) remain outside intervention scope. The analysis revealed that use of resolution fund resources only is insufficient, because there would still remain a big group of institutions, for which successful restructuring actions would be impossible due to lack of funds.

Nevertheless, the analysis of deposit insurance agency inclusion in resolution procedures revealed that an increase of successful restructuring interventions by 34 institutions in the favorable, and 42 in the unfavorable scenario, may be expected in the EU. The results are important not only seemingly for as many as 4,000 analyzed entities— it must be kept in mind that the increase also concerns the biggest of institutions. Still, the prominent diversification of potential intervention scope among EU countries, as well as the fact that despite resolution procedures, 226 or 126 entities (in the unfavorable and favorable scenario, respectively) still remain outside intervention scope, deserves special recognition. Even if costs of potential restructuring will be lower than assumed by the author, and part of responsibilities will be taken over by the SRB and its single financing mechanism, it leads to the conclusion that most EU banks and investment companies still remain outside successful intervention reach. Hence, resolution intervention planned on a union level indicates deficiencies toward the biggest entities. This, in turn, potentially casts the banking union in unfavorable light and hinders its proper functioning in the first years. Therefore, it is crucial that country calibration of target levels of the resolution organ and deposit guarantee scheme takes place, so that they correspond to the specificity of the local financial sector, and the levels declared in the BRR Directive are perceived as the minimum. An example of calibration is Poland, where higher target levels than those required by the DGS and

BRR Directives were proposed, thus enhancing the potential for effective resolution intervention.

In light of the studies above, proposing a new deposit insurance agency functioning model through its inclusion to resolution procedures is of practical significance. The validity of deposit insurance agency participation in resolution has been verified with quantitative measures, with consideration of intervention scope toward banks in different scenarios. Confirmation of the validity of participation of the above institutions in restructuring and orderly liquidation of financial institutions provides a partial solution to the problem of insufficient financial potential of deposit guarantee schemes and is a guideline for country target level calibration.

The BRR Directive imposes changes of the financial safety net structure through the addition of a new entity—the resolution organ. Member states are at liberty to select the institutional shape of the financial safety net. In light of crisis management experiences of the financial safety net of EU countries, it seems necessary that sound cooperation of the supervisor, deposit insurer, and resolution organ be provided during attempts at restructuring a failing bank. Still, due to former development politics of the above institutions in the EU, the role of the deposit guarantee scheme is still overlooked and unappreciated throughout the process. Meanwhile, successful resolution intervention analyses indicate that deposit insurance agencies may play a key role in the restructuring of big and mid-sized financial institutions in accordance with restrictive postcrisis reforms introduced by the BRR Directive, which prohibits the use of public funds for bank rescue, and obliges bank owners to participate in restructuring costs.

EU countries have started resolution organ creation efforts in 2015, nevertheless their activity has not been tested in practice in most cases. Despite the recent commencement of the process of financial resources accumulation for the sake of future resolution actions, funds still remain very modest. Thus, the role of the deposit guarantee scheme rises, especially during the process of acquiring full operability of resolution mechanisms, because, most often, it only has at its disposal funds collected from banks through *ex ante* procedures, which work toward the same goal. Additionally, part of EU deposit insurance agencies possesses authoritative forms of action or restructuring intervention capabilities. Still, due to the earlier indicated institutional diversification among deposit insurance agencies in the EU, and the different positions in the financial safety net, their readiness to support resolution varies greatly.

The above-mentioned facts justified the problem of measuring resolution preparedness of deposit insurance agencies in the EU, analyzed in the following book. The proposed index includes basic deposit guarantee scheme characteristics that express their restructuring readiness. These include, among others, financial potential, management methods, and political position. The analysis of index results allows to distinguish three basic groups on the basis of their deposit insurance agencies' readiness for the participation in resolution.

The first group of countries represents a guarantee scheme properly prepared for resolution actions (for instance, Spain, Denmark, and Poland). In these countries, significant support of financial institution restructuring through the participation of the deposit guarantee scheme, and its strong authority or previously accumulated funds, is realistic. The clearly outlined political position of the deposit insurer in part of the countries above may even allow for the performance of the dominant role in the process, as well as the acquisition of resolution authority functions by the entity mentioned above. The second group of countries represents moderate readiness of the guarantee scheme for the participation in resolution. In this group, three subcategories may be singled out. The first is characterized by its strengthened key specifications as the deposit insurer, such as accumulation of available funds or public governance. This subcategory includes such countries as Bulgaria and Romania. The subcategory of countries with moderate readiness indicators includes, among others, Belgium and the Czech Republic. Countries, such as Ireland and Portugal, ranked below average mainly due to their *ex post* financing variants, or the marginalized institutional position in the financial safety net. Affiliation to the middle group with moderate deposit insurance agency readiness for participation in resolution means that some reforms are required in order for resolution participation provisions to be fulfilled by the deposit insurer. The last group of countries includes such states as the Netherlands, France,

Germany, and Italy, whose guarantee schemes are least ready for participation in resolution. In these countries, the guarantee scheme is deeply unprepared for the postcrisis realm of the financial safety net, and their situation requires radical changes and application of new methods, because, in many spheres, the deposit guarantee scheme does not meet new, regulatory agenda of postcrisis reality.

The analysis of each of the three mentioned groups leads to the conclusion that EU countries may chose between two target scenarios of financial safety net development in regard to the role of the deposit guarantee scheme. It may either take on the role of the risk minimizer entity or—even more radically—resolution organ with the dominant role in the process. Alternatively, the insurance agency may perform paybox model operations with its financial contributions to the procedure only. The fact that other scopes (hence, scenarios of role development) of deposit insurance agencies will, in light of upcoming reform, be impossible to maintain is an important conclusion. In a resolution procedure with an independent deposit insurance agency with broad authority in place, restructuring competences would be duplicated. Thus, the right moment for intervention would not be indicated, nor would its relation to the resolution organ be regulated. Hence, it was concluded that a big diversification in deposit insurance agency readiness for resolution exists in EU countries. Still, the extension of competences of deposit insurance agencies through the inclusion of resolution participation functions will strengthen the financial safety net, enhance depositor protection, and allow for the increase of resolution effectiveness.

Further thematic fields related to deposit insurance agencies and resolution include the monitoring of advancements in postcrisis reform implementation and their influence on the institutional shape of the financial safety net. It is also crucial that relations of the new resolution organ and other participants of the safety net be analyzed in the future. Once first practical experiences come to light, the evaluation of new regulations will also be determinant for future research challenges.

Annex I Deposit guarantee schemes across the world

© The Author(s) 2017
J. Kerlin, *The Role of Deposit Guarantee Schemes as a Financial Safety Net in the European Union*, Palgrave Macmillan Studies in Banking and Financial Institutions, DOI 10.1007/978-3-319-54163-1

Table A.1 Countries where a formalized deposit guarantee scheme is existent, along with year of establishment of the first deposit insurance agency in the given country

Country	Scheme establishment year	Country	Scheme establishment year
United States (2)	1934	Bosnia and Herzegovina	1998
India	1961	Ecuador	1998
Norway	1961	Estonia	1998
Dominican Republic	1962	Gibraltar	1998
Philippines	1963	Indonesia	1998
Germany (7)	1966	Jamaica (2)	1998
Canada (11)	1967	Latvia	1998
Lebanon	1967	Malaysia	1998
Finland	1969	Ukraine	1998
Japan (2)	1971	Guatemala	1999
Belgium	1974	Honduras	1999
Marshall Islands	1975	Kazakhstan	1999
Spain	1977	El Salvador	1999
Netherlands	1978	Bahamas	1999
Argentina	1979	Cyprus (2)	2000
Austria (5)	1979	Jordan	2000
France	1980	Turkmenistan	2000
United Kingdom	1982	Vietnam	2000
Turkey	1983	Bolivia	2001
Bangladesh	1984	Montenegro	2001
Switzerland	1984	Nicaragua	2001
Iceland	1985	Serbia	2001
Colombia (2)	1985	Slovenia	2001
Taiwan	1985	Albania	2002
Venezuela	1985	Uruguay	2002
Chile	1986	Uzbekistan	2002
Mexico (3)	1986	Malta	2003
Trinidad and Tobago	1986	Paraguay	2003
Denmark	1987	Russia	2003
Italy (2)	1987	Zimbabwe	2003
Kenya (2)	1988	Hong Kong	2004
Nigeria	1988	Moldova	2004
Ireland	1989	Tajikistan	2004
Luxembourg	1989	Armenia	2005
Peru	1991	Singapore	2006
Isle of Man	1991	Azerbaijan	2007
Liechtenstein	1992	Barbados	2007

Table A.1 (continued)

Country	Scheme establishment year	Country	Scheme establishment year
Portugal (2)	1992	Australia	2008
Bahrain	1993	Yemen	2008
Hungary	1993	Kyrgyzstan	2008
Czech Republic	1994	Guernsey	2008
Tanzania	1994	Jersey	2008
Uganda	1994	Mauretania	2008
Brazil	1995	Afghanistan	2009
Greece	1995	Libya	2010
Oman	1995	Nepal	2010
Poland	1995	Brunei	2011
Belarus	1996	British Virgin Islands	2011
Bulgaria	1996	Central African Republic	2011
South Korea (6)	1996	Chad	2011
Lithuania	1996	Democratic Republic of Congo	2011
Macedonia	1996	Equatorial Guinea	2011
Morocco	1996	Gabon	2011
Romania	1996	Bermuda	2012
Slovakia	1996	Kosovo	2012
Sudan	1996	Sri Lanka	2012
Sweden	1996	Mongolia	2013
Algeria	1997	Palestine	2013
Croatia	1997	Laos	2014
Thailand	1997	China	2015

Numbers in parentheses express the number of deposit insurance agencies in the given country with a multi-entity deposit guarantee scheme (in this case, the year of establishment of the first deposit insurance agency was featured)

Source: IADI (2013, 2015d), Demirgüç-Kunt et al. (2014), and author's own research

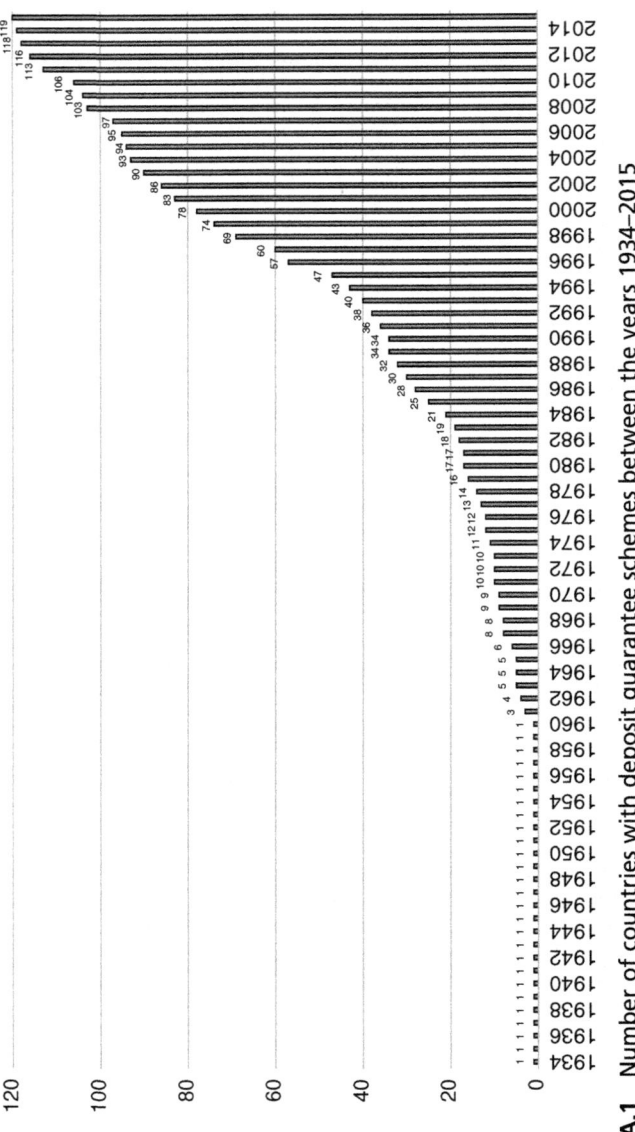

Fig. A.1 Number of countries with deposit guarantee schemes between the years 1934–2015

Source: IADI (2013, 2015d), Demirgüç-Kunt et al. (2014) and author's own research

Annex II   Deposit insurance agencies in the European Union

© The Author(s) 2017   **293**
J. Kerlin, *The Role of Deposit Guarantee Schemes as a Financial Safety Net in the European Union*, Palgrave Macmillan Studies in Banking and Financial Institutions, DOI 10.1007/978-3-319-54163-1

Table A.2 Specification of EU deposit insurance agency names and their website addresses

Country	Name in English	Name in the establishment country's language	Website
Austria	Deposit Protection Company of the Austrian Commercial Banks	Sparkassen-Haftungs Aktiengesellschaft	www.einlagensicherung.at
	Cooperative Guarantee Fund	Schulze-Delizsche-Haftungsgenossenschaft	www.hypoverband.at/einlagensicherung.htm
	Austrian Raiffeisen Deposit Guarantee	Oesterreichische Raiffeisen-Einlagensicherung	www.raiffeiseneinlagensicherung.at
	Hypo-Liability Association	Hypo-Haftungsgesellschaft m.b.H	www.volksbankeinlagensicherung.at
	Deposit Insurance for Banks	Einlagensicherung der Banken und Bankiers GmbH	www.sparkasse.at/sgruppe/Wirueberuns/Einlagensicherung
Belgium	Deposit and Financial Instrument Protection Fund	Beschermingsfonds voor deposito's en financiële instrumenten	www.protectionfund.be
Bulgaria	Bulgarian Deposit Insurance Fund	Фонут за гарантиране на влоговете в банките	www.dif.bg
Croatia	State Agency for Deposit Insurance and Bank Rehabilitation	Državne agencije za osiguranje štednih uloga i sanaciju banaka	www.dab.hr
Cyprus	Deposit Protection Scheme	Σχέδιο Προστασίας Καταθέσεων για Συνεργατικών Εταιρείών	www.centralbank.gov.cy
Czech Republic	Deposit Insurance Fund	Fond pojištění vkladů	www.fpv.cz

Country	Agency	Name	Website
Denmark	The Danish Guarantee Fund for Depositors and Investors	Garantifonden for Indskydere og Investorer	www.indskydergarantifon den.dk
Estonia	Guarantee Fund	Tagatisfond	www.tf.ee
Finland	The Deposit Guarantee Fund	Insättningsgarantifonden i Finland	www.talletussuojarahasto.fi
France	Deposit Guarantee and Investors Guarantee Fund	Fonds de Garantie des Dépôts	www.garantiedesdepots.fr
Germany	Deposit Protection Fund	Einlagensicherungsfonds des Bundesverbandes deutscher Banken	https://bankenverband.de/service/einlagensicherung
	Depositor Compensation Scheme of the Association of German Public Sector Banks GmbH	Entschädigungseinrichtung deutscher Banken Gmbh	www.voeb.de
	Deposit-Protection Fund of the Association of German Public Sector Banks e.V.	Einlagensicherungsfonds des Bundesverbandes deutscher Banken	www.voeb.de
	German Saving Banks Association	Entschädigungseinrichtung deutscher Banken	www.sparkassenfinanz gruppe.de/Haftungsverbun
	National Association of German Cooperative Banks	The Deutscher Sparkassen- und Giroverband	www.bvr.de
	The German Private Commercial Banks Compensation Scheme for Investors	Bundesverband der Deutschen Volksbanken	https://edbbanken.de
	Deposit Insurance Fund for Building Societies	Bausparkassen-Einlagensicherungsfonds e.V.	www.bausparkassen.de

(continued)

Table A.2 (continued)

Country	Name in English	Name in the establishment country's language	Website
Great Britain	Financial Services Compensation Scheme	Financial Services Compensation Scheme	www.fscs.org.uk
Greece	Hellenic Deposit and Investment Guarantee Fund	ΚΑΛΩΣ ΗΛΘΑΤΕ ΣΤΗΝ ΙΣΤΟΣΕΛΙΔΑ ΤΟΥ ΤΑΜΕΙΟΥ ΕΓΓΥΗΣΗΣ ΚΑΤΑΘΕΣΕΩΝ & ΕΠΕΝΔΥΣΕΩΝ	www.hdigf.gr
Hungary	National Deposit Insurance Fund of Hungary	Országos Betétbiztosítási Alap	www.oba.hu
Ireland	Irish Deposit Protection Scheme	Irish Deposit Protection Scheme	www.centralbank.ie
Italy	Guarantee Fund for Bondholders	Fondo di Garanzia degli Obbligazionisti	www.fgo.bcc.it
	Guarantee Fund for Cooperative Financial Institutions	Fondo di Garanzia dei Depositanti del Credito Cooperativo	www.fgd.bcc.it
	Interbank Deposit Protection Fund	Fondo Interbancario di Tutela dei Depositi	www.fitd.it
Latvia	Financial and Capital Market Commission of Latvia	Finanšu un kapitāla tirgus komisija	www.fktk.lv/en
Lithuania	Deposit and Investment Insurance	Indėlių ir investicijų draudimas	www.iidraudimas.lt
Luxembourg	Deposit Guarantee System	Association pour la Garantie des Dépôts Luxembourg	www.abbl.lu
Malta	Depositor Compensation Scheme	Depositor Compensation Scheme	www.compensationschemes.org.mt
Netherlands	Deposit Guarantee Scheme	Deposito Garantie Stelsel	www.dnb.nl
Poland	Bank Guarantee Fund	Bankowy Fundusz Gwarancyjny	www.bfg.pl

Country			
Portugal	Guarantee Fund for Mutual Agricultural Credit Institutions	Fundo de Garantia do Crédito Agrícola Mútuo	www.fgcam.pt
	Guarantee Deposit Fund	Fundo de Garantia de Depósitos	www.fgd.pt
Romania	Bank Deposit Guarantee Fund	Fondul de Garantare a Depozitelor in Sistemul Bancar	www.fgdb.ro
Slovakia	Deposit Protection Fund	Fond ochrany vkladov	www.fovsr.sk
Slovenia	The Bank of Slovenia	Banka Slovenije	www.bsi.si
Spain	Deposit Guarantee Fund of Credit Institutions	El Fondo De Garantía De Depósitos De Entidades De Crédito	www.fgd.es
Sweden	Swedish National Debt Office	Riksgälden	www.riksgalden.se

Source: EFDI (2015) and author's own research

Annex III   Chosen data on deposit insurance agencies in the European Union

© The Author(s) 2017   **299**
J. Kerlin, *The Role of Deposit Guarantee Schemes as a Financial Safety
Net in the European Union*, Palgrave Macmillan Studies in Banking
and Financial Institutions, DOI 10.1007/978-3-319-54163-1

Table A.3 Description of authorization of deposit guarantee schemes that exceed the paybox model

Country	Authorization model	Scope of above-standard authority
Austria	*paybox plus*	– Acting as forced administrator – Capability of excluding the institution from the guarantee scheme
Belgium	*paybox plus*	– Remedial measures (early intervention)
Bulgaria	*paybox plus*	– Remedial measures (decision on the rise of bank capital) – Acting as forced administrator
Croatia	*paybox plus*	– Capability of financially supporting restructuration of financial institutions
Cyprus	*paybox*	None
Czech Republic	*paybox*	None
Denmark	*paybox plus*	– Capital participation capabilities for restructuring of financial institutions (if such an action serves depositor protection)
Estonia	*paybox*	None
Finland	*paybox*	None
France	*loss minimizer*	– Remedial and restructuring interventions
Greece	*paybox plus*	– Capability of financing acquisition or sale of assets of financial institutions
Spain	*risk minimizer*	– Remedial interventions (supplying direct financial assistance and grants; providing guarantee and loans on more favorable conditions than available on the market)– Leading reorganization efforts of financial institutions' activities
Netherlands	*paybox*	None
Ireland	*paybox*	None
Lithuania	*paybox*	None
Luxembourg	*paybox plus*	– Capability of insolvent bank takeover
Latvia	*paybox*	None
Malta	*paybox*	None
Germany	*paybox plus*	– Application of various support forms (mainly liquidity and restructuring)
Poland	*paybox* plus	– Granting financial aid in the form of grants, loans, and guarantee– Possibility of acquiring debt from financial institutions
Portugal	*paybox plus*	– Commencing actions crucial for the restoration of solvency and liquidity
Romania	*paybox plus*	

Table A.3 (continued)

Country	Authorization model	Scope of above-standard authority
Slovakia	*paybox plus*	– Performing the role of temporary or forced administrator – Performing the role of legal or administrative liquidator
Slovenia	*paybox*	None
Sweden	*paybox*	None
Hungary	*paybox*	None
Great Britain	*paybox plus*	– Capital participation in financial institutions' restructuring efforts
Italy	*paybox*	None

Data aggregated for all insurance agencies in the EU; provided for unified deposit guarantee schemes of the given countries

Source: Iwanicz-Drozdowska (2014), Iwanicz-Drozdowska et al. (2015), EC (2011a), IADI (2008a, 2013)

Table A.4 Number of employees and expenses of deposit insurance agencies

Country	Number of full-time employees as of the end of 2007	Administrative expenses as of the end of 2008, expressed in thousands of euros
Austria	10	569
Belgium	5	803
Bulgaria	24	823
Croatia	20	No data
Cyprus	0	2
Czech Republic	4	489
Denmark	1.5	183
Estonia	3	142
Finland	1.5	246
France	4	1,800
Germany	77	No data
Great Britain	168	No data
Greece	10	891
Hungary	7	869
Ireland	0	No data
Italy	22	4,302
Latvia	2	No data

(*continued*)

Table A.4 (continued)

Country	Number of full-time employees as of the end of 2007	Administrative expenses as of the end of 2008, expressed in thousands of euros
Lithuania	2	No data
Luxembourg	10	No data
Malta	0	18
Median-UE-13	13	541
Median-UE-15	24	1,314
Median-UE-28	18	920
Netherlands	0	No data
Poland	65	No data
Portugal	9	102
Romania	30	1,667
Slovakia	5	339
Slovenia	0	0
Spain	16	3,360
Sweden	3	883

Data aggregated for all insurance agencies constituting unified deposit guarantee schemes of the given countries. Number of employees expresses full-time employment rates

Sources: EC (2006b, 2011a) and IADI (2008a, 2013)

Annex IV   Value of chosen depositor categories in EU countries

© The Author(s) 2017
J. Kerlin, *The Role of Deposit Guarantee Schemes as a Financial Safety Net in the European Union*, Palgrave Macmillan Studies in Banking and Financial Institutions, DOI 10.1007/978-3-319-54163-1

Table A.5 Information on the value of chosen depositor categories in EU countries as of the end of 2012 (expressed in millions of euros)

Countries	Deposits (in total)	Eligible deposits	Covered deposits	Covered-to-eligible deposit ratio
Austria	324,900	242,275	173,369	72%
Belgium	529,000	342,700	229,149	67%
Bulgaria	28,972	26,373	18,382	70%
Croatia*	38,291	No data	21,901	No data
Cyprus	104,392	77,679	51,941	67%
Czech Republic	123,620	98,223	65,347	67%
Denmark	166,900	124,191	105,473	85%
Estonia	10,825	8,601	5,255	61%
EU	14,645,559	10,491,227	6,922,418	67%
Finland	136,538	128,463	77,759	61%
France	1,577,301	1,536,912	1,103,482	72%
Germany	3,171,800	2,361,206	1,575,248	67%
Great Britain	2,922,200	2,174,428	1,218,760	56%
Greece	175,000	140,338	104,769	75%
Hungary	60,048	44,180	30,266	69%
Ireland	194,000	140,000	80,000	57%
Italy	1,511,600	724,822	490,471	68%
Latvia	17,765	14,391	5,951	41%
Lithuania	13,400	9,971	6,667	67%
Luxembourg	215,900	160,653	30,440	19%
Malta	28,004	9,478	7,025	74%
Netherlands	863,684	575,455	447,001	78%
Poland	278,563	175,645	103,209	59%
Portugal	221,500	164,820	110,208	67%
Romania	64,295	33,089	27,410	83%
Slovakia	45,940	26,890	24,201	90%
Slovenia	23,512	17,433	14,877	85%
Spain	1,568,800	934,260	674,892	72%
Sweden	267,100	198,751	140,866	71%

*Data on Croatia as of the end of 2013

Source: Iwanicz-Drozdowska et al. (2015), EC (2011a), FSB (2012), IADI (2008a, 2013), Cannas et al. (2014, p. 9, 12) and DAB (2015), and author's own research

Annex V   Scope of successful deposit insurance agency intervention

© The Author(s) 2017
J. Kerlin, *The Role of Deposit Guarantee Schemes as a Financial Safety Net in the European Union*, Palgrave Macmillan Studies in Banking and Financial Institutions, DOI 10.1007/978-3-319-54163-1

Table A.6 Scope of successful deposit insurance agency intervention in case guarantee requirements are fulfilled in a single bank

1. Country	2. Deposit guarantee scheme intervention scope–0.8% level	3. Percentage of entities outside the scope of deposit guarantee scheme intervention–0.8% level	4. Deposit guarantee scheme intervention scope–levels as of the end of 2012	5. Percentage of entities outside the scope of deposit guarantee scheme intervention–levels as of the end of 2012	6. Influence of the DGS Directive on intervention scope
Austria	41	16.53%	None	100.00%	207
Belgium	20	43.48%	19	41.30%	–1
Bulgaria	20	80.00%	5	20.00%	–15
Croatia	14	41.18%	13	38.24%	–1
Cyprus	11	68.75%	15	93.75%	4
Czech Republic	19	70.37%	15	55.56%	–4
Denmark	21	25.30%	21	25.30%	0
Estonia	8	100.00%	2	25.00%	–6
Finland	9	28.13%	7	21.88%	–2
France	35	11.11%	97	30.79%	62
Germany	38	2.20%	145	8.38%	107
Great Britain	29	16.29%	None	100.00%	149
Greece	8	61.54%	4	30.77%	–4
Hungary	13	52.00%	12	48.00%	–1

Ireland	16	69.57%	19	82.61%	3
Italy	37	6.48%	None	100.00%	534
Latvia	15	88.24%	8	47.06%	–7
Lithuania	9	100.00%	None	100.00%	1
Luxembourg	37	52.11%	None	100.00%	34
Malta	8	80.00%	7	70.00%	–1
Netherlands	25	50.00%	None	100.00%	25
Poland	20	52.63%	14	36.84%	–6
Portugal	14	50.00%	16	57.14%	2
Romania	17	70.83%	8	33.33%	–9
Slovakia	13	86.67%	12	80.00%	–1
Slovenia	None	0.00%	None	0.00%	0
Spain	27	20.77%	42	32.31%	15
Sweden	11	12.36%	7	7.87%	–4

Source: Author's own research.

Table A.7 Interpretation of study results

Number and name of column in Tables A.6	Results achievement method	Interpretation
1. Country	–	–
2. Deposit guarantee scheme scope—0.8% level	Comparison of country deposit guarantee fund levels (0.8 per cent of covered funds' value of the country financial sector) with the value of possessed covered deposits of ordered crediting institutions—starting from those with the biggest number of covered deposits.	The value represents the number of the bank, in which payouts of covered deposits are possible. For instance, 20 indicates that in case guarantee requirements of a given country are fulfilled, payout of covered deposits is possible for the 20th biggest credit institution (measured by the size of aggregated deposits). The remaining 19 entities with higher covered deposits' values do not fall under the scope of possible payout. "None" means that no institution covered by the study is under the scope of successful intervention of the deposit insurance agency.
3. Percentage of entities outside the scope of deposit guarantee scheme intervention —0.8% level	Ratio of the number of credit institutions, where payouts from the resources of the deposit guarantee scheme are not possible due to the exceeding value of covered deposits under governance of the given institution, divided by the number of all credit institutions that are	The value expresses the percentage of banks outside the scope of successful deposit insurance agency intervention. For example, a result of 5 per cent means that such percentage of all banks participating in the guarantee scheme remains outside the factual scope of

Table A.7 (continued)

Number and name of column in Tables A.6	Results achievement method	Interpretation
	under the authority of the deposit insurance agency.	intervention due to insufficient funds aggregated in the deposit guarantee fund.
4. Deposit guarantee scheme intervention scope—levels as of the end of 2012	Comparison of the value of country deposit guarantee fund's current budget (as of the end of 31 December 2012) with the value of covered deposits of subsequent credit institutions (starting from those with the biggest deposit value).	As in the second column of Tables A.6—scope of deposit guarantee scheme intervention— 0.8 per cent.
5. Percentage of entities outside the scope of deposit guarantee scheme intervention —levels as of the end of 2012	Ratio of credit institutions, which are not eligible for payouts from the resources of the deposit guarantee scheme due to the exceeding value of covered deposits, divided by the number of all credit institutions that are under the authority of the deposit insurance agency.	As in the third column of Tables A.6—percentage of entities outside deposit guarantee scheme intervention.
6. Influence of the DGS Directive on intervention scope	Comparison of results from the second and fourth columns of Tables A.6, providing the difference between the two variants (current and DGS Directive anticipated accumulation levels).	The number expresses the change of successful intervention scope in a given country, accredited to the introduction of the DGS Directive. For example, a result of (+2) means that intervention

(*continued*)

Table A.7 (continued)

Number and name of column in Tables A.6	Results achievement method	Interpretation
		capabilities of the deposit guarantee scheme will increase by two banks (successful intervention scope extended to two additional institutions). Marking with (–) symbol indicates that the DGS Directive introduces less restrictive conditions than those already existent in the given country.

Source: Author's own formulation

Annex VI Costs of bank restructuring in the European Union

© The Author(s) 2017
J. Kerlin, *The Role of Deposit Guarantee Schemes as a Financial Safety Net in the European Union*, Palgrave Macmillan Studies in Banking and Financial Institutions, DOI 10.1007/978-3-319-54163-1

Table A.8 Costs of state aid in relation to own capital of financial institutions in the EU between the years 2008 and 2014

Bank name	Country of registration	Intervention year	Gross aid amount expressed in millions of euros	Participation of aid in own capital in the year of intervention	Participation of aid in own capital a year before intervention
Komunalkredit Austria AG	Austria	2008	250	–	50%
Erste Bank Group	Austria	2008	2,700	24%	24%
Hypo Alpe-Adria Bank AG ("Hypo in Kärnten")	Austria	2008	1,600	63%	96%
BAWAG	Austria	2009	550	29%	48%
Raiffeisen Bank International AG	Austria	2009	1,750	17%	20%
Österreichische Volksbanken AG	Austria	2010	1,000	51%	47%
Hypo Tirol	Austria	2012	220	41%	63%
Dexia	Belgium/France/ Luxembourg	2008	3,000	53%	18%
KBC	Belgium	2008	3,500	23%	–
Grupa FORTIS	Belgium/Netherlands/ Luxembourg	2008	4,700	643%	14%
Bank of Cyprus	Cyprus	2012	500	149%	21%
Cyprus Popular Bank (Laiki Bank)	Cyprus	2012	1,800	186%	77%
Roskilde Bank	Denmark	2008	603		171%
Crédit Agricole	France	2008	4,664	7%	7%
Crédit Mutuel	France	2008	1,914	20%	17%
Groupe Banque Populaire	France	2008	7,050	74%	76%

Société générale (SocGen)	France	2008	2,414	6%	8%
Agricultural Bank of Greece (ATE)	Greece	2009	675	73%	–
Alpha Bank	Greece	2009	940	16%	–
EFG Eurobank Ergasias S.A	Greece	2009	950	15%	–
National Bank of Greece (NBG)	Greece	2009	350	4%	–
Piraeus Bank	Greece	2009	370	10%	–
Proton Bank/Nea Proton Bank	Greece	2009	80	25%	–
TT Hellenic Postbank S.A./New TT Hellenic Postbank	Greece	2009	225	18%	–
Catalunya Banc (Caixa)	Spain	2008	10,760	331%	–
Caja3	Spain	2009	327	20%	–
Caja Castilla La Mancha	Spain	2009	1,650	157%	–
Banco Ceiss	Spain	2010	3,718	216%	–
Banco Mare Nostrum (BMN)	Spain	2010	5,339	227%	–
Bankia-BFA	Spain	2010	4,465	71%	–
NCG Banco	Spain	2010	1,162	66%	–
UNNIM Banc	Spain	2010	380	54%	–
Banco CAM	Spain	2011	5,970	241%	–
Banco de Valencia	Spain	2011	1,000	272%	–
Liberbank	Spain	2012	4,999	455%	–
ING Groep N.V.	Netherlands	2008	10,000	–	25%
SNS REAAL	Netherlands	2008	750	–	21%
Fortis NL	Netherlands	2008	20,800	–	–
ABN Amro Group	Netherlands	2009	2,500	–	15%
Allied Irish Bank	Ireland	2009	3,500	34%	–

(continued)

Table A.8 (continued)

Bank name	Country of registration	Intervention year	Gross aid amount expressed in millions of euros	Participation of aid in own capital in the year of intervention	Participation of aid in own capital a year before intervention
Anglo-Irish Bank	Ireland	2009	4,000	96%	–
Bank of Ireland	Ireland	2009	3,500	55%	–
Irish Nationwide Building Society (INBS)	Ireland	2010	5,400	–	–
Educational Building Society (EBS)	Ireland	2010	875	–	217%
Irish Life & Permanent Group Holdings (IL&P)	Ireland	2011	3,800	–	235%
Parex Bank	Latvia	2009	35	–	44%
Mortgage and Land Bank (LHZB)	Latvia	2009	102	–	170%
Commerzbank	Germany	2008	8,200	41%	–
IKB	Germany	2008	2,300	198%	–
BayernLB	Germany	2008	3,000	27%	–
HSH Nordbank	Germany	2009	3,000	–	150%
Landesbank Baden Württemberg	Germany	2009	5,000	–	83%
Aareal Bank	Germany	2009	525	–	36%
West LB	Germany	2009	700	19%	–
NordLB	Germany	2011	500	–	9%
Banco BPI (BPI)	Portugal	2012	1,400	–	299%
	Portugal	2012	3,000	–	78%

Bank	Country	Year	Amount		
Banco Comercial Português (BCP)					
Banco Portugues de Negocios (BPN)	Portugal	2012	560	157%	–
Caixa Geral de Depósitos (CGD)	Portugal	2012	1,650	–	38%
Banco Internacional do Funchal S.A. (Banif)	Portugal	2013	1,100	136%	–
Banco Espirito Santo	Portugal	2014	4,900	–	78%
Nordea	Sweden	2009	518	–	3%
Northern Rock	Great Britain	2007	1,579	240%	–
HBOS	Great Britain	2008	14,761	110%	–
Lloyd's	Great Britain	2008	23,500	231%	–
RBS	Great Britain	2008	25,672	30%	–
Banca Monte dei Paschi di Siena (MPS)	Italy	2009	1,900	42%	–
Banca Popolare di Milano (BPM)	Italy	2009	500	14%	–
Banco Popolare	Italy	2009	1,450	13%	–
Credito Valtellinese	Italy	2009	200	27%	–
Nova Ljubljanska Banka	Slovenia	2011	250	26%	–
Nova Kreditna Banka Maribor	Slovenia	2012	873	345%	–
Factor Banka	Slovenia	2013	285	–	341%
Probanka	Slovenia	2013	236	–	454%
Abanka Vipa	Slovenia	2013	348	–	210%
AB Ukio Bankas	Lithuania	2013	231	182%	–

Source: Author's own research and Iwanicz-Drozdowska et al. (2016)

Annex VII   Scope of successful resolution intervention

© The Author(s) 2017
J. Kerlin, *The Role of Deposit Guarantee Schemes as a Financial Safety Net in the European Union*, Palgrave Macmillan Studies in Banking and Financial Institutions, DOI 10.1007/978-3-319-54163-1

Table A.9 Scope of intervention in the unfavorable scenario (financial requirements on the level of 100 per cent of own capital of the restructured institution) in case a single institution becomes insolvent

1.	2.	3.	4.	5.	6.	7.
	RF variant		RF+DGS variant			
Country	Intervention scope	Percentage of entities outside intervention	Intervention scope	Percentage of entities outside intervention	Influence of the deposit guarantee scheme on the procedure	Relation of deposit guarantee scheme funds to deposits of the restructured institution
Austria	14	5.04%	12	4.32%	+2	11.90%
Belgium	10	14.93%	10	14.93%	None	9.99%
Bulgaria	11	40.74%	8	29.63%	+3	3.34%
Croatia	8	23.53%	8	23.53%	None	9.30%
Cyprus	6	35.29%	5	29.41%	+1	9.89%
Czech Republic	8	22.22%	7	19.44%	+1	6.81%
Denmark	16	16.84%	12	12.63%	+4	5.66%
Estonia	6	66.67%	5	55.56%	+1	16.16%
Finland	5	12.20%	5	12.20%	None	No deposits
France	13	3.39%	13	3.39%	None	5.68%
Germany	10	0.56%	7	0.39%	+3	44.63%
Great Britain	18	5.06%	16	4.49%	+2	14.83%
Greece	2	14.29%	2	14.29%	None	2.02%
Hungary	10	31.25%	9	28.13%	+1	3.56%
Ireland	14	43.75%	12	37.50%	+2	20.48%
Italy	10	1.69%	7	1.18%	+3	18.44%
Latvia	9	47.37%	8	42.11%	+1	23%
Lithuania	5	50.00%	4	40.00%	+1	6.40%

Luxembourg	32	38.10%	31	36.90%	+1	17%
Malta	9	69.23%	7	53.85%	+2	5.09%
Median-UE-13	9	–	7	–	+2	–
Median-UE-15	12	–	11	–	+1	–
Median-UE-28	11	–	9	–	+2	–
Netherlands	9	12.86%	8	11.43%	+1	100.00%
Poland	12	27.91%	9	20.93%	+3	6.91%
Portugal	8	21.05%	8	21.05%	None	6.47%
Romania	9	34.62%	6	23.08%	+3	10.61%
Slovakia	10	62.50%	9	56.25%	+1	5.38%
Slovenia	11	52.38%	8	38.10%	+3	3.31%
Spain	8	5.16%	7	4.52%	+1	4.63%
Sweden	13	12.87%	11	10.89%	+2	10.99%

Source: Author's own formulation

Table A.10 Scope of intervention in the favorable scenario (financial requirements on the level of 50 per cent of own capital of the restructured institution) in case a single institution becomes insolvent

1.	2.	3.	4.	5.	6.	7.
	RF variant		RF+DGS variant			
Country	Intervention scope	Percentage of entities outside intervention	Intervention scope	Percentage of entities outside intervention	Influence of the deposit guarantee scheme on the procedure	Relation of deposit guarantee scheme funds to deposits of the restructured institution
Austria	9	3.24%	7	2.52%	+2	4.09%
Belgium	8	11.94%	7	10.45%	+1	2.34%
Bulgaria	6	22.22%	4	14.81%	+2	4.74%
Croatia	5	14.71%	5	14.71%	None	5.44%
Cyprus	4	23.53%	4	23.53%	None	100.00%
Czech Republic	6	16.67%	4	11.11%	+2	5.10%
Denmark	8	8.42%	8	8.42%	None	3.21%
Estonia	3	33.33%	3	33.33%	None	15.17%
Finland	5	12.20%	5	12.20%	None	No deposits
France	10	2.61%	9	2.35%	+1	2.83%
Germany	5	0.28%	5	0.28%	None	4.02%
Great Britain	12	3.37%	10	2.81%	+2	3.08%
Greece	1	7.14%	1	7.14%	None	No deposits
Hungary	7	21.88%	3	9.38%	+4	876.81%*
Ireland	9	28.13%	7	21.88%	+2	6.18%
Italy	6	1.01%	5	0.84%	+1	5.83%
Latvia	7	36.84%	5	26.32%	+2	2.21%
Lithuania	4	40.00%	4	40.00%	None	6.40%

Luxembourg	22	26.19%	15	17.86%	+7	10.87%
Malta	6	46.15%	6	46.15%	None	10.97%
Median-UE-13	5		4		+1	
Median-UE-15	8		7		+1	
Median-UE-28	7		6		+1	
Netherlands	7	10.00%	7	10.00%	None	28.69%
Poland	5	11.63%	3	6.98%	+2	5.10%
Portugal	6	15.79%	4	10.53%	+2	3.35%
Romania	5	19.23%	3	11.54%	+2	3.46%
Slovakia	6	37.50%	5	31.25%	+1	2.64%
Slovenia	3	14.29%	2	9.52%	+1	47.06%
Spain	5	3.23%	5	3.23%	None	5.48%
Sweden	8	7.92%	8	7.92%	None	No deposits

*The high result of Hungary, which stands out from remaining countries, is a result of the specificity of the institution, which does not widely accept covered deposits

Source: Author's own formulation

Table A.11 Scope of intervention in the unfavorable and favorable scenarios, in the RF and RF+DGS variants, in case two subsequent financial institutions become insolvent

1.	2.	3.	4.	5.	6.	7.
	Unfavorable scenario			Favorable scenario		
Country	Resolution fund intervention scope	Resolution fund and deposit guarantee scheme intervention scope	Influence of the deposit guarantee scheme on the procedure	Resolution fund intervention scope	Resolution fund and deposit guarantee scheme intervention scope	Influence of the deposit guarantee scheme on the procedure
Austria	20–21	17–18	+3	13–14	12–13	+1
Belgium	17–18	12–13	+5	10–11	9–10	+1
Bulgaria	13–14	12–13	+1	11–12	8–9	+3
Croatia	9–10	8–9	+1	7–8	7–8	None
Cyprus	10–11	8–9	+2	5–6	4–5	+1
Czech Republic	9–10	8–9	+1	7–8	7–8	None
Denmark	21–22	19–20	+2	15–16	11–12	+4
Estonia	6–7	6–7	None	5–6	4–5	+1
Finland	7–8	6–7	+1	5–6	5–6	None
France	16–17	14–15	+2	13–14	12–13	+1
Germany	14–15	12–13	+2	10–11	6–7	+4
Great Britain	24–25	20–21	+4	18–19	15–16	+3
Greece	2–3	2–3	None	1–2	1–2	None
Hungary	12–13	11–12	+1	10–11	9–10	+1
Ireland	21–22	17–18	+4	14–15	10–11	+4
Italy	17–18	13–14	+4	10–11	7–8	+3
Latvia	14–15	11–12	+3	9–10	7–8	+2

Lithuania	6–7	5–6	+1	5–6	4–5	+1
Luxembourg	46–47	39–40	+7	32–33	29–30	+3
Malta	10–11	9–10	+1	9–10	6–7	+3
Median-UE-13	11–12	9–10	+2	8–9	6–7	+2
Median-UE-15	17–18	14–15	+3	12–13	10–11	+2
Median-UE-28	14–15	12–13	+2	10–11	8–9	+2
Netherlands	13–14	10–11	+3	9–10	7–8	+2
Poland	15–16	12–13	+3	11–12	8–9	+3
Portugal	11–12	10–11	+1	8–9	7–8	+1
Romania	15–16	12–13	+3	9–10	6–7	+3
Slovakia	11–12	10–11	+1	9–10	7–8	+2
Slovenia	13–14	11–12	+2	10–11	7–8	+3
Spain	11–12	9–10	+2	8–9	6–7	+2
Sweden	15–16	14–15	+1	12–13	9–10	+3

Source: Author's own formulation

Table A.12 Interpretation of sample study results of Tables A.9 and A.10

	Number of column and name of indicator in Tables A.9 and A.10	Result achievement method	Interpretation
RF variant	2. Intervention scope	Comparison of country resolution fund level of 1 per cent of covered funds of a given country with own capital values of subsequent financial institutions (starting from those with the highest own capital).	The value represents the number of the financial institution that may be restructured. For instance, 20 indicates that resolution procedures allow for resolution of the 20th biggest financial institution (measured by the size of own capital). The remaining 19 entities with higher covered deposits' values do not fall under the scope of resolution organ intervention.
	3. Percentage of entities outside resolution fund intervention	Ratio of the number of entities, which may not be restructured with resolution fund resources due to the exceeding value of own capital, divided by the number of all entities under the procedure authority.	The value expresses the percentage of financial institutions outside the scope of successful resolution fund intervention. For example, a result of 5 per cent means that such percentage of all entities under resolution authority remains outside the factual scope of intervention due to insufficient resources aggregated in the resolution fund.

RF+DGS variant		
4. Intervention scope	Comparison of the value of resources of the country resolution fund acting with the deposit guarantee scheme (paybox fund), with a total budget of 1.4 per cent of covered deposits value of the financial sector of the given country, with the value of own capital of subsequent financial institutions (starting from those with the highest own capital)	The value represents the number of the financial institution which may be restructured. For instance, 20 indicates that resolution procedures allow for restructuration of the 20th biggest financial institution (measured by the size of own capital). The remaining 19 entities with higher covered deposits' values do not fall under the scope of resolution organ intervention.
5. Percentage of entities outside resolution fund intervention	Ratio of the number of entities which may not be restructured in the RF +DGS variant due to their exceedingly high own capital levels, divided by the number of all entities under the procedure authority.	The value expresses the percentage of financial institutions outside the scope of successful resolution fund intervention. For example, a result of 5 per cent means that such percentage of all entities under resolution authority remains outside the factual scope of intervention due to insufficient resources aggregated in the resolution fund.

(continued)

Table A.12 (continued)

Number of column and name of indicator in Tables A.9 and A.10	Result achievement method	Interpretation
6. Influence of the deposit guarantee scheme on the procedure	Comparison of results in the second and fourth columns, providing the difference between the two variants in the given scenario (comparison of the RF and RF+DGS variants).	The number expresses the change of successful intervention scope in a given country, accredited to the inclusion of the deposit guarantee scheme in resolution. For example, a result of (+2) means that intervention capabilities in the financial safety net increased by two financial institutions (successful intervention scope extended to two additional institutions). A "none" remark indicates the lack of deposit insurance agency engagement in resolution procedures in the given country.
7. Relation of deposit guarantee scheme funds to deposits of the restructured institution	Ratio of the number deposit of guarantee scheme funds available for the procedure, divided by the value of covered deposits of the first obtainable financial institution.	The number expresses the value of deposit guarantee scheme funds within covered deposits' value of the restructured institution. For example, a percentage of 6.91 per cent in the case of Poland means that in the 9th biggest entity in terms of own capital size (hence, the first in which successful resolution intervention is expected) deposit

guarantee scheme funds designated for intervention are equal to nearly 7 per cent of covered deposits of the given institution. A "no deposits" remark means that the restructured institution is an investment company without covered deposits. Therefore, the deposit guarantee scheme is not legitimized to act in its case.

The interpretation method of Tables A.11 is similar to that expressed in Tables A.9 and A.10, nevertheless, the part with percentage calculations has been excluded, and studies were limited solely to two basic variants and scenarios

Source: Author's own formulation

Annex VIII   Values of Deposit Insurance Agency Readiness for Resolution Index

© The Author(s) 2017
J. Kerlin, *The Role of Deposit Guarantee Schemes as a Financial Safety Net in the European Union*, Palgrave Macmillan Studies in Banking and Financial Institutions, DOI 10.1007/978-3-319-54163-1

Table A.13 Evaluation of component study results (component numbers 1–4)

| Country | 1. | | 2. | | 3. | | | 4. | |
	Mandate scope	Points	Position in the financial safety net	Points	Coverage ratio	Ratio evaluation	Points	Restructuring experience	Points
Austria	Paybox plus	1	A separate entity of private law	0	0.00%	None	0	None	0
Belgium	Paybox plus	1	A separate entity of public law	3	0.90%	Good	3	None	0
Bulgaria	Paybox plus	1	A separate entity of public law	3	8.60%	Very good	4	None	0
Croatia	Paybox plus	1	A separate entity of public law	3	0.49%	Scarce	1	None	0
Cyprus	Paybox	0	Part of the central bank	3	0.04%	Scarce	1	None	0
Czech Republic	Paybox	0	A separate entity of public law	3	1.50%	Very good	4	None	0
Denmark	Paybox plus	1	A separate entity of public law	3	0.73%	Moderate	2	Significant	4

Country									
Estonia	Paybox	0	A separate entity of public law	3	3.27%	Very good	4	None	0
Finland	Paybox	0	A separate entity of private law	0	1.17%	Good	3	None	0
France	Loss minimizer	2	A separate entity of private law	0	0.19%	Scarce	1	None	0
Germany	Paybox plus	1	A separate entity of private law	0	0.15%	Scarce	1	None	0
Great Britain	Paybox plus	1	A separate entity of public law	3	−0.08%	None	0	Significant	4
Greece	Paybox plus	1	A separate entity of private law	0	3.80%	Very good	4	Moderate	2
Hungary	Paybox	0	A separate entity of public law	3	0.88%	Good	3	None	0
Ireland	Paybox	0	Part of the central bank	2	0.50%	Moderate	2	None	0
Italy	Paybox	0	Part of the central bank	2	0.00%	None	0	None	0
Latvia	Paybox	0	Part of the financial market supervisor	1	4.40%	Very good	4	None	0

(continued)

Table A.13 (continued)

Country	1. Mandate scope	Points	2. Position in the financial safety net	Points	3. Coverage ratio	Ratio evaluation	Points	4. Restructuring experience	Points
Lithuania	Paybox	0	A separate entity of public law	3	−9.90%	None	0	None	0
Luxembourg	Paybox plus	1	A separate entity of private law	0	0.00%	None	0	None	0
Malta	Paybox	0	Part of the financial market supervisor	1	0.23%	Scarce	1	None	0
Netherlands	Paybox	0	Part of the central bank	2	0.00%	None	0	None	0
Poland	Paybox plus	1	A separate entity of public law	3	1.73%	Very good	4	Moderate	2
Portugal	Paybox plus	1	A separate entity of public law	3	0.22%	Scarce	1	None	0
Romania	Paybox plus	1	A separate entity of public law	3	2.41%	Very good	4	None	0

Slovakia	Paybox plus	1	A separate entity of public law	3	0.80%	Good	3	None	0
Slovenia	Paybox	0	Part of the central bank	2	0.00%	None	0	None	0
Spain	Risk mini-mizer	3	A separate entity of public law	3	0.13%	Scarce	1	Significant	4
Sweden	Paybox	0	Department of the ministry of finance	1	2.32%	Very good	4	None	0

Source: Author's own formulation

Table A.14 Evaluation of component study results (component numbers 5–8) and final results

Country name	5. Governance method	Points	6. Number of employees*	Organizational background	7. Deposit guarantee scheme structure	Points	8. Integration of the deposit guarantee scheme	Points	9. Points	Result
Austria	Private	0	10	Sufficient	2	Multi-entity	0	Integrated	0	1	4
Belgium	Mixed	1	5	Scarce	1	Unified	1	Integrated	1	1	11
Bulgaria	Mixed	1	24	Good	3	Unified	1	Solo	1	0	13
Croatia	Public	3	20	Good	3	Unified	1	Solo	1	0	12
Cyprus	Public	3	0	None	0	Unified	1	Solo	1	0	7
Czech Republic	Mixed	1	4	Scarce	1	Unified	1	Solo	1	0	10
Denmark	Public	3	1,5	Scarce	1	Unified	1	Integrated	1	1	16
Estonia	Mixed	1	3	Scarce	1	Unified	1	Solo	1	0	10
Finland	Private	0	1,5	Scarce	1	Unified	1	Solo	1	0	5
France	Private	0	4	Scarce	1	Unified	1	Integrated	1	1	6
Germany	Private	0	77	Good	3	Multi-entity	0	Integrated	1	1	6
Great Britain	Public	3	168	Good	3	Unified	1	Integrated	1	1	12
Greece	Mixed	1	10	Sufficient	2	Unified	1	Integrated	1	1	12
Hungary	Mixed	1	7	Sufficient	2	Unified	1	Solo	1	0	10
Ireland	Public	3	0	None	0	Unified	1	Solo	1	0	8
Italy	Private	0	22	Good	3	Multi-entity	0	Solo	0	0	5
Latvia	Public	3	2	Scarce	1	Unified	1	Solo	1	0	10

Lithuania	Public	3	2	Scarce	1	Unified	1	Solo	0	8
Luxembourg	Private	0	10	Sufficient	2	Unified	1	Integrated	1	5
Malta	Mixed	1	0	None	0	Unified	1	Integrated	1	5
Netherlands	Public	3	0	None	0	Unified	1	Solo	0	6
Poland	Mixed	1	65	Good	3	Unified	1	Solo	0	15
Portugal	Mixed	1	9	Sufficient	2	Multi-entity	0	Solo	0	8
Romania	Mixed	1	30	Good	3	Unified	1	Solo	0	13
Slovakia	Mixed	1	5	Scarce	1	Unified	1	Solo	0	10
Slovenia	Public	3	0	None	0	Unified	1	Solo	0	6
Spain	Public	3	16	Good	3	Unified	1	Solo	0	18
Sweden	Public	3	3	Scarce	1	Unified	1	Integrated	1	11

*Measured in reference to full-time employment rates; a detailed description of components may be found in Section 7.2

Source: Author's own formulation

Bibliography

Archer, D. (2009). *Roles and Objectives of Modern Central Banks, Issues in the Governance of Central Banks*, BIS, Basel, May.

Bafia, P.S. (2011). *Kazus Icesave. Problem gwarancji depozytów gromadzonych w zagranicznych oddziałach instytucji kredytowych na podstawie sporu brytyjsko-islandzkiego*, "Bezpieczny Bank", nr 2(44), BFG, Warszawa.

Bartholdy J., Boyle G., Stover R. (2001). *Deposit Insurance and Market Assessment of Banking System Stability: Evidence from Denmark*, "European Journal of Finance", vol. 27.

BCBS. (2002). *Supervisor Guidance on Dealing with Weak Banks. Report of the Task Force on Dealing with Weak Banks*, March.

BIS, BCBS. (2014). *Consultative Document Supervisory Guidelines for Identifying and Dealing with Weak Banks*, 19 September.

Boccuzzi, G. (2015). *The European Banking Union: Supervision and Resolution*, Palgrave Macmillan UK.

Bureau van Dijk. (2015). *Bankscope database, World banking information source*, www.bvdinfo.com.

Burke, V.J. (2012). *Developing Europe's Financial 'Safety Net' in a Time of Crisis*, Administración e Cidadanía, vol. 7, no. 1, Escola Galega de Administración Pública (EGAP).

© The Author(s) 2017   **337**
J. Kerlin, *The Role of Deposit Guarantee Schemes as a Financial Safety Net in the European Union*, Palgrave Macmillan Studies in Banking and Financial Institutions, DOI 10.1007/978-3-319-54163-1

Campbell, A.; Brosse, J.L.; Mayes, D.; Singh, D.; La Brosse, J.R. (2007). *Deposit Insurance*, Palgrave Macmillan UK.

CASE. (2013). *Procedura restrukturyzacji i uporządkowanej likwidacji banku – doświadczenia światowe, rozwiązania dla UE i dla Polski*, Warszawa, 25 lutego.

CASE. (2015). *Unia Bankowa – gdzie jesteśmy*, Materiały Seminaryjne, Warszawa, 17 kwietnia.

Claessens S. (2001). *Experiences of Resolution of Banking Crises*, BIS.

Claessens, S.; Kose, M.A. (2013). *Financial Crises: Explanations, Types, and Implications*, IMF Working Paper WP/13/28, January.

Cull, R.; Senbet, L.; Sorge, M. (2003). *Deposit Insurance and Financial Development*, World Bank Policy Research, Working Paper no. 2682, March 2003.

Dash E.; Sorkin A. (2008). *Government Seizes WaMu and Sells Some Assets*, "New York Times", 26.09.2008.

Demirgüç-Kunt A., Huizinga H. (2009). *Market Discipline and Deposit Insurance*, World Bank.

Demirgüç-Kunt A., Kane E., Laeven L. (2004). *Determinants of Deposit-Insurance Adoption and Design*, December 2004.

Dermine J. (2005). *European Banking Integration: Don't put the Cart before the Horse*, Cross-Border Banking, Regulatory Challenges, Federal Reserve Bank of Chicago, Fontainebleau, October 2005.

Di Giorgio G., Di Noia C. (2001). *Which Deposit Insurance in the E-Banking World?* Mimeo.

Drehmann M. (2002). *Will an Optimal Deposit Insurance Always Decrease the Probability of Systematic Banking Crisis?*, Bank for International Settlements, February 2002.

EBA. (2016). *BRRD/DGSD transposition and designation of National Authorities*, EBA Resolution Unit, London, 5 April.

EC. (2006b). *Screening Report. Financial Services. Croatia*, 28 November.

EC. (2008). *Report on the Minimum Guarantee Level of Deposit Guarantee Schemes Directive 94/19/EC*.

EC. (2015a). *Towards the Completion of the Banking Union*, Strasbourg, COM (2015) 587.

EC. (2015c). *Proposal for a Regulation of the European Parliament and of the Council amending Regulation (EU) 806/2014 in order to establish a European Deposit Insurance Scheme*, COM(2015) 586 final, 2015/0270 (COD), Strasbourg.

EC. (2015d). *Financial Services: Commission requests 11 Member States to apply EU rules on Bank Recovery and Resolution*, Brussels, 28 May.

ECB. (2006). *EU Banking Structures*, October.

ECB. (2008). *EU Banking Structures*, October.

ECB. (2014). *EU Banking Structures*, October.

EFDI. (2015). *Full-members*, www.efdi.eu, (dostęp: 18.08.2015 r.).

EFDI. (2006). *Deposit Guarantee Systems: EFDI's First Report*, Rome, October 2006.

England C. (1985). *Private Deposit Insurance: Stabilizing The Banking System*, Cato Policy Analysis, no. 54.

Enoch C., Garcia G., Sundararajan V. (2001). *Recapitalizing Banks with Public Funds: Selected Issues*, IMF.

European Council. (2013). *Conclusions of the European Council* (14/15 March), EUCO 23/13, Brussels, 14 March.

Europejska Unia Bankowa, red. M. Zaleska, Difin, Warszawa 2015.

FDIC. (1998). *A Brief History of Deposit Insurance in the United States*, September.

FDIC. (1984). *The First Fifty Years: A History of the FDIC 1933–1983*, FDIC, Washington.

FINREG. (2014). *II Polski Kongres Regulacji Rynków Finansowych*, Warszawa, 15–16 października.

Frolov M. (2003). *Funding Deposit Insurance: Designing Options and Practical Choices*, Keio University.

Global Economics Crisis Resource Center, (2009). *Global Economic Watch: Impact on Economics*, Cengage Learning, March 2009.

Goodhart C. (1998). *Financial Regulation: Why, How and Where Now?*, Routledge, London, New York.

Goodhart C. (2004). *Some New Directions for Financial Stability?*, Per Jacobsson Lecture, LSE.

Gospodarowicz M. (2013). *Skorygowana o ryzyko opłata za gwarancje depozytowe a ryzyko systemowe banku*, "Zarządzanie i Finanse" 2013, nr 2.

Grafton, J. (ed.) (1999). *Franklin Delano Roosevelt – Great Speeches*, Dover Publications, New York.

Gropp R., Vesala J. (2004). *Deposit Insurance, Moral Hazard and Market Monitoring*, ECB Working Paper no. 302, February 2004.

Gros D., Schoenmaker D., (2014). *European Deposit Insurance and Resolution in the Banking Union*, December 2013, "Journal of Common Market Studies", vol. 52, no. 3,.

Grzegorczyk F. (2005). *Pojęcie instytucji kredytowej w świetle polskiego prawa*, "Zeszyty Naukowe Akademii Ekonomicznej w Krakowie" 2005, nr 690.

Hagfræðistofnun Háskóla Íslands, (2012). *The Financial Strength of the Deposit Guarantee Schemes in the EU and Iceland*, Reykjavík, Júlí 2012.

Handschke J., Monkiewicz J. (2008). *Ubezpieczenia*, Poltext, Warszawa.

House of Commons Treasury Committee, *The Run on the Rock*, Fifth Report of Session 2007–08, vol. I.

Hüpkes E. (2005). *Too Big to Save – Towards a Functional Approach to Resolving Crises in Global Financial Institutions*, September 2004, World Scientific Publishing,.

IADI. (2008b). *Funding of Deposit Insurance Systems*, BIS, Basel.

IADI. (2009b). *General Guidance for the Resolution of Bank Failures*, BIS, Basel.

IADI. (2009c). *Governance of Deposit Insurance Systems*, BIS, Basel.

IADI. (2010). *Annual Survey*, BIS, Basel.

IADI. (2011a). *Annual Survey*, BIS, Basel.

IADI. (2011b). *Funding Mechanisms of Deposit Insurance Systems in the Asia-Pacific Region*, July.

IADI. (2012a). *Annual Survey*, BIS, Basel.

IADI. (2012b). *Comparative Analysis of Deposit Insurance System* in CIS Countries, June.

IADI. (2012c). *Core Principles for Effective Deposit Insurance Systems and the Compliance Assessment Methodology*, Basel.

IADI. (2012e). *Bibliography of Papers Related to Deposit Insurance*, www.iadi. org, (dostęp: 20.10.2015 r.).

IADI. (2014b). *Systems under Construction*, BIS, Basel.

IADI. (2014c). *The Revised Core Principles for Effective Deposit Insurance Systems*, Basel.

IADI. (2015). *Glossary*, www.iadi.org (dostęp: 11.06.2015 r.).

IADI. (2015a). *Enhanced Guidance for Effective Deposit Insurance Systems: Ex Ante Funding*, June.

IADI. (2015d). *Deposit Insurance Systems Worldwide*, www.iadi.org, 2015 (dostęp: 21.08.2015 r.).

IMF. (2013). *European Union: Technical Note on Deposit Insurance*, Country Report no. 13/66, March 2013.

Ioannidou V., de Dreu J. (2006). *The Impact of Explicit Deposit Insurance on Market Discipline*, DNB Working Paper, no. 89, February 2006.

Iwanicz-Drozdowska. (2014). *Systemy gwarancyjne w sektorze finansowym i ich znaczenie dla stabilności finansowej*, Badania Statutowe SGH, Warszawa.

Iwanicz-Drozdowska. (2015). *Analiza wielkości i struktury sektorów finansowych w wybranych krajach Europy Środkowej i Wschodniej oraz w krajach wysoko rozwiniętych. Konwergencja czy własna droga?*, Badania Statu22towe SGH, Warszawa.

Iwanicz-Drozdowska. (2015b). *Analiza wielkości i struktury sektorów finansowych w wybranych krajach Europy Środkowej i Wschodniej oraz w krajach wysoko rozwiniętych. Konwergencja czy własna droga?*, Badania Statutowe SGH, Warszawa.

Iwanicz-Drozdowska, M. (2011a). *Deposit Insurance Systems – Lessons from the Crisis for CESEE Banking Systems*, The Future of Banking in CESEE after the Financial Crisis, SUERF Studies 2011/1.

Iyer R., Puri M. (2008). *Understanding Bank Runs: the Importance of Depositor-Bank Relationships and Networks*, August 2008, NBER Working Paper no. 14280.

Jones K., Nguyen C. (2004). *Increased Concentration in Banking: Megabanks and Their Implications for Deposit Insurance*, FDIC, Washington, June.

Jurkowska-Zeidler A. (2008). *Bezpieczeństwo rynku finansowego w świetle prawa Unii Europejskiej*, Wolters Kluwer, Warszawa,.

Kahn C., Santos J. (2003). *Allocating Bank Regulatory Powers: Lender of Last Resort, Deposit Insurance and Supervision*, BIS.

Kane E. (1986). *Appearance and Reality in Deposit Insurance: The Case for Reform*, "Journal of Banking & Finance", vol. 10, no. 2.

Kane E. (1985). *The Gathering Crisis in Federal Deposit Insurance*, MIT Press,.

Kaufman G.; Wallison, P. (2001). *The New Safety Net. Regulation*, vol. 24, no. 2, Summer 2001.

KDPW. (2013). *System Rekompensat. Podstawy prawne oraz zasady funkcjonowania Systemu Rekompensat w Polsce*, Warszawa.

Kerlin, J. (2014a). *Ewolucja systemów gwarantowania depozytów – rozwój uprawnień i ich znaczenie w sieci bezpieczeństwa finansowego*, Badania Młodych Naukowców SGH, Warszawa.

Kerlin, J. (2015). *Rozwój systemów gwarantowania depozytów na świecie*, [w:] *Badania naukowe z zakresu nauk ekonomicznych a praktyka gospodarcza*, Oficyna Wydawnicza SGH, Warszawa.

KNF. (2014). *Przejęcie SKOK im. Św. Jana z Kęt przez Alior Bank*, Komunikat, 14 sierpnia.

KNF. (2014). *Przejęcie SKOK Kopernik przez Bank Pekao*, Komunikat, 5 grudnia

KNF. (2015). *Przejęcie SKOK Siarkopol przez SKOK im. E. Kwiatkowskiego*, Komunikat, 29 września.

KNF. (2015). *Przejęcie SKOK Wesoła przez PKO Bank Polski*, Komunikat, 18 czerwca.

Koleśnik, J. (2013). *Institutional Protection Scheme w sektorze banków spółdzielczych w Polsce – modelowe rozwiązania*, Annales, Universitatis Mariae Curie-Skłodowska, Lublin-Polonia, vol. XLVII, no. 3.

Kouassi T., Distinguin I., Tarazi A. (2011). *Bank Deposit Insurance, Moral Hazard and Market Discipline: Evidence from Central and Eastern Europe*, Université de Limoges, LAPE, June 2011.

Krimminger M. (2006). *Controlling Moral Hazard in Bank Resolutions: Comparative Policies & Considerations in System Design*, July 2006.

Kuritzkes A., Weiner S., Schuermann T. (2002). *Deposit Insurance and Risk Management: How Much? How Safe? Who Pays?*, Wharton Financial Inst. Working Paper no. 02–02, June 2002.

Kwiatkowski W. (2014). *System rezerwy federalnej*, Wydawnictwo Naukowe Scholar, Warszawa.

Laeven L.(2008). Valencia F., *The Use of Blanket Guarantees in Banking Crises*, IMF.

Mayes D.G., Wood G. (2008). *Lessons from the Northern Rock Episode*, CASS 2008.

McCoy P. (2007). *The Moral Hazard Implications of Deposit Insurance: Theory and Evidence*, IMF.

Monkiewicz M. (2013). *Bezpieczeństwo rynku ubezpieczeniowego UE a systemy gwarancyjne pewności ochrony ubezpieczeniowej. Teoria i praktyka*, Poltext, Warszawa.

Morrison A., White L. (2006). *Is Deposit Insurance a Good Thing, and if so, Who Should Pay for It?*, Oxford Financial Research Centre Working Paper no. 2004-FE-08; EFA 2006 Zurich Meetings, June 2006.

NBP. (2013). *Financial Stability Report*, December 2013.

Obal T. (2004). *Teoretyczne aspekty systemu gwarantowania depozytów*, "Bezpieczny Bank", nr 2(23), BFG, Warszawa.

Obal, T. (2004). *Podstawowe cechy systemów gwarantowania depozytów i działalności pomocowej w państwach Unii Europejskiej – wnioski dla Polski*, "Bezpieczny Bank", nr 1(22), BFG, Warszawa.

Oliveira R., Schiozer R., Barros L. (2012). *Depositors Perception of "Too-Big-To-Fail"*, "Review of Finance", December 2012.

Pawlikowski A. (2005). *Polski system gwarantowania depozytów na tle rozwiązań zastosowanych w innych państwach UE*, Zeszyt nr 193, Materiały i Studia, NBP, Warszawa, czerwiec.

Pennacchi G. (2004). *Risk-Based Capital Standards, Deposit Insurance and Procyclicality*, FDIC Center for Financial Research Working Paper no. 2004–05, November 2004.

Peria M., Schmukler S. (1999). *Do depositors Punish Banks for "Bad" Behavior?*, WPS2058, World Bank.

Pierce J. (1983). *Some Public Policy Issues Raised by the Deregulation of Financial Institutions*, "Contemporary Economic Policy", vol. 1, no. 2, January.

Polijaniuk H. (2000). *Zagraniczne systemy gwarantowania depozytów – rozwiązania zalecane i praktykowane*, "Bezpieczny Bank", nr 1(8), Warszawa.

Pruski, J. (2014b). *Ewolucja światowego systemu ochrony depozytów oraz systemu recovery i resolution*, BFG, Warszawa.

Pruski, J. (2014c). *The rationale and benefits of a deposit insurance system – from the standard setter perspective*, Nairobi, 15 May.

Ratowanie instytucji finansowych w Unii Europejskiej w latach 2007–2013 – koszty, skuteczność i konsekwencje, Badania Statutowe SGH, kierownik: M. Iwanicz-Drozdowska, Warszawa 2015.

Restrukturyzacja banków w Unii Europejskiej w czasie globalnego kryzysu finansowego, red. M. Iwanicz-Drozdowska, Oficyna Wydawnicza SGH, Warszawa 2015.

Russel C., Ross T. (1991). *Bank Runs: Liquidity and Incentives*, NBER, Working Paper no. 3921, November 1991.

Santomero A.M. (1997). *Deposit Insurance: Do We Need It and Why?*, University of Pennsylvania – The Wharton School, August 1997.

Sato R., Ramachandran R.V., Kang B. (1990). *Risk Adjusted Deposit Insurance for Japanese Banks*, NBER, no. 3314, 1990.

Shibut L. (2002). *Should Bank Liability Structure Influence Deposit Insurance Pricing?*, FDIC Working Paper no. 2002–01, January 2002.

Shy O., Stenback R., Yankov V. (2014). *Limited Deposit Insurance Coverage and Bank Competition*, Finance and Economics Discussion Series Divisions of Research & Statistics and Monetary Affairs Federal Reserve Board, Washington D.C.

Słownik języka polskiego, red. W. Doroszewski, Państwowe Wydawnictwo "Wiedza Powszechna", Warszawa 1958–1962.

Smaga P. (2014). *Paneuropejski system gwarantowania depozytów – część II (propozycja konstrukcji)*, "Bezpieczny Bank", nr 1(54), BFG, Warszawa.

Szczepańska O. (2005). *Podstawowe przesłanki, założenia i struktura sieci bezpieczeństwa finansowego w świetle teorii i doświadczeń międzynarodowych*, "Bezpieczny Bank", nr 1(26), BFG, Warszawa.

Talley S. (1990). *Deposit Protection and the Spread of Deposit Insurance: Some Guidelines for Developing Countries*, World Bank.

Urrutia J.L., Mishra C., *Deposit Insurance Subsidies, Moral Hazard, and Bank Regulation*, "Journal of Economics and Finance", vol. 19, no. 1.

Waxman M. (1998). *A Legal Framework for Systemic Bank Restructuring*, World Bank – Bank and Financial Restructuring, June 1998.

White E. (1995). *Deposit Insurance*, World Bank.

White E. (1997). *The Legacy of Deposit Insurance: The Growth, Spread, and Cost of Insuring Financial Intermediaries*, NBER April 1997.

Wierzba R. (2005). *System gwarantowania depozytów jako element sieci bezpieczeństwa finansowego. Doświadczenia francuskie*, "Bezpieczny Bank", nr 1(26), BFG, Warszawa.

Wilmarth A. (2010). *Reforming Financial Regulation to Address the Too-Big-To-Fail Problem*, "Brooklyn Journal of International Law", vol. 35, March.

World Bank. (2003). *Banking Regulation Database*.

Yehoue, E. B. (2009). *Emerging Economy Responses to the Global Financial Crisis of 2007–09: An Empirical Analysis of the Liquidity Easing Measures*, IMF Working Paper, WP/09/265.

Yuk-Shee Ch., King-Tim M. (1985). *Depositors Welfare, Deposit Insurance, and Deregulation*, American Finance Association, "Journal of Finance", vol. 40, no. 3, July.

Zaleska M. (2010). *Zmiany zasad gwarantowania depozytów w odpowiedzi na globalny kryzys finansowy*, [w:] *Instrumenty i regulacje bankowe w czasie kryzysu*, red. J. Nowakowski, Difin, Warszawa.

Zdanowicz, B. (2007). *Podstawowe dylematy i kryteria wyboru formuły systemu gwarantowania depozytów w świetle teorii i doświadczeń międzynarodowych*, "Bezpieczny Bank", nr 1(34), BFG, Warszawa.

Law Acts

Banking (Special Provisions) Act (2008, c. 2).

Commission Recommendation 87/63/EEC of 22 December 1986 concerning the introduction of deposit-guarantee schemes in the Community, OJ L 33, 4.2.1987, p. 16.

Council Regulation (EU) No 1024/2013 of 15 October 2013 conferring specific tasks on the European Central Bank concerning policies relating to the prudential supervision of credit institutions, OJ L 287, 29.10.2013, p. 63.

Directive 2001/24/EC of the European Parliament and of the Council of 4 April 2001 on the reorganisation and winding up of credit institutions, OJ L 125, 05.05.2001, p. 15.

Directive 2009/14/EC of the European Parliament and of the Council of 11 March 2009 amending Directive 94/19/EC on deposit-guarantee schemes as regards the coverage level and the payout delay (Text with EEA relevance), OJ L 68, 13.3.2009, p. 3.

Directive 2014/49/EU of the European Parliament and of the Council of 16 April 2014 on deposit guarantee schemes Text with EEA relevance, OJ L 173, 12.6.2014, p. 149.

Directive 2014/59/EU of the European Parliament and of the Council of 15 May 2014 establishing a framework for the recovery and resolution of credit institutions and investment firms and amending Council Directive 82/891/EEC, and Directives 2001/24/EC, 2002/47/EC, 2004/25/EC, 2005/56/EC, 2007/36/EC, 2011/35/EU, 2012/30/EU and 2013/36/EU, and Regulations (EU) No 1093/2010 and (EU) No 648/2012, of the European Parliament and of the Council Text with EEA relevance, OJ L 173, 12.6.2014, p. 190.

Directive 94/19/EC of the European Parliament and of the Council of 30 May 1994 on deposit-guarantee schemes, OJ L 135, 31.5.1994, p. 5.

Regulation (EU) No 806/2014 of the European Parliament and of the Council of 15 July 2014 establishing uniform rules and a uniform procedure for the resolution of credit institutions and certain investment firms in the framework of a Single Resolution Mechanism and a Single Resolution Fund and amending Regulation (EU) No 1093/2010, OJ L 225, 30.7.2014, p. 1.

The Banking Act (2009, c. 1).

The Banking Act of 1933 (L. Pub. 73–66, 48 Stat. 162, enacted 16 June 1933).

The Dodd-Frank Wall Street Reform and Consumer Protection Act (Pub. L. 111–203, H.R. 4173).

Internet Sources

CNBC, *In Cyprus, the Bank Run That Wasn't*, Europe: Economy, www.cnbc.com, 1.04.2013 (access 18.01.2016).

CNBC, *Latvia's Biggest Bank Fights Off Deposit Run*, Europe: Economy, www.cnbc.com, 12.12.2011 (access 18.01.2016).

Dutch News, *DSB Client to Sue Lakeman over Run*, http://dev.dutchnews.nl, 14.10.2009 (access 18.01.2016).

ECB, *The List of Significant Supervised Entities and the List of Less Significant Institutions*, www.ecb.europa.eu (access 21.10.2015).

European Parliament, *ECON Committe*, www.europarl.europa.eu (access 20.10.2015).

FDIC, *Research & Analysis*, www.fdic.gov (access 19.10.2015).

FDIC, *Understanding Deposit Insurance*, www.fdic.gov (access 23.06.2015).

FGDR, *The Fonds de Garantie des Dépôts et de Résolution, Law 99–235 of 25 June 1999 Relating to Savings and Financial Security*, www.garantiedesde pots.fr (access 24.06.2015).

FSCS, *Information Charter*, www.fscs.org.uk (access 23.06.2015).

Reuters, *Bulgaria Ready to Rescue Corpbank after Bankrun*, www.reuters.com, 27.06.2014 (access 18.01.2016).

Why the run on banks, "The Economist", www.economist.com, 1.07.2014 (access 18.01.2016).

Index

© The Author(s) 2017   **347**
J. Kerlin, *The Role of Deposit Guarantee Schemes as a Financial Safety
Net in the European Union*, Palgrave Macmillan Studies in Banking
and Financial Institutions, DOI 10.1007/978-3-319-54163-1

Printed by Printforce, the Netherlands